STRATEGIC

PLANNING

for

CATHOLIC

SCHOOLS

A Diocesan Model of Consultation

About the Authors

Dr. John Convey is a professor at The Catholic University of America, where he is the chair of the Department of Education and the holder of the St. Elizabeth Ann Seton Chair in Education. He has been on the faculty since 1974, teaching courses in statistics, evaluation, and psychometric theory. Dr. Convey received a B.A. in mathematics from LaSalle College in 1962, a M.Sc. in mathematics from The Ohio State University in 1968, and a Ph.D. in research and evaluation from The Florida State University in 1974. During the 1986-87 academic year, he was a Senior Research Fellow in the Office of Research at the United States Department of Education. Dr. Convey was the 1991 recipient of the C. Albert Koob Award, given by the National Catholic Educational Association for outstanding service to Catholic schools. He was a member of the Committee on Education of the United States Catholic Conference from 1992 to 1994. Dr. Convey is the author of *Catholic Schools Make A Difference: Twenty-Five Years of Research,* and he writes a column on research for NCEA Notes.

Dr. Maria J. Ciriello, OP, is an associate professor at The Catholic University of America, where she coordinates the master and doctoral programs in education administration, policy, and foundations in the Department of Education. She is also active in the teacher education program, where she teaches "Foundations of Education" and supervises student teachers. She joined the faculty in 1987 after completing her doctoral studies at The Catholic University. Sr. Maria earned a B.S.E. in Elementary Education from St. John College of Cleveland in 1966 and a M.S.E. in Education Administration from the University of Dayton in 1971. She has also been an elementary school teacher and served as a Catholic school administrator at the elementary and secondary levels. Sr. Maria is the project director and editor of the *Formation and Development Series for Catholic School Principals.* This self-study program for prospective and newly hired Catholic school administrators includes volumes addressing the principal as educational leader, spiritual leader, and managerial leader.

STRATEGIC PLANNING

for

CATHOLIC SCHOOLS

A Diocesan Model of Consultation

John J. Convey

and

Maria J. Ciriello

UNITED STATES CATHOLIC CONFERENCE ✦ WASHINGTON, D.C.

In its plans and programs, as approved by the general membership of the United States Catholic Conference in November 1993, the Department of Education was authorized to prepare materials to assist dioceses in strategic planning so they may be better able to ensure that Catholic elementary and secondary schools provide high quality education to parents who wish to send their children to them. This volume, *Strategic Planning for Catholic Schools*—which is intended to assist in the attaining of this goal as outlined in the bishops' statement issued in November 1990, *In Support of Catholic Elementary and Secondary Schools*—was reviewed by the Most Reverend Robert J. Banks, Chairman of the Bishops' Committee on Education, and is authorized for publication by the undersigned.

Monsignor Dennis M. Schnurr
General Secretary
NCCB/USCC

ISBN 1-57455-055-1

TABLE OF CONTENTS

■ These appendices appear on the disk included with this volume.

LIST OF EXHIBITS

◼ These exhibits appear on the disk included with this volume.

Long-range or strategic planning is as essential for Catholic elementary and secondary schools as it is for the business world, higher education, and public schools. The strategic planning process helps a diocese or an individual school identify present needs, develop strategies to help it adjust to changing conditions, make current decisions that are future-oriented, and make future decisions more effectively.

This book is a resource for a diocese, a group of schools, or individual schools to assist them in conducting a strategic planning study for the future of Catholic schools. The consultative approach to long-range planning described in this book directly involves the schools' stakeholders, those people on whom the schools depend for success. The reasons for involving stakeholders in the planning process are to understand their concerns and values, to take advantage of their experience and insights, and to secure their cooperation in the implementation of recommendations.

Since 1983, the Catholic University of America has assisted dioceses around the country with long-range strategic planning for Catholic schools. The purpose of these planning studies has been to assess the needs of Catholic education in the particular diocese and to develop a comprehensive plan for the use of limited resources to meet those needs. Typically, these studies have produced a five- to fifteen-year strategic plan regarding the placement of schools within the diocese, as well as a series of recommendations concerning Catholic identity, curriculum, finances, governance, marketing and public relations, parental involvement, and the structure and organization of the diocesan school office

Our initial studies were conducted for the Archdiocese of Washington. The first study for Washington lasted twelve months and produced a strategic plan for the twenty-four high schools of the archdiocese, while the second study lasted twenty months and resulted in a fifteen-year strategic plan for the seventy-six archdiocesan elementary schools. After Washington, we assisted the Diocese of Corpus Christi, Texas, with a study of its elementary and secondary schools, and the Archdiocese of Baltimore with a study concerning the financing and governance of its elementary schools. Each of these studies lasted two years, both ending in 1989. These studies were followed by strategic planning studies for all of the schools of the Archdiocese of Boston (1989-1991), the Diocese of Honolulu (1990-1992), the Diocese of Brooklyn (1991-1993), and the Diocese of Providence (1992-1994).

Except for the high school study for the Archdiocese of Washington, each study employed extensive consultation of relevant constituencies as an integral part of the development of the strategic plan. In this book we describe the planning model that we developed during the course of these studies. This model differs from some approaches to long-range planning in that it prescribes the use of widespread consultation from the very beginning of the planning process. Although it developed within the context of planning studies for schools, the model is applicable to general planning situations. The model also is useful for planning for individual schools or groups of schools. In addition, the parish planning process described in Chapter 5 is useful for general parish planning.

The contributions and encouragement of a number of people helped to make this book a reality. We extend our deep appreciation to all who assisted along the way, particularly the following:

❖ The Department of Education of the United States Catholic Conference provided the funding for the book. Sr. Lourdes Sheehan, RMS, and Msgr. Thomas McDade were particularly supportive of this project as one means to assist dioceses in their efforts to engage in long-range planning for their schools.

❖ Much of the strategic planning model presented in this book developed during the elementary school study for the Archdiocese of Washington. Dr. Leonard DeFiore, Dr. Claire Helm, Mr. Vance Johnson, and Dr. Jerome Porath made significant contributions to the development of the model.

❖ We also acknowledge the contributions made to the refinement of the model during subsequent planning studies by Msgr. Vincent Breen, Mr. Lawrence Callahan, Bro. Daniel Casey, FSC, Msgr. Daniel Dever, Rev. Michael Hardiman, Dr. Rosemarie Kamke, Sr. David Ann Niski, OSF, Mrs. Grace Rank, Sr. Ann Dominic Roach, OP, and Sr. Mary Jude Waters, OP.

❖ Finally, we are indebted to Dr. Shelly Convey for her editorial review and suggestions, and for the efforts of the Office for Publishing and Promotion Services of the United States Catholic Conference in helping to bring this book to its completion.

John J. Convey, Ph.D.
Maria J. Ciriello, OP, Ph.D.
Department of Education
The Catholic University of America

CHAPTER 1
Introduction to Strategic Planning

Chapter Objectives

In this chapter you will learn the following:

1. What strategic planning is, why it is important, and how it differs from conventional planning

2. How to design a diocesan strategic planning study that is based upon extensive consultation

3. Whom to consult during the course of a diocesan strategic planning study

4. What a typical timeline is for a full diocesan strategic planning study

Need for Planning

Planning is indispensable for the future welfare of all schools. Schools must adapt to economic conditions, shifts in the number of school-age children, changes in students' racial/ethnic backgrounds, the availability of qualified teachers, and curricular innovations. Public schools have planning departments and school boards have a long-range planning function precisely to anticipate changing conditions and to develop plans to address them.

Planning is especially critical for Catholic schools, both for the diocese and for individual schools. Demographic changes, including decreasing enrollments and shifting populations, and rapidly increasing costs are among the factors that contribute to a need to identify areas of a diocese where the opening, expansion, consolidation, or closing of schools may be necessary. In some dioceses, increasing numbers of non-Catholic students in the schools may require an examination of their evangelization mission. Some dioceses are struggling to deal with new immigrants, many of whom are poor and do not have the financial means to afford Catholic schools. In addition, all dioceses continually need to address issues regarding finances, governance, curriculum, staffing, programs, services, marketing, and public relations. Dioceses and individual Catholic schools across the nation are experiencing similar challenges and face the need to address these same issues.

In their 1990 statement *In Support of Catholic Elementary and Secondary Schools,* the United States Catholic bishops (1) reaffirmed their conviction from the 1972 pastoral *To Teach as Jesus Did* to maintain and strengthen Catholic schools and (2) invited the entire Catholic community to join them in addressing the challenges that face Catholic schools. The bishops committed themselves to achieve four goals:

1. Catholic schools will continue to provide high-quality education for all their students in a context infused with gospel values.

2. Serious efforts will be made to ensure that Catholic schools are available for Catholic parents who wish to send their children to them.

3. New initiatives will be launched to secure sufficient financial assistance from both private and public sectors for Catholic parents to exercise this right.

4. The salaries and benefits of Catholic school teachers and administrators will reflect the bishops' teaching, as expressed in *Economic Justice for All.*

To achieve these goals, the bishops pledged to accomplish the following actions:

❖ Call upon all Catholics in a spirit of stewardship to support Catholic schools financially.

❖ Create diocesan development offices to establish endowments and raise funds for Catholic schools.

❖ Support the formation of diocesan, state, and national organizations of Catholic school parents to join in a coordinated effort to support federal and state legislation to provide financial assistance to parents, so that they can afford to choose the type of schools they desire for their children.

❖ Engage in strategic planning to ensure the future viability of Catholic schools.

This book is a response to this last action.

An Approach to Planning

Planning will help ensure the continuation of quality Catholic schools. A comprehensive planning study produces a blueprint that describes the policies governing the schools of a diocese and any changes in the configuration of those schools during the next three to five to ten years. The blueprint also specifies how resources will be used to ensure the viability of Catholic schools, as well as what additional resources are needed to implement the policies that affect schools and the projected configuration of schools.

Sr. Lourdes Sheehan in *Building Better Boards* (1990) lists the steps commonly used for long-range planning:

❖ Develop ideal goals.

❖ Gather preliminary data and identify constraints, including any technical, financial, legal, moral, political, social, or demographic limitations.

❖ Set attainable goals in light of the constraints.

❖ Develop alternatives for reaching the goals.

❖ Perform a cost-benefit analysis to determine the best alternatives.

❖ Establish alternatives to deal with contingencies.

❖ Implement and evaluate the plan.

Strategic planning goes beyond conventional long-range planning. In addition to developing a plan for the future, the goal of strategic planning is to engage the planners, the decision-makers, and their constituents in a dialogue that will produce a series of decisions designed to ensure the future vitality of the schools. Because strategic planning anticipates the inevitability of change and the instability that may result from change, emphasis shifts from product to process (Patterson, Purkey, and Parker, 1986).

The definition of strategic planning provided by McCune (1986) provides a context in which to understand the planning model proposed in this book. According to McCune, strategic planning has four characteristics:

❖ *It assumes an open system whereby organizations must constantly change as the needs of the larger society change.*

Change is inevitable, and some changes provide specific challenges to Catholic schools:

❖ Declining enrollment threatening a school's existence.

❖ Increasing numbers of non-Catholic and non-Christian students, requiring the school to examine how it will maintain its Catholic identity.

❖ Increasing numbers of new immigrants, dictating a review of the appropriateness of a school's curriculum.

❖ Increasing numbers of lay teachers, requiring the school to ensure that these teachers understand the school's mission, its Catholic identity, and their role in promoting them.

❖ Increasing costs straining the resources of parents, parishes, and the diocese.

❖ Increasing participation of parents in the life of the school, dictating the exploration of new governance structures and other forms of parental involvement.

❖ *It is conducted by a small group of planners with widespread involvement of stakeholders, rather than a planning department or professionals.*

The model presented in this book places the responsibility for overseeing the design and management of the study and for developing its final recommendations with a planning committee composed of individuals from representative groups within the diocese. Some members of the Catholic school department, as well as the diocesan planning department, are on the planning committee, but these individuals are not exclusively, nor primarily, responsible for developing the strategic plan. The stakeholders—including parents, clergy, principals, teachers, religious congregations, and diocesan officials—are represented on the diocesan planning committee and are consulted frequently during the course of the study. Finally, external consultants are not required to implement this model. However, some dioceses and schools may benefit by employing a professional evaluator, planner, or management consultant to monitor the process and provide objective, disinterested advice.

❖ *It uses current and projected trends to make current decisions.*

The model makes extensive use of data concerning enrollments, school and parish financial data, and past demographic trends and future projections. In addition, the attitudes of parents, clergy, principals, and teachers help to formulate recommendations and develop strategies for their implementation.

❖ *It focuses on what decision is appropriate today, based on an anticipation of the situation in five years, as opposed to focusing on organizational goals and objectives in five years.*

The model results in a strategic plan for the schools for the next five to fifteen years. In attempting to anticipate future conditions, the model concentrates on the present structures, personnel, financial resources, and other resources to identify strategies that will ensure the future vitality of the schools. The planning process challenges pastors, parents, educators, and others to view Catholic schools in a new way. The wide participation of various interested groups galvanizes support for Catholic schools and promotes a new awareness of them.
As Lunenburg and Ornstein (1991) state:

Strategic planning goes beyond a mechanistic series of planning procedures. Its power lies in its capacity to create dissonance in people, upset traditional views, identify new possibilities, and pose new questions.

A Diocesan Model for Strategic Planning

Philosophy of the Model

The planning model described in this book assumes that the diocese and the schools are committed to a consultation process. The consultation provides an opportunity for input by the various stakeholders whose members would be most affected by the results of the study. The proposed model promotes grassroots participation. The planners include representatives from the schools and their constituencies, especially parents, in addition to diocesan personnel such as individuals from the Catholic school office and clergy.
The following characteristics of the model are particularly beneficial:

❖ *The model adopts a philosophy of consultation at all stages of the planning process.*

The use of widespread and frequent consultation has several advantages.

❖ The diocesan planning committee is exposed to a larger, richer source of ideas and suggestions than either it or the task forces may have assembled without the consultation.

❖ The diocesan planning committee avoids having to defend final recommendations, but rather can test preliminary proposals, assess reactions to them, and make appropriate modifications, if it deems necessary.

❖ Participants develop a sense of ownership of the problems, potential solutions, and recommendations. The consultation empowers people to take responsibility and encourages them to be more actively involved in planning for the future of Catholic schools.

❖ People are educated about the realities facing Catholic schools. The consultation challenges their assumptions and possible stereotypes concerning the schools.

❖ Stakeholders' involvement makes it easier to secure their cooperation for the acceptance and implementation of the final recommendations.

❖ *The planners wait until they have fully consulted with members of various constituencies before they formulate their preliminary proposals.*

In traditional approaches to planning, an external consultant or a team of experts is hired to assist a diocese or a school in planning. After collecting and analyzing the data, the consultant prepares a report that contains, at a minimum, a description of the present condition of the school or schools, the consultant's views on future prospects, and the consultant's recommendations.

The model proposed in this book has the planners establish an extensive network of consultation that provides them with grassroots perceptions about the study's issues and their possible solutions. After studying the feedback from this network, the planners develop the preliminary proposals and encourage public debate concerning them. Because the preliminary proposals reflect the discourse developed during the consultation, this methodology has a high likelihood of producing recommendations that propose significant changes in the diocese and are likely to be implemented.

❖ *The planners evaluate reaction to the preliminary proposals to determine if adjustments must be made before final recommendations are developed and presented to the decision-maker.*

In traditional planning studies, often little or no consultation regarding the recommendations occurs prior to their presentation to the decision-maker. Thus, a decision-maker usually will consult with advisers and, perhaps, with constituents before making a final decision about the recommendations. The bishop or, depending upon the circumstances in the study, another decision-maker then must decide whether to accept the recommendations as presented, to reject them, or to modify them appropriately.

The opportunity to adjust final recommendations on the basis of widespread consultation, which the proposed model provides, not only increases the potential success of the planning study, but also avoids placing the bishop or another decision-maker in a position to have to reject or substantially modify recommendations.

❖ *The model promotes a tactic of compromise and negotiation regarding preliminary proposals in order to engender greater ownership of the recommendations that the decision-maker eventually accepts and implements.*

Many traditional approaches to planning are "top-down." A consultant studies an individual school's situation or the schools in an entire diocese and makes recommendations. The strength of this approach rests in the expertise of the consultant and his or her experience with similar situations. The very fact that a consultant is external to the situation and can offer a professional, unbiased view is another important advantage. A potential weakness of this model can be its failure to engender ownership of the recommendations in those affected by them. Decision-makers, sensing a lack of grassroots participation and support, may reject the recommendations or fail to act on them. In other cases, implementation of recommendations is thwarted by constituents' resentment because they never had significant input into the formation of the recommendations.

On the other hand, the proposed planning model is designed to build consensus. Preliminary proposals generally do not develop into final recommendations until a consensus is reached regarding them—or at least until a substantial majority of constituents supports them. An additional strength of the model is that the bishop is apprised of the degree of the consensus reached and the nature of any disagreement when he receives the recommendations, which enables him to assess both the extent and source of the support or opposition.

Components of the Diocesan Model

Exhibit 1-1 is a schematic representation of a diocesan model for strategic planning. The model is easily adapted for use with individual schools or groups of schools. The remainder of this chapter and much of this book describe the use of this model in diocesan planning. Chapter 7 portrays how the model can be adapted for high schools, particularly when several high schools with different types of ownership (diocesan, private, parish, or board of trustees) are involved in a joint planning effort. Chapter 8 describes the adaptation of the model for local school planning.

Study Team

A study team of four to eight individuals familiar with the schools is assembled at the very beginning of the study and serves as the executive committee for the planning effort. The study team is responsible for the design, scheduling, and daily management of the study.

The study team normally includes the following individuals:

❖ The chairperson of the diocesan planning committee

❖ The superintendent of schools

❖ An assistant superintendent

❖ Other individuals familiar with and committed to Catholic schools (e.g., pastors, principals, parents, or prominent community leaders)

❖ As applicable, the consultant that the diocese has secured

The following are the major responsibilities of the study team:

❖ To act as a clearinghouse for ideas

❖ To maintain contact with the task forces

❖ To make critical decisions regarding the design of the study

❖ To schedule its events

❖ To initially discuss the nature of the proposals that will be developed for the consultation phase of the study

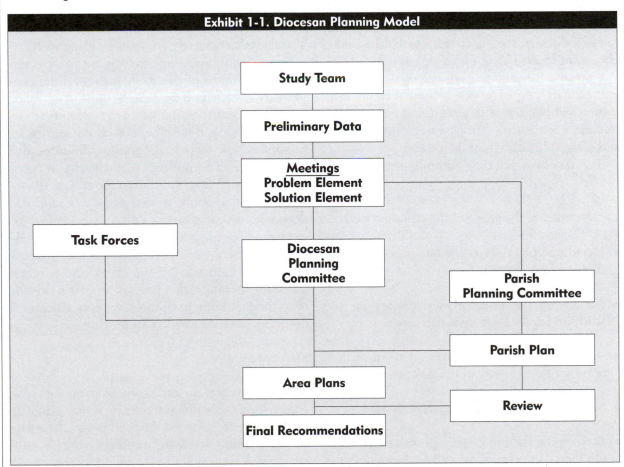

Exhibit 1-1. Diocesan Planning Model

❖ To initially review the parish plans

❖ To discuss any major changes in the number, type, and location of schools in different parts of the diocese

❖ To draft initial area proposals for the parishes

❖ To prepare drafts of diocesan proposals for discussion by the diocesan planning committee

The study team forms the nucleus of a larger planning group, called the diocesan planning committee.

Diocesan Planning Committee

The diocesan planning committee consists of approximately eighteen to twenty-four individuals who oversee the conduct of the planning study and make the final recommendations to the bishop. The chair of the diocesan planning committee, who normally is appointed by the bishop, should be a person held in high esteem and well known throughout the diocese. An auxiliary bishop, the vicar or secretary for education, a prominent pastor, or a distinguished lay person would be a good choice for chair. The other members of the diocesan planning committee are selected to provide approximately equal representation of clergy, educators, and parents, with attention given to representation from the various racial/ethnic groups and geographical areas of the diocese.

The diocesan planning committee is responsible for

❖ Determining the scope of the planning study

❖ Deciding upon the type of data needed and the method for collecting them

❖ Identifying the task forces necessary for the study and appointing their members

❖ Acting as a sounding board and agent of final approval for the work of the task forces

❖ Safeguarding the interests of the diocese

❖ Developing the preliminary proposals concerning diocesan policies, as well as developing the area plans for the consultation phase of the study

❖ Conducting an extensive consultation of the parishes and schools regarding the area plans and preliminary proposals

❖ Keeping individuals and groups in the diocese apprised of the progress of the study and consulting with them at strategic times during the study

❖ Educating those being consulted about the significant issues in the study and assisting them in the accomplishment of their assigned tasks

❖ Keeping the study on a timely course

❖ Deciding upon the final recommendations of the study

❖ Approving the final report before it is submitted to the bishop

Preliminary Data

The diocesan planning committee, along with any external consultants, spends approximately the first four months of the study gathering the preliminary data. The data include present and past enrollment statistics, including the enrollments of non-Catholics and members of ethnic and racial minorities. The diocesan planning committee also gathers financial information, including tuitions, parish financial contributions to the school, diocesan financial support, tuition assistance, and endowment disbursements. Other data consist of demographic projections concerning the availability of school-age children for as many years as possible and attitudes of the clergy and parents, including reasons why parents send or do not send their children to Catholic schools. Chapter 2 describes the data needed for planning.

Major Meetings

After the study team and diocesan planning committee have determined the scope of the planning study and have gathered the preliminary data, two all-day meetings involving pastors, principals, parents, parish representatives, and others concerned with education are held for the purpose of consulting with these groups about the schools. The first meeting, called the problem element meeting, informs the participants about the design of the study, reviews with them the preliminary data, and solicits their opinions about the problems they perceive are facing the schools. Approximately four to six weeks later the same participants are invited to a second meeting, the solution element meeting, at which they suggest solutions to the problems they identified at the problem element meeting. Chapter 3 describes the methodology for these two meetings.

Task Forces

Near the date for the problem element meeting and based on the problems identified by the participants at that meeting, the diocesan planning committee forms several task forces to assist it in developing recommendations for the study. Although the exact number of task forces is determined by the problems that emerge during the problem element meeting, usually a diocese has the following task forces: Catholic identity, finance, governance, curriculum, marketing and public relations, parental involvement, and secondary schools. Each task force studies the data from the problem element meeting and the solution element meeting and collects other information concerning the issues it is charged to examine. The diocesan planning committee acts as a sounding board and agent of final approval for the work of the task forces. Chapter 4 contains more information about the task forces.

Parish Planning Committees

Concurrent with the work of the task forces, each parish in the diocese, whether it has a school or not, is asked to form a parish planning committee. This committee examines the parish's relationship to Catholic schools and its efforts to provide for the Catholic education of its youth. The diocesan planning committee also requests each parish committee to make recommendations concerning the number of Catholic schools needed in its immediate area of the diocese. The parish planning committee makes its recommendations to the diocesan planning committee in the form of a parish plan, which includes a description about how the parish intends to support Catholic schools. Chapter 5 describes the parish planning process.

Area Plans

The diocesan planning committee divides the diocese into geographical areas and develops an area plan for the schools and parishes in each area. The proposals in the area plan, which are based on the parish plans submitted by the parishes and other information available to the diocesan planning committee, contain specific recommendations regarding the future of each current school and, as appropriate, the opening of new schools. The diocesan planning committee seeks reactions regarding these area plans, as well as the preliminary diocesan proposals, by conducting an extensive consultation of all parishes and schools in the diocese. Chapter 6 describes the development of area plans.

Final Recommendations

The task force reports, parish plans, responses to area plans, and the results of the consultation that occurs throughout the planning study form the basis for the final recommendations presented to the bishop at the end of the planning study. Chapter 6 describes how the final recommendations are developed.

Who Is Consulted?

After the design of the planning study is finalized, the focus of consultation shifts to the parish level and ultimately involves all groups in a diocese. In addition to parishioners who complete surveys, are represented by their parish planning committees, or attend the major meetings of the study, the stakeholders consulted most often are (1) the presbyteral council or diocesan priest senate, (2) the deans of each deanery or the vicars of each vicariate, (3) the pastors of the parishes, (4) the principals of the schools, (5) boards of trustees, and (6) the representatives of the parish planning committees. Others consulted often include (1) heads of diocesan agencies and departments and other diocesan leaders, (2) teachers, (3) representatives of the religious congregations that serve the schools, and (4) parents of children in the schools.

Bishop

The ordinary of the diocese does not formally participate in the consultation because he will ultimately decide which recommendations to accept. However, since the bishop must approve the initiation of the study, he is consulted about its design and methodology. The bishop usually is also present at the meeting of the presbyteral council to review the study's preliminary proposals. Finally, since the bishop always reserves a preemptive veto regarding any proposal, the chair of the diocesan planning committee, the consultant, or some diocesan official should brief the bishop periodically throughout the course of the study, not to secure his approval for what is happening but to determine if there are any proposals that he feels he must veto if they were made as recommendations to him.

Pastors

Because of their canonical responsibility for the welfare of the school, especially in the areas of finances and spiritual leadership, pastors of parishes with schools are consulted often during the planning study. In addition, since Catholic schools are a ministry of the diocese and all parishes share the responsibility for stewardship of diocesan ministries, pastors of parishes without schools are included in the consultation.

Ordinarily, the first consultations are held with the pastors. During the first month of the study, one or more meetings, depending upon the size of the diocese, are held with the pastors to inform them about the study and to seek their advice regarding its design and timeline. As a result of these meetings, some minor changes in the proposed design of the planning study may occur. In some studies, pastors have suggested changes in the timing of major meetings or particular deadlines; however, to date, pastors have not suggested any substantial changes in the proposed study design.

In addition, the pastors have the opportunity to participate in subsequent consultations by

❖ Completing a clergy survey during the gathering of the preliminary data

❖ Attending the problem element meeting and solution element meeting

❖ Serving on the parish planning committee

❖ Attending special meetings, sometimes specifically for pastors, to discuss the diocesan proposals and area plans

Vicars or Deans

Depending on the organization of the diocese, vicars or deans have special leadership roles. In addition, these priests may also be pastors who participate in the consultation in the same way as other pastors. In some cases, however, the diocesan planning committee may want to hold special meetings for the vicars or deans to receive their special counsel regarding the conduct of the study, its preliminary proposals, or its final recommendations.

Principals

Principals, along with pastors in the case of parish schools, are responsible for the welfare of local Catholic schools. The principal shares with the pastor the responsibility for the spiritual leadership of the school, which includes fostering a community of faith. As a professional educator and administrator, the principal is the school's instructional leader, who is responsible for its daily operation and management, curriculum, personnel, and budget.

Because of their key role, principals are consulted often during the planning study. As was done with the pastors, a consultation is held with the principals early in the study. Depending on the size of the diocese and its traditions, the consultation with principals may be combined with the one for pastors. The principals also will have the following opportunities to participate in subsequent consultations:

❖ Completing a principal survey

❖ Attending the problem element meeting and solution element meeting

❖ Serving on a parish planning committee

❖ Attending special meetings, sometimes specifically with principals, to discuss diocesan proposals and area plans

Teachers

Every diocese in the country has been blessed with excellent, dedicated religious and lay teachers. In addition to exercising their professional role as educators, individuals choose to teach in Catholic schools to serve the Church, to share their faith and values, and to fulfill their special ministry. Clearly, the caliber of the schools' academic and religious formation programs depends upon the quality of the teachers that the schools attract and retain.

The teachers have opportunities to participate in the consultation in various ways:

❖ All teachers are invited to complete a teacher survey.

❖ One teacher from each school is invited to attend the problem element meeting and solution element meeting.

❖ Some teachers serve as group facilitators at the problem element meeting and solution element meeting.

❖ One teacher from each school is invited to serve on the parish planning committee in parishes with schools.

❖ Teachers are consulted during the development of the report that each school may submit to the diocesan planning committee in addition to the plan submitted by its parish.

Religious Congregations

The religious congregations whose members serve as administrators, teachers, or other staff in the schools have a keen interest in the outcomes of a planning study. All or some of these congregations may have a long history of involvement in the schools of the diocese. Many of these congregations may have been primarily responsible for establishing the early schools in the diocese, and their interest will be even higher if they currently own and operate schools. The diocesan planning committee seeks opportunities to consult with the leadership of these congregations and keeps them informed of the progress of the study. Several opportunities exist for special consultation with the religious congregations:

❖ At regular meetings of major superiors in the diocese

❖ At meetings of the sisters' senate and brothers' senate, when these or similar groups exist in the diocese

❖ At special meetings of representatives from congregations to discuss the study's design and methodology and later during the consultation on the preliminary proposals

Boards of Trustees

Some schools in the diocese may have a separately incorporated board of trustees, which, by law, is responsible for the welfare of the particular school. Most often these boards of trustees are associated with schools that are privately owned; however, in some cases, parish schools may have separately incorporated boards of trustees. The consultation of these boards is essential. Many dioceses invite the private schools to participate in the planning study.

The consultation of boards of trustees may occur in the following ways:

❖ One or two members from each board may attend the problem element meeting and solution element meeting.

❖ An entire board is consulted during the development of the report submitted by the school to the diocesan planning committee.

❖ If high schools are a particular focus of the diocesan planning study and special meetings are held specifically for high schools, the entire board of trustees could be invited to attend meetings that deal specifically with high school issues.

❖ Depending on the circumstances of the school, the diocesan planning committee may want to have a special meeting with the members of a particular board of trustees.

Parents

Parents are the consumers of Catholic education. They choose the school for their children, pay the bills, and, in most cases, financially support the parish that sponsors the school. Parents deserve to know about the planning study. Their advice should be sought often by the diocesan planning committee and the parish committees.

The opportunities for parents to be consulted occur when

❖ Some parents, either randomly sampled from around the entire diocese or selected from each school and parish religious education program, are invited to complete a parent survey during the gathering of the preliminary data for the study.

❖ At least one parent from each parish is ordinarily invited to attend the problem element meeting and solution element meeting.

❖ Several parents are invited to serve on each parish planning committee.

❖ All parents have the opportunity to complete a parish survey distributed by the parish planning committee.

❖ Parents have the opportunity to attend special parish meetings during the consultation phase of the study.

Parishioners

Parishioners should be consulted regarding the future of Catholic schools in the diocese. Catholic schools are a diocesan ministry and deserve the attention and support of all Catholics in the diocese. In addition, the parish may have specific financial obligations for a school or may be asked to provide some financial support for the schools throughout the diocese. In both cases, the parish is accountable to the parishioners for the use of their parish contributions and should consult them regarding major decisions involving schools.

The opportunities for the consultation of parishioners include the following:

❖ Some parishioners attend the problem element meeting and solution element meeting.

❖ Some parishioners serve on the parish planning committee.

❖ All parishioners have the opportunity to complete a parish survey distributed by the parish planning committee.

❖ Parishioners also have the opportunity to attend special parish meetings during the consultation phase of the study.

Presbyteral Council

The presbyteral council is a canonically established group of priests that provides advice to the bishop. Because of its advisory role, the presbyteral council is one of the most important groups that the diocesan planning committee consults during the study. As both a courtesy to the council in recognition of its role and an opportunity for the diocesan planning committee to test the council's reaction to the preliminary proposals, it is recommended that the first consultation with the presbyteral council occur immediately before the public consultation on the preliminary proposals. A second consultation with the presbyteral council occurs ideally just prior to developing the final recommendations for the bishop. The necessity of this second consultation increases when serious objections have been raised to some of the preliminary proposals. This consultation often helps the diocesan planning committee develop compromise proposals that are more widely accepted throughout the diocese.

Diocesan Agency and Department Heads

In order to build consensus and ownership, the diocesan planning committee should keep other diocesan officials, especially those responsible for ministries other than Catholic schools, apprised of the progress of the study. Soliciting their advice regarding both the preliminary proposals and the final recommendations will keep them aware of the study's proceedings.

Some Caveats and Practical Considerations

At this point, it is important to stress that widespread consultation at all phases of the strategic planning process is very demanding of time and resources. Those responsible for seeking the consultation need to agree that this approach is what they really want. Before a final decision is made, the following issues should be carefully considered.

❖ The bishop, in particular, and the superintendent of schools must be comfortable with permitting the consultation to occur.

❖ The consultation may produce ideas that encroach on diocesan traditions or strongly held beliefs. Once embarking on the consultation, those in authority must be willing to let the process evolve naturally.

❖ Extensive consultation results in a generalized expectation on the part of those being consulted that their advice will be utilized in some form or another in the development of the recommendations. Those in authority risk the possibility that a decision they would be required to make and which goes against recommendations received in the consultation would be unpopular and would result in resentment and resistance, instead of support and cooperation.

❖ The superintendent of schools plays a key role in the planning study. The superintendent as a member of the diocesan planning committee and, ordinarily, of the study team has equal status with the other members of these groups. However, it is very important that the superintendent carefully assess the developments in the planning study and be comfortable with them, since he or she will most likely be responsible for implementing the recommendations. If a study proceeds in a direction that makes the superintendent uncomfortable, its recommendations may not have the superintendent's full support and enthusiasm. This situation diminishes the likelihood of a successful implementation of these recommendations if the current superintendent remains in office.

❖ The diocese must be willing to hire an additional staff person or identify a current staff person from the Catholic school office to act as the project director for the planning study. Because of the extent and ongoing nature of the consultation, an on-site project director whose primary responsibility is the local coordination of the planning study is absolutely necessary. If finances permit, hiring an additional staff person as the project director enables the current staff of the Catholic school office to attend to their usual full-time responsibilities. In addition, the project director, when not working directly on the planning study, can assist with the normal operations of the Catholic school office.

❖ The diocese can expect to incur additional costs because of the highly consultative nature of the study. The costs for paper, xeroxing, postage, and refreshments will be significantly higher because of the type and extent of the consultations held during the study.

❖ The diocesan planning committee, which ordinarily will consist of individuals with busy schedules, must be willing to spend a substantial amount of time in planning, gathering, and analyzing the data resulting from the consultation. A strategy of widespread and frequent consultation extends considerably the time necessary to complete the study. For example, previous diocesan planning studies lasted twenty to twenty-four months. Because the planning committee may meet as many as twenty or twenty-five times during the course of the study, the early coordination of members' calendars to schedule meetings is recommended. Exhibit 1-2 shows the meetings for the Boston study, which is a typical schedule of meetings for a diocesan planning committee. Generally, the study team will have more meetings than those shown in Exhibit 1-2.

❖ The members of the diocesan planning committee must be willing to devote their energies and resources to ensure the highest quality input from the consultation. Except in unusual cases, members of the diocesan planning committee will be more knowledgeable about the salient issues than those consulted. The diocesan planning committee will be more expert in the processes and tasks that they request task forces and parish planning committees to perform. Therefore, it is incumbent upon the diocesan planning committee to educate those being consulted about the issues and to assist them in the accomplishment of their assigned tasks.

❖ The diocesan planning committee must provide tangible evidence that the feedback obtained during the consultation has been thoroughly evaluated and, when appropriate, included into either the planning process or the recommendations. When the actions of the planning committee demonstrate that it has seriously considered the advice offered, the likelihood of receiving quality input from future consultations is increased and notions like "there's already a plan," "the decisions have already been made" or "no one is going to listen, so why waste my time" are effectively countered.

Job Descriptions

Superintendent

1. Participates as a voting member of the study team and the diocesan planning committee
   a. Oversees the major responsibilities of the study team
   b. Facilitates the major responsibilities of the planning committee
   c. Assists in the development of recommendations

Exhibit 1-2. Schedule of Meetings from Boston Study

September 13, 1989	Design of the study
October 23, 1989	Finalize design and arrange pastor/principal briefings
November 2, 1989	Parent survey results; prepare problem element meeting; finalize task forces
January 11, 1990	Problem element results; design process for secondary schools
April 26, 1990	Briefings by task forces
June 14, 1990	Preliminary task force reports
June 21, 1990	Preliminary task force reports
September 20, 1990	Task force reports: Catholic identity/curriculum, marketing/public relations, finance
October 11, 1990	Task force reports: governance, finance
November 2-3, 1990	Initial discussion of area proposals
December 3, 1990	Discussion of area proposals
December 17, 1990	Discussion of archdiocesan proposals
January 10, 1991	Discussion of consultation document
March 21, 1991	Discussion of reactions to archdiocesan proposals
April 18, 1991	Revision of area proposals
May 6, 1991	Discussion of area proposals and high school proposals
May 23, 1991	Revision of finance proposals
June 26, 1991	Task force reports: Catholic school office, secondary schools
July 10, 1991	Discussion of final recommendations

2. Works with the project director to ensure the smooth progress of the study
   a. Expedites the scheduling and daily management of the study
   b. Expedites the collection and distribution of the data needed for the study
   c. Signs letters of invitation to pastors, principals, and facilitators for problem and solution meetings

3. Facilitates the gathering and analysis of data
   a. Assists in determining the content of the surveys
   b. Provides for the analysis of data collected at the problem and solution element meetings

4. Acts as the official representative of the diocese
   a. Keeps the bishop apprised of the progress of the study
   b. Ensures the cooperation of the schools in all aspects of the study
   c. Communicates with the parishes to encourage their participation
   d. Monitors the developments of the study, especially with an eye to future implementation
   e. Safeguards the interests of the diocese

Consultant (if applicable)

1. Designs the planning study and participates in all of its phases
   a. Seeks input from various diocesan groups about the design of the planning study
   b. Attends all meetings of the study team and the diocesan planning committee
   c. Conducts meetings of the study team and the diocesan planning committee, when requested
   d. Maintains communication with the study team, diocesan planning committee, and the chairpersons of task forces throughout the study

2. Conducts orientations for the following groups regarding their roles in the study:
   a. Study team and diocesan planning committee
   b. Pastors and principals
   c. Task forces
   d. Parish planning committees

3. Attends to all of the technical issues in the study
   a. Determines the type of data needed for the study
   b. Prepares statistical reports on the preliminary data obtained from the diocese
   c. Designs all surveys and analyzes their results

4. Conducts the problem element meeting and the solution element meeting
   a. Analyzes and prepares reports on the data from the problem element meeting and the solution element meeting
   b. Assists in the preparation of training materials for facilitators

5. Participates in the development of recommendations
   a. Reviews parish plans and task force reports
   b. Assists in the development of area plans
   c. Reviews and edits area plans from the diocesan planning committee
   d. Attends major consultation meetings regarding the recommendations
   e. Assists in the development of final recommendations
   f. Writes the final report and presents the final recommendations to the bishop

Project Director (on site)

1. Coordinates all procedural details of the study
   a. Schedules meetings of the study team and diocesan planning committees
   b. Arranges for meetings of pastors and principals
   c. Schedules problem element meeting and solution element meeting
   d. Schedules consultation meetings with parishes and diocesan groups
   e. Organizes the distribution and collection of surveys from the various constituencies

2. Participates as a voting member of the study team and the diocesan planning committee

3. Manages public relations and communications concerning the study
   a. Handles routine questions about the study's progress and acts as the study's troubleshooter
   b. Maintains contacts with the parishes throughout the study

c. Coordinates the consultation phase of the study

4. Prepares for the problem element and solution element meetings
   a. Makes pre-arrangements
   b. Determines membership of small groups
   c. Makes arrangements on-site
   d. Trains small group facilitators
   e. Oversees the systematic collection of data

5. Coordinates all activity between diocesan planning committee and the parish planning committees
   a. Organizes the preparation and distribution of materials to the parish planning committees
   b. Oversees the collection and filing of the parish plans
   c. Arranges for the distribution of the preliminary recommendations and areaplans
   d. Oversees the collection and filing of the responses to area plans

6. Coordinates all activity between the diocesan planning committee and the task forces
   a. Organizes the preparation and distribution of the task force materials
   b. Distributes the data collected at the problem and solution element meetings to the appropriate task forces
   c. Oversees the collection and filing of the task force reports and their distribution to the diocesan planning committee

7. Coordinates the development of the recommendations
   a. Oversees the preparation of the preliminary recommendations and the area plans
   b. Oversees the writing of the final report

Diocesan Planning Committee Chairperson

1. Manages the work of the diocesan planning committee
   a. Presides over the meetings of the diocesan planning committee
   b. Assists in the development of agendas for meetings
   c. Appoints subcommittees and their chairs
   d. Appoints a recording secretary to keep accurate records of the diocesan planning committee's activities

e. Oversees the preparation of the area plans
f. Keeps the study on a timely course
g. Oversees the preparation of the final report

2. Maintains communication with other individuals and groups in the planning study
   a. Ensures that communication is maintained with the task forces
   b. Works with the study team to review parish plans and discuss any major proposals

3. Acts as the bishop's representative
   a. Oversees the direction of the planning study
   b. Safeguards the interests of the diocese
   c. Communicates with the bishop periodically and presents the final report to him

Task Force Chairperson

1. Manages the work of the task force
   a. Presides over the meetings of the task force
   b. Appoints subcommittees and their chairpersons
   c. Ensures that someone acts as recording secretary and keeps accurate records
   d. Assists in the identification and gathering of appropriate data
   e. Oversees the preparation of the task force report

2. Acts as the official liaison with the diocesan planning committee
   a. Maintains communication with the diocesan planning committee
   b. Represents the task force at meetings of the diocesan planning committee, when requested

Parish Planning Committee Chairperson

1. Manages the work of the parish planning committee
   a. Manages the meetings of the PPC
   b. Ensures that someone records the actions of the PPC
   c. Arranges for the appropriate materials to be present at the meetings of the PPC
   d. Appoints individuals to carry out PPC assignments
   e. Ensures that the PPC meets its deadlines

2. Acts as the official spokesperson for the parish planning committee
   a. Communicates with the project director and the diocesan planning committee
   b. Ensures that the parish pastoral council and the parish finance committee are consulted and kept apprised of the PPC's activities and discussions
   c. Arranges for cooperative endeavors with PPCs from neighboring parishes, if appropriate

Pastor

1. Participates in important planning meetings
   a. Attends special briefing meeting at the beginning of the study
   b. Participates in the problem element meeting and solution element meeting
   c. Attends special meetings that are held during the consultation phase

2. Provides data needed for planning
   a. Completes a clergy survey during the gathering of the preliminary data
   b. Provides parish financial data to the diocesan planning committee

3. Ensures the participation of the parish in the planning study
   a. Arranges for parish representation at the problem element and solution element meetings
   b. Arranges for the formation of the parish planning committee
   c. Appoints the chairperson and the members of the parish planning committee
   d. Serves on the parish planning committee
   e. Facilitates the work of the parish planning committee and the production of its parish plan
   f. Monitors the progress and consultation process of the parish planning committee
   g. Ensures that the parish planning committee prepares a written reaction to the area plan

Principal

1. Participates in important planning activities
   a. Attends a special briefing meeting at the beginning of the study
   b. Participates in the problem element meeting and solution element meeting
   c. Serves on a parish planning committee
   d. Attends special meetings that are held during the consultation phase

2. Provides data needed for planning
   a. Completes a principal survey during the course of the study
   b. Distributes and coordinates the collection of teacher surveys
   c. Provides the appropriate school data requested by the diocesan planning committee and/or the parish planning committee
   d. Distributes and collects surveys of parents

3. Ensures the participation of the school in the planning study
   a. Arranges for a teacher to attend the problem element and solution element meeting
   b. Arranges for a teacher to be on the parish planning committee
   c. Oversees the preparation of the school's response to the area plan, if requested by the diocesan planning committee

Timeline

Exhibit 1-3 shows a typical timeline for a diocesan planning study. Ordinarily, we have started studies in September at the beginning of the school year and completed them by the end of the following school year. Local circumstances and issues will determine the exact length of a particular study, so the timeline in Exhibit 1-3 is simply offered as a general guide.

Summary

The model presented in this chapter is useful for dioceses, groups of schools, and individual schools to plan for the future of Catholic schools. The model is fully participatory and relies on widespread consultation in all of its phases. Key elements of the model are its extensive consultation sought on preliminary proposals prior to developing final recommendations and its philosophy of negotiation and compromise.

Chapters 2 through 6 describe in more detail the various components of this model. Chapter 7 shows the adaptation of the model for planning for the high schools in a diocese. Chapter 8 illustrates the use of the model for strategic planning by individual Catholic schools. The next chapter describes the types of data required for good planning and offers suggestions on how to gather and analyze these data.

Exhibit 1-3. Timeline for Diocesan Planning Study

	Diocesan Planning Committee	Task Force	Parish Planning Committee
September	Preliminary Data		
October			
November			
December			
January	Problem Element		
February	Solution Element	Establish	Establish
March	Discussion of Issues		Parishioners' Survey
April			Development of Proposals
May			Consultation of Parishioners
June		Preliminary Report	Submission of Parish Plan
July			
August			
September	Development of Area Plans	Final Report	
October			
November			
December	Final Area Plans		
January	Consultation		Area Plan Consultation
February			
March			Reaction to Diocesan Planning Committee
April	Final Report		
May			
June	Report to Bishop		
July	Discussion of Final Recommendations		

CHAPTER 2
Gathering and Analyzing Data

Chapter Objectives

In this chapter you will learn the following:

1. What kinds of enrollment, demographic trend, financial, staffing, and attitudinal and opinion data are needed for a planning study, how to gather these data, and how to display them

2. What types of surveys are useful for gathering attitudinal and opinion data from parents, clergy, teachers, and principals, including examples of specific survey questionnaires

3. What other resources are helpful to a diocesan planning committee

Introduction

This chapter describes data essential for good planning. While the data are quantitative in nature—traditionally, this type of data has been the staple of long-range planning—we wish to stress that qualitative data also play an important role in strategic planning. We agree with Patterson and his associates that "because the future is uncertain, subjective judgment, intuition, and even hunches become important pieces of data in planning for the future" (Patterson, Purkey, and Parker, 1986). Chapter 3 will describe the collection and analysis of the qualitative data obtained during the problem element meeting and the solution element meeting.

The primary purpose of gathering extensive empirical data is to help the diocesan planning committee understand the school situation in the diocese and make informed recommendations. A secondary purpose is to provide information to those not on the diocesan planning committee but who take part in the study, either as members of task forces or parish committees, attendees at major meetings, or interested participants in the consultations. Because these individuals will differ in their awareness of the issues to be examined, it is critical that some baseline data be made available to them. A body of data that all can study and refer to provides a common frame of reference and a basis for discussion among those with different experiences and expertise.

What data should be collected? We recommend that the diocesan planning committee gather at least the data regarding enrollment, demo-graphic trends and projections, school finances, staffing of the schools, and attitudes and opinions of various groups in the diocese concerning the issues that the study will address. The following sections contain more details concerning these data and some guidelines on how the data might be displayed to facilitate interpretation.

Enrollment Data

Data Gathering

Information concerning the history of student enrollment numbers in the diocese enables the diocesan planning committee to examine how the enrollment has changed over a certain number of years, whether these changes have been uniform in each part of the diocese, whether the changes have affected elementary and secondary schools differently, and what the prospects are for changes in the future. In addition, the diocesan planning committee will be able to identify particular schools that are either underenrolled or at capacity, as well as those that have experienced significant declines or increases.

The diocesan planning committee gathers the following data about enrollment:

- Total diocesan enrollment for the past twenty years for
  - All schools
  - Elementary schools
  - High schools
  - Each racial/ethnic group
  - Non-Catholics

Traditional racial/ethnic categories are American Indian/Alaskan Native; African American/Black; Asian/Pacific Islander; Hispanic; and White, Non-Hispanic. In some cases, a diocese may want a more detailed breakdown of race/ethnicity to include Chinese, Cuban, Haitian, Hawaiian, Portuguese, Vietnamese, and so forth, as appropriate.

These data, which are ordinarily part of the permanent records kept by the Catholic school department, are also available from the summary statistics that the diocese reports annually to the National Catholic Educational Association.

❖ Annual enrollment for each school for each of the past five to eight years by
  ❖ Grade and gender
  ❖ Each racial/ethnic group
  ❖ Non-Catholics

These data, which also are ordinarily part of the permanent records kept by the Catholic school department, could be obtained from a summary form distributed to individual schools.

Data Display

The following displays will be helpful to the members of the diocesan planning committee, task forces, parish planning committees, attendees at the problem element meeting, and others interested in examining the enrollment trends in the diocese.

❖ *Listing of each school grouped by vicariate or deanery and its location, grades served, current enrollment, change in enrollment over the past five or six years, current percentage of minority students, and current percentage of non-Catholic students.*

This listing provides a quick overview of trends in each school over the past five or six years (see Exhibit 2-1).

❖ *Graph (or table) showing the annual diocesan-wide total enrollment for the past twenty years.*

This graph permits the tracking of enrollment trends in the diocese, including periods when the enrollment decline or increase accelerated, leveled, or decelerated. Exhibit 2-2 shows an example of such a graph from the Diocese of Providence planning study.

❖ *Graphs (or tables) showing the total annual elementary school enrollment and the total annual high school enrollment for the past five to eight years.*

This graph helps examine the effect that changes in elementary school enrollment have on high school enrollment.

❖ *Graph (or table) showing the annual preschool enrollment for the entire diocese over the past five to eight years.*

Exhibit 2-1. Enrollment Summary from Providence North Deanery							
School	Location	Grades	Type	Students 1992-93	Change 1986-92	Percent Non-Cath. 1992-93	Percent Minority 1992-93
Msgr. Bove	Providence	K-8	Parish	212	-94	5.7	2.8
St. Augustine	Providence	PK-8	Parish	302	59	1.7	3.3
Bl Sacrament	Providence	PK-8	Parish	224	-111	8.0	14.7
Holy Name	Providence	K-8	Parish	173	22	44.5	100.0
St. Patrick	Providence	K-8	Parish	144	34	22.9	61.8
St. Pius V	Providence	PK-8	Parish	183	0	6.6	15.3
St. Thomas	Providence	K-8	Regional	237	-6	4.6	4.2
St. Philip	Smithfield	K-8	Parish	204	-43	5.4	3.9

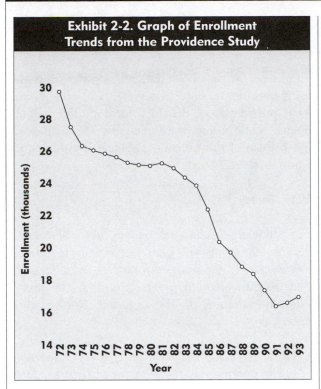

Exhibit 2-2. Graph of Enrollment Trends from the Providence Study

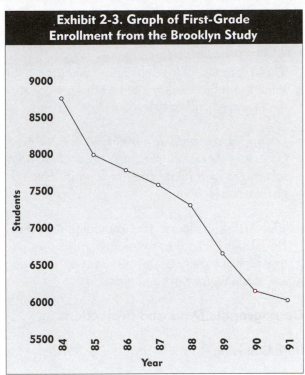

Exhibit 2-3. Graph of First-Grade Enrollment from the Brooklyn Study

This graph helps determine the effect of preschool enrollment on first-grade enrollment, which can be a good predictor of total school enrollment.

❖ *Graph (or table) showing the annual first-grade enrollment for the entire diocese over the past five to eight years.*

This graph ordinarily is a good predictor of the trend in elementary school enrollment. Exhibit 2-3 shows the first-grade enrollment in the Diocese of Brooklyn.

❖ *Graph (or table) showing the year-to-year enrollment from kindergarten or first grade to eighth grade for at least five cohort groups of students. (For example, one cohort group might be those in kindergarten in 1980, in first grade in 1981, in second grade in 1982, and so forth.)*

This graph enables the diocesan planning committee and others to examine the retention pattern of students from grade to grade and to identify key grades where the pattern changes.

❖ *Graph (or table) showing changes in the annual enrollment of minority students and non-*

Catholic students and their percentage of the total enrollment over the past five to eight years.

This graph permits the examination of changes in the enrollment of minority students and non-Catholic students and the detection of departures from expected trends, if they occur.

❖ *Graph (or table) showing changes in the total annual enrollment of elementary schools for each vicariate or deanery for the past five to eight years.*

This graph facilitates the comparison of enrollment changes across the various vicariates or deaneries in the diocese.

❖ *Listing of the annual enrollment for the past five to eight years for each elementary school grouped by vicariate or deanery.*

This listing helps the diocesan planning committee concentrate on the enrollment patterns in each deanery when discussing the future of particular schools.

❖ *Graphs (or tables) showing the total annual high school enrollment for the past five to eight years of the different types of high schools: by* gender (all-boy, all girl, coed) and by ownership (diocesan, parish, private).

These graphs help determine whether high school enrollment is related to the type of students served and/or to a school's ownership.

❖ *Listing of the annual enrollment for the past five to eight years for each individual high school grouped by whether it is an all-boy, all-girl, or coed school.*

This listing facilitates the examination of individual high school enrollments and the extent to which a variety of enrollment opportunities are available for boys and girls.

Demographic Data and Projections

Data Gathering

Some of the fluctuations in enrollment within a diocese are due to changes in the birth rate. Indicators of the availability of the number of school-aged children include the number of births in the previous ten to fifteen years, changes in public school enrollment, and migration into and out of the area.

The diocesan planning committee obtains the following information:

❖ Number of births annually in the nation or in the state for at least the past ten to fifteen years

❖ Total annual enrollment in the local public schools for the past five to eight years

❖ Name and location of any local public school that has closed during the past ten years

❖ Additional public schools planned within diocesan boundaries over the next ten to fifteen years

❖ Census data regarding the number and racial/ethnic distribution of children between ages five and eighteen who live within the geographical boundaries of the diocese, including changes during the past twenty years

❖ Projected enrollment in the public schools and/or projected number of school-age chil-

dren or changes in the population for as many years into the future as available

Sources for the above data include state and local governments, state departments of education, local public school districts, local public school boards, county and state planning departments, the Bureau of the Census, and local Chambers of Commerce.

Data Display

The following displays will be helpful to the members of the diocesan planning committee, task forces, parish planning committees, attendees at the problem element meeting, and others interested in examining the demographic trends in the area.

❖ *Graph showing the number of births annually in the nation or in the state for at least the last ten to fifteen years.*

This graph enables the planning committee to examine the potential impact of the changing birth rate on the availability of students for the elementary and secondary grades. Exhibit 2-4 shows the number of births nationally in five-year increments from 1960 to 1990. Exhibit 2-5 shows a graph of the number of births in Massachusetts used in the Boston planning study.

❖ *Graph (or table) showing the annual enrollment in the public schools (local or statewide) during the past five to eight years.*

Exhibit 2-4. Births in the United States	
Year	**Births**
1960	4,257,850
1965	3,760,358
1970	3,731,386
1975	3,144,198
1980	3,612,258
1985	3,760,581
1990	4,179,000

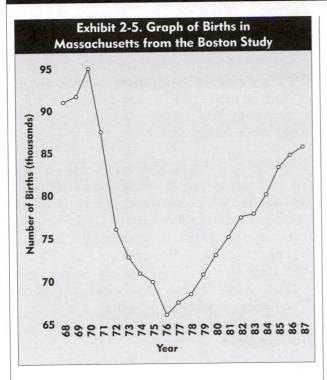

Exhibit 2-5. Graph of Births in Massachusetts from the Boston Study

Depending on its similarity to the corresponding data for the Catholic schools, this graph assists in determining the extent to which birth rate and migration influence the enrollment of Catholic schools. A different pattern for the enrollment of Catholic schools would signal the presence of other factors such as finances, location, or parental preferences that may be influencing the enrollment.

❖ *Tables showing the projected number of public school students and/or students of school age or the general population over the next five to ten to twenty years, listed by specific geographical regions of the diocese, if available.*

These tables help the diocesan planning committee identify areas of the diocese where additional schools may be necessary or where consolidation of existing schools may be warranted over the next five to ten years. (See Exhibit 2-6.)

Financial Data

Data Gathering

The diocesan planning committee gathers the following financial data for the current school year, if available, and at least the three previous years:

❖ Tuition rates for parish families, out-of-parish Catholic families, and non-Catholic families

❖ Total income, broken down by tuition, fund raising, parish subsidy, and diocesan subsidy, for each school

❖ Average cost per student for each school and for the entire diocese

❖ Amount of parish funds given as subsidy for the support of the school, for each parish

❖ Amount of parish funds given in tuition assistance, for each parish

❖ Ordinary income (receipts from offertory collection or stewardship program) for each parish

❖ Amount of diocesan funds given as subsidy to support a school or to help a parish support a school, for each school/parish that receives such funds

Exhibit 2-6. Demographic Projections for Selected Cities in the Providence Study								
	Age 5-9			Age 10-14			Age 15-19		
	1990	1995	2000	1990	1995	2000	1990	1995	2000
Barrington	913	1037	1080	844	904	1041	995	839	909
Bristol	1291	1406	1369	1101	1303	1420	1217	1112	1315
Burrillville	1069	1149	1195	1262	1083	1156	1407	1278	1090
Central Falls	1121	1153	1108	1155	1092	1134	1072	1125	1076

- Average salaries of lay teachers by school and for the entire diocese

- Diocesan average compensation package for teachers from religious congregations

- Diocesan average salaries for principals

Data Display

The following displays help the members of the diocesan planning committee, task forces, parish planning committees, attendees at the problem element meeting, and others interested in examining the financial trends for the schools in the diocese.

- *Listing, by school, of tuition for in-parish students for the current school year and latest available data on cost per student, total parish subsidy, percentage of parish ordinary income represented by parish subsidy, total parish support for tuition assistance, fund-raising net revenue, diocesan subsidy, and average salary for lay teachers.*

This summary listing provides the diocesan planning committee and others with a quick overview of the important financial data for each school. (See Exhibit 2-7.)

- *Tables showing the following averages for each vicariate or deanery of the diocese and for the entire diocese:*

  - *Tuition for in-parish students, for Catholic students who are not parishioners, and for non-Catholic students*

- *Cost per student*
- *Parish subsidy and percent of ordinary parish income that this represents*
- *Percentage of total school revenue from tuition income, parish subsidy, diocesan subsidy, and fund raising*
- *Salaries for lay teachers*

These tables permit the identification of differences in these various financial indexes across the diocese. In addition, the diocesan averages can be compared with national financial averages for Catholic schools contained in various reports from the National Catholic Educational Association, for example *United States Catholic Elementary Schools and Their Finances* and *Catholic High Schools and Their Finances*, each published periodically.

Staffing Data

Data Gathering

The diocesan planning committee gathers the following data on teachers and administrators:

- Number of full-time and part-time teachers per school

- Number of lay teachers and teachers from religious congregations per school

- Number of Catholic and non-Catholic teachers per school

- Diocesan percentage of teachers and administrators with advanced degrees

		Cost Per		Percent	Parish		Average
School	Tuition 1991-92	Student 91 Budgt	Subsidy 1989-90	Assessmt Base	Contrib 91 Budgt	Fund-R Net	Teacher Salaries
St. A	$1,300	$1,732	$50,659	17.6	$15,000	$30,000	$20,777
St. B	$1,440	$1,685	$30,000	15.2	$5,000	$12,000	$22,313
St. C	$1,800	$2,973	$211,361	40.6	$174,808	$25,380	$25,591
St. D	$1,500	$2,288	$69,334	15.4	$45,000	$124,600	$23,848
St. E	$1,550	$1,934	$98,160	35.1	$93,000	$27,000	$24,589

Exhibit 2-7. Financial Data from the Brooklyn Study

Data Display

The following display will be helpful to the members of the diocesan planning committee, task forces, parish planning committees, attendees at the problem element meeting, and others interested in the statistics regarding teachers and administrators.

❖ *Table showing the following averages for each vicariate or deanery of the diocese and for the entire diocese:*

  ❖ *Number of full-time teachers*
  ❖ *Percentage of full-time teachers who are lay teachers, who are Catholic, and who possess at least a master's degree*
  ❖ *Percentage of lay administrators who possess at least a master's degree*

This table permits the identification of differences in these statistics regarding teachers and administrators across the diocese. In addition, the diocesan averages can be compared with national averages for Catholic schools available from the National Catholic Educational Association and published annually in the *Annual Statistical Report on Schools, Enrollment and Staffing.*

Data Concerning Attitudes and Opinions

Collecting attitude and opinion data from those intimately involved with the schools of the diocese not only provides an opportunity for participation in the planning study, but also helps develop a sense of ownership regarding the study's outcomes. The diocesan planning committee should survey at least the following groups: parents, pastors, teachers, and principals.

Parent Survey

Audience

The target populations for the parent survey should be the Catholic and non-Catholic parents of children in Catholic schools and the parents of Catholic children in other schools. These populations tend to provide the most useful information for the planning study. However, in some cases,

the diocesan planning committee may wish to identify all Catholic adults in the diocese or all adults in the area covered by the diocese, depending on what information the committee wishes to obtain.

Form

We recommend use of a simple two-page questionnaire (or one page copied back-to-back). Translations of surveys may be needed for parents in various racial/ethnic groups. A sample questionnaire is included in Appendix A.

In some cases, the diocesan planning committee may decide that a telephone survey of parents is preferable to a printed questionnaire. If so, the committee should employ a professional firm that has experience conducting telephone surveys.

Sample

In most dioceses, surveying all parents of school-age children is not feasible because of the large numbers involved. Therefore, the diocesan planning committee will need to identify an appropriate sample of parents. We have found that the following method is both feasible and efficient:

❖ We recommend that the committee distribute the surveys through the Catholic schools and through either the parishes or the parish religious education programs.

  ❖ Surveys sent to parents through their children in the Catholic schools generally will have a very high response rate. In our studies, this rate has ranged from 40 to 90 percent; rates in elementary schools were higher than in high schools.

  ❖ To reach the parents of children not in Catholic schools, the surveys may be distributed through the parish religious education programs. Although the response rate is typically low (10 to 25 percent in our experience), it is probably higher than distributing surveys through the parishes. One advantage, however, of using the parishes as points for distribution is the possibility of reaching parents who do not send their children to parish religious education programs.

- The committee must decide how many schools and parishes or religious education programs to sample. We recommend that the committee attempt to get at least seven hundred completed surveys. Because the rate of return will vary, two to three times as many surveys should be distributed. The total number of surveys to distribute will then determine the number of schools and parishes or religious education programs that should be sampled.

    For example, in the Archdiocese of Boston planning study, the diocesan planning committee distributed 2,700 surveys: 750 to parents of fourth graders in twenty-eight elementary schools, 750 to parents of eleventh graders in eleven high schools, and 1,200 to parents of children in thirty-one parish religious education programs. Completed surveys were received from 1,140 parents: 623 of the elementary school parents (83 percent return), 316 of the high school parents (42 percent return), and 201 of the parents with children in the parish religious education program (17 percent return).

- If the diocesan planning committee wants to sample every school and parish or religious education program, we suggest that one or two or more classes within each school and parish religious education program be identified for the sample, and all children in these classes receive a survey to bring home to their parents.

    For example, the Diocese of Brooklyn distributed surveys in one class in each of its 161 elementary schools, 22 high schools, and 220 parish religious education programs and received 4,709 completed surveys.

    In another example, the Diocese of Providence distributed surveys in two classes in each of its 53 elementary schools, 10 high schools, and 160 parishes and received 2,783 completed surveys.

Content

The parent survey should include demographic information about the parents, their reasons for choosing or not choosing Catholic schools for their children, and their attitudes and opinions concerning key issues being addressed by the planning study.

The **demographic information** should include at least the following:

- Number of school-age children
- Catholic schools attended by children
- Intentions to send children to a Catholic school
- Highest educational level of the parent
- Racial/ethnic background of the parent
- Parent's educational background in Catholic schools
- Annual family income
- Whether the parent is a single parent
- Zip code of the family's residence
- Parish attended by the family

The **reasons for choosing or not choosing Catholic schools** should include the following options:

- **Reasons for sending their children to Catholic schools.** In the dioceses we have studied, parents chose the following reasons as most important:

    - The three most commonly chosen reasons:
        - Discipline and safe, caring environment
        - Academic reasons (good curriculum, effective teachers)
        - Religious reasons (Catholic tradition, religion, teaching values)

    - A frequently chosen reason:
        - Alternative to public schools

    - Less commonly chosen reasons:
        - Location of the school
        - Family tradition
        - School facilities
        - School activities (sports, clubs, and so forth)
        - Friends attend

- **Reasons for not sending their children to Catholic schools.** In the dioceses we have studied, parents selected the following reasons as most important:

- The most commonly chosen reason:
  - Finances (unable or unwilling to pay tuition)

- A frequently chosen reason:
  - Academics (other schools as good or better)

- Less commonly chosen reasons:
  - Prefer public schools
  - Location of the schools (more frequently chosen in certain dioceses)
  - Child has special needs
  - Poorer facilities than other schools
  - Fewer activities than other schools
  - Class size is too large
  - Teachers not as competent as teachers in other schools
  - Friends attend other schools
  - Child has poor grades

Parents' **attitudes and opinions concerning key issues** include the following:

- Need for and importance of Catholic schools
- Perceived effectiveness and quality of Catholic schools
- Number of schools needed in diocese
- Parish religious education programs and public schools
- Financial support of Catholic schools

Analysis and Report of Results

We suggest that the data be analyzed for at least the following groups of parents: all parents, Catholic parents of elementary school students, Catholic parents of high school students, non-Catholic parents, and parents with children attending other schools.

The results could be reported in three major sections: demographic characteristics, attitudes and opinions, and reasons for school choice.

Demographic characteristics. Display tables that show the percentage of respondents in each parent group according to their

- Race/ethnicity
- Annual family income
- Level of education
- Own attendance at Catholic schools
- Status as single parents (see Exhibit 2-8)

Attitudes and opinions. Display tables (see Exhibit 2-9) that show the percent agreement and the average (mean) score from the four-step strongly agree-strongly disagree Likert scale (the **Don't Know** response should be coded as a missing value and not included in the calculation of the average score) for the respondents in each parent group for each item in the themes shown in Exhibit 2-10.

Reasons for school choice. Present tables that show the percentage of parents in each parent group who selected a reason as the most important and the percentage who selected a reason as an important factor in choosing or not choosing a Catholic school for their children.

- **Reasons for choosing a Catholic school.** The most relevant data will come from those parents who send their children to Catholic schools. On the other hand, the ratings from the parish religious education parents or parents of children in other schools who respond to these factors can be viewed as their

Exhibit 2-8. Race/Ethnicity Summary from the Brooklyn Study

	Total	Cath Elem	Cath HS	Non-C Elem	Non-C HS	Not In Cath S
White, non-Hispanic	52	51	66	12	14	70
Hispanic	24	28	16	9	4	18
Black, non-Hispanic	16	14	12	50	42	8
Asian/Pacific Islander	8	6	5	28	31	4
Alaskan/Amer Indian	<1	<1	1	1	9	<1

Exhibit 2-9. Selected Data from Parent Survey

	Total	Cath Elem	Cath HS	Non-C Elem	Non-C HS	Not In Cath S
Percent Agreement						
Schools Essential to Church Mission	92	96	95	86	85	81
Schools Needed More Today	87	92	90	81	78	72
Schools Worth Cost	72	78	75	72	65	50
Average Scale Score*						
Schools Essential to Church Mission	4.41	4.54	4.50	4.22	4.07	4.01
Schools Needed More Today	4.36	4.51	4.47	4.20	4.18	3.88
Schools Worth Cost	3.88	4.01	3.99	3.84	3.68	3.39

* Means are based on a five-point scale.

impressions about what prompts a parent to select a Catholic school. In our studies, we have found that parents with children in the parish religious education program accurately estimate the importance that Catholic school parents place on academics and religion, but underestimate the importance these parents place on the environmental factors.

❖ **Reasons for not choosing a Catholic school.** The data from the parents whose children do not attend Catholic schools are the most relevant. On the other hand, the ratings from Catholic school parents who responded to these items can be viewed as their impressions as to why Catholic parents do not send their children to Catholic schools. In our studies we have found that Catholic school parents overestimate the importance that parents with children in the parish religious education program place on finances and underestimate the importance they place on academics in deciding not to send their children to Catholic schools.

Clergy Survey

Audience

The clergy survey is intended for all clergy in the diocese, or if the diocese is large, at least all pastors and a sample of parochial vicars (assistant pastors), priests in other ministries, and retired priests.

Content

The clergy survey should include demographic information about the priests and their attitudes and opinions concerning key issues being addressed by the planning study. A copy of a clergy survey that we have used in previous studies appears in Appendix B.

The **demographic information** from the priests should include at least the following:

❖ Type of ministry (pastor, parochial vicar, special ministry, retired)
❖ Diocesan or religious order priest
❖ Location of parish

- Responsibility of parish for a school (parish school, regional school, none)
- Age and number of years ordained
- Number of years as pastor in general and for this parish in particular
- Race/ethnicity and educational background in Catholic schools

The priests' **attitudes and opinions concerning key issues** include the following:

- Need and importance of Catholic schools
- Quality and effectiveness of Catholic schools
- Number and location of schools in the diocese
- Effectiveness of teachers, suitability to teach religion, and compensation

- Parental involvement and motivations
- Relation of the school to the parish
- Diocesan commitment to schools for the disadvantaged
- Financial support of Catholic schools
- Governance of Catholic schools

Analysis and Report of Results

We suggest that the data be analyzed for at least the following groups of priests: pastors with parish schools, pastors of parishes associated with regional schools, pastors of parishes without schools, parochial vicars, priests in other ministries, retired priests, and all priests.

First, the report should contain a brief descrip-

Exhibit 2-10. Themes for Parent Survey
(Item numbers are from sample parent survey)

Need for/importance of Catholic schools

1. Essential part of Church's educational mission
2. Needed more than 25 years ago
3. Worth operation costs

Financial issues

4. Increase salaries, even if tuition increases
11. I can increase my parish contribution to support schools
12. Diocese should establish school endowment

Quality/effectiveness of Catholic schools

8. All lay teachers can provide effective Catholic education
9. Those I know have good reputations
10. Those I know effectively teach Catholic doctrine
13. Public views as among best schools in the area
14. Those I know have well-prepared and effective principals
16. Those I know establish foundation of moral and ethical values
17. Those I know have well-prepared and effective teachers

Number of schools

6. Elementary school needed in area
7. High school needed in area

Parish religious education programs and public schools

5. Parish religious education program functioning well
15. Good area public schools

tion of the demographic characteristics of the priests that responded, including

- ❖ Number of priests in each category who completed a survey
- ❖ Number of priests in parishes with schools, with regional schools, or without schools
- ❖ Percentage of priests from different regions of the diocese
- ❖ Number of priests in each age group
- ❖ Number of priests in each racial/ethnic group
- ❖ Percentage of priests that attended various levels of Catholic schools

Next, the report should contain a series of tables that show the percent agreement and the average (mean) scale score (Exhibit 2-11) for the different groups of priests on all survey items on **attitudes and opinions concerning key issues,** which are listed in Exhibit 2-12.

In our previous studies, the pastors of parishes with schools and the retired clergy have shown the highest levels of support for Catholic schools and the pastors of parishes without schools have shown the lowest.

Teacher Survey

Audience

The teacher survey is intended for all teachers in the elementary schools and high schools of the diocese. If it is not feasible to survey all teachers,

the diocesan planning committee should select an appropriate sample. We urge, however, that all teachers be surveyed. We have found that completing this survey helps teachers examine different facets of their commitment and satisfaction and provides them with the opportunity to express their opinions about the issues being explored in the study.

We suggest that no names appear on the teacher surveys and that survey distribution and return be arranged to ensure anonymity.

Content

The teacher survey should include demographic information about the teachers and their attitudes and opinions concerning reasons for teaching in a Catholic school, working conditions, instructional goals, attributions for student success, and key issues being addressed by the planning study. A sample copy of a teacher survey that we have used in previous studies is included in Appendix C.

The **demographic information** from the teachers should include at least the following:

- ❖ Employment status, religion, and state in life
- ❖ Race/ethnicity, sex, and age
- ❖ Level of education and educational background in Catholic schools
- ❖ Type of school in which they teach and their certification status
- ❖ Their tenure in Catholic schools and in other schools

Exhibit 2-11. Display of Data from Clergy Survey							
	School Pastor	Region Pastor	Other Pastor	Assoc Pastor	Other Ministry	Retired Clergy	All Clergy
Percent Agreement							
Poor Areas Top Priority	97	72	53	66	78	82	74
Greater Role Educ Disadvan	94	79	65	85	86	71	80
Average Score							
Poor Areas Top Priority	3.33	2.96	2.40	3.00	3.00	3.24	2.96
Greater Role Educ Disadvan	3.33	3.06	2.65	3.24	3.18	3.12	3.09

Exhibit 2-12. Themes for Clergy Survey
(Item numbers are from sample clergy survey)

Need for/importance of Catholic schools

10. Essential to Church's educational mission
11. Needed more than 25 years ago
12. Worth operational costs
15. Effective use of Church's resources
16. Best for religious education of young
44. Catholic-public school differences don't justify Catholic schools

Quality/effectiveness of Catholic schools

13. Quality in my area is high
30. Effectively teach Catholic doctrine
35. Public views as among best schools
36. Clear goals and priorities
38. Strong Christian communities
56. Establish a foundation of moral and ethical values

Administrators/teachers

27. All lay teachers can provide effective Catholic education
31. Well-prepared and effective teachers
32. Well-prepared and effective principals
37. Only Catholics should teach religion
9. Lack of teachers from religious congregations is serious problem

Number of schools

19. Schools should be available in all parts of the diocese
26. Area has too many elementary schools
53. Build new schools where population growth warrants
54. Area needs elementary school
55. Area needs high school

Parents

28. Most parents settle for average religion if school has good academics
29. Most parents place at least equal emphasis on religion as on academics
41. Finances is main reason for parents not sending child

Service to the poor

14. Greater role in educating disadvantaged
24. Schools in poor areas should be top priority

Parish-related

17. Many parish leaders are Catholic school graduates
18. Schools are excellent sources of vocations
22. School is one of highest parish priorities
39. Pastor and principals share responsibility for spiritual leadership
45. Schools strengthen parish unity
52. Enjoy or would enjoy being pastor of parish with a school

Governance

34. Parents should have more voice in governance of Catholic schools
42. Pastor should leave daily operation of school to principal
50. All Catholic schools should have school boards
51. Interparish schools should have representative boards

Financial

20. All Catholics have responsibility for financially supporting schools
21. Every parish should provide financial support for schools
23. When there is one school and several parishes, all parishes should support
25. Teachers should receive just wages according to their duties
33. Diocese should establish endowment fund for schools
40. Each parish financing its own school is still best policy
43. Take special collections in each parish for schools
46. Parishes without schools should support schools attended by parishioners
47. Schools drain money that other parish ministries should get
48. Lay teachers are not paid adequate salaries

❖ Recency of formal graduate coursework and professional updating

Their **attitudes and opinions concerning reasons for teaching, their working conditions, and key issues being addressed by the planning study** should include at least the following:

❖ Reasons for working in their particular schools
❖ Reasons they remain in their particular schools
❖ Satisfaction with their present situation
❖ Any serious threats to their remaining in the schools
❖ Importance of religion in their lives
❖ Relationships between faculty and administrators
❖ Goals and priorities of their schools
❖ Involvement of clergy and parents in the schools
❖ Strengths and weaknesses of their schools
❖ Importance of instructional goals
❖ Factors contributing to a student's success in school
❖ Need for and importance of Catholic schools
❖ Perceived effectiveness and quality of Catholic schools
❖ Financial support of Catholic schools
❖ Governance of Catholic schools

Analysis and Report of Results

We suggest that the data be analyzed and reported separately for elementary school teachers and secondary school teachers, as well as for teachers from religious congregations, lay Catholic teachers, and non-Catholic teachers. The teacher survey provides a rich database for research and could form the basis for many types of reports. In this section, we describe only a basic report.

The basic report should begin with a demographic profile of the teachers, followed by sections dealing with a discussion of (1) the factors that influenced their decisions to work at their schools; (2) the factors that influenced their decisions to remain at their schools; (3) their satisfaction with various aspects of their work; (4) the factors that constituted serious threats to their continuing at their schools; (5) their attitudes and opinions concerning various issues pertaining to the study; and (6) their personal instructional goals.

❖ **Demographic profile.** The committee should prepare a table containing the percentage of all teachers, elementary school teachers, and secondary school teachers with regard to the demographic information requested above.

❖ **Reasons for teaching at the school.** In this section it is helpful to classify the teachers into

Exhibit 2-13. Primary Orientation Groups for Teachers (Item numbers are from sample teacher survey)		
Mission-related	**Profession-related**	**Job-related**
1. Commitment to Catholic education	2. Professional qualifications	4. Salary offered
3. Teaching as ministry	8. Teachers' influence	7. Only teaching job available
5. Faith witness	9. Teach in expertise area	10. Gain experience
6. Catholic environment	13. Social environment	12. Schedule compatible with family situation
11. Community assignment	15. Work with young	14. Benefits
18. Share values	16. Love teaching	17. School request
19. God's choice	20. Personal growth	22. Close to home
23. Catholic school background	21. School's academic philosophy	25. Contribute to household income
24. School's religious philosophy	26. School's size	

three primary orientation groups based on the reasons they identified.

❖ A table should show the percentage of teachers from religious congregations, lay Catholic teachers, and non-Catholic teachers in each of three basic orientation groups, as defined by the reasons listed in Exhibit 2-13. The orientation groups are defined as follows:

❖ **Mission-related:** Teachers who desire to teach in the school primarily because of its Catholic or religious nature. Teachers in this group emphasize sharing of values, witnessing their faith, ministry, a sense of vocation or God's call, or commitment to the mission of Catholic schools.

❖ **Profession-related:** Teachers who teach in the school primarily because of the opportunity to engage in teaching young people; that is, a view of teacher primarily as professional rather than as minister or witness. Teachers in this group emphasize the love of teaching, a desire to work with young people, their own personal growth and development, or a desire to teach in their area of expertise.

❖ **Job-related:** Teachers who work in the school primarily because of the particular school itself or simply because a job was available. Teachers in this group emphasize gaining experience, earning extra money, supporting their families, the unavailability of other jobs, the compatibility of schedule, the salary offered, or the school's request for their assistance.

❖ In our previous studies, the most important reasons for teaching in the school ordinarily included love of teaching, desire to work with young people, commitment to Catholic education, opportunity to work in this type of environment, and view of teaching as ministry.

❖ Another table (see Exhibit 2-14) might show the average importance score attached to each theme and the items within each theme by the different types of teachers and those from the

Exhibit 2-14. Sample Display of Two Themes from Teacher Survey

Average Importance of Reasons for Teaching in the School
(on a scale of 1-5)

	Catholic Essence	Teaching Process
Elementary	3.28	3.30
Religious	3.81	3.43
Lay Catholics	3.22	3.28
Non-Catholics	3.10	3.39
Mission	3.57	3.36
Profession	2.93	3.17
Job	3.10	3.30
Secondary	3.13	3.44
Religious	3.69	3.45
Lay Catholics	2.97	3.27
Non-Catholics	2.35	3.33
Mission	3.52	3.41
Profession	2.81	3.07
Job	2.75	3.30

Exhibit 2-15. Reasons for Teaching in School
(Item numbers are from sample teacher survey)

Catholic essence	Teaching process
1. Commitment to Catholic education	2. Professional qualifications
3. Teaching as ministry	9. Teach in expertise area
5. Faith witness	13. Social environment
6. Catholic environment	15. Work with young
23. Catholic school background	16. Love teaching
24. School's religious philosophy	21. School's academic philosophy

Exhibit 2-16. Efficacy Themes
(Item numbers are from sample teacher survey)

Mission efficacy	Professional efficacy
6. Help students develop faith	7. Personal growth
17. Work with committed people	9. Work satisfaction
18. Help create Christian community	10. Help others
19. School's faith community	12. Relationships with students
	16. Regard for opinion
	24. Feeling of accomplishment
	25. Autonomy enjoyed
	26. Satisfied students' achievement
	27. Teaching subjects I like

different orientation groups. Exhibit 2-15 shows two themes we have used in past studies.

❖ **Factors influencing remaining at the school.** In addition to reporting the percentage of different types of teachers (religious, lay Catholic, and non-Catholic) and those from the different commitment orientations on each of the thirty factors included in this section, it is useful to report the average importance scores on those items that constitute the themes we define as mission efficacy and professional efficacy (see Exhibit 2-16). Teachers with a high sense of efficacy, those who feel they effectively contribute to stu-

dent learning and the school community, are most likely to remain teaching at a particular school.

❖ **Mission efficacy** represents a teacher's belief that he or she has made or can make a contribution to the religious aspects of the school.

❖ **Professional efficacy** represents a teacher's perceived contribution to the academic nature of the school.

❖ **Satisfaction.** The satisfaction items are divided into seven themes as shown in Exhibit 2-17.

Exhibit 2-17. Satisfaction Composites for Teachers
(Item numbers are from sample teacher survey)

Religious nature

6. School's religious philosophy
25. Helping students grow spiritually
29. Recognition of ministerial role
41. Comfort with religion

Personal relationships

2. Discipline in the school
4. Relationships with my students
11. Relationships with other teachers
20. Communication in the school
40. Student attitudes
42. Community among faculty and students

Educational aspects

1. Professional stimulation
8. Challenge of my work
13. Ability to help students learn
18. Creativity possible in work
19. Ability with gifted students
21. My sense of accomplishment

24. Amount of autonomy I have
26. Self-esteem as a teacher
28. My professional qualifications
31. Amount of responsibility I have
32. My professional competence
33. My interest in my work

Political climate

15. School's academic philosophy
17. Amount of bureaucracy in school
23. Relationship with principal
30. Principal's philosophy
38. My voice in school affairs
44. Teacher evaluation policy
45. Administration's supervision

Personal rewards

3. My salary
9. Recognition of my teaching
14. Staff development opportunities
16. Recognition of contributed services
22. My benefits
34. Work-family compatibility
39. Advancement opportunities

Teaching factors

5. Students' academic ability
10. Discipline in my classes
12. Size of my classes
36. Class preparation time
37. Ability to work with slow learners

Community support

7. Pastor's interest in the school
27. Parents' support of the school
43. Parish's support of the school

Overall satisfaction

All forty-five satisfaction factors from item 20 on the sample teacher survey

Exhibit 2-18. Attitude Themes for Teachers
(Item numbers are from sample teacher survey)

Need for/importance of Catholic schools

46. Importance of Catholic-educated leaders
47. Essential to Church's educational mission
48. Needed more than 25 years ago

School community

67. Students proud and happy
69. Different backgrounds get along
76. Strong Christian community among faculty and students

Quality/effectiveness of schools

51. School's religious program effective
52. All lay teachers can provide effective Catholic education
54. School has good academic reputation
61. Public views Catholic schools as among best
77. Local community has positive perception of this school
78. School develops awareness of Church's social teachings

Goal consensus

72. School's goals/priorities are clear
74. Most colleagues share vision of school's mission
80. Support principal's vision
81. Parents understand school's mission and philosophy

The principal

58. Supports teachers in discipline
70. Fair assigning responsibilities
71. Effective leader
79. Encourages me to achieve my potential

Financial issues

49. Increase salaries, even if tuition must rise significantly
50. Make personal contributions to support school
53. Diocese should establish endowment fund
63. Paid as much as school can afford
66. Cannot afford to teach in Catholic schools much longer

Teacher self-esteem

55. Important role in students' spiritual development
60. Satisfied with current position
62. Feel respected in society
64. Imam effective
68. Still would choose teaching as career

Governance

56. Teachers have adequate voice
57. Parents should have more voice

Teacher morale

65. Teacher morale is high
73. Teachers continually learn and seek new ideas

Two themes, religious aspects and educational aspects, represent internal sources of satisfaction, which deal with the nature of the work itself. The remaining five themes represent external sources of teacher satisfaction, which are related to the school and its environment. Most research shows that teachers are more satisfied with internal sources than with external sources. In addition to reporting the percentage of teachers who indicated they were satisfied or very satisfied with each satisfaction item by teacher type (religious, lay Catholic, and non-Catholic) and primary orientation (mission, professional, and job), we have found it useful to report the average satisfaction scores for the seven themes and the overall satisfaction score.

❖ **Serious threats.** We suggest a table showing the factors that the different groups of teach-ers identified as serious threats to their continuation at their schools (item 21 on the sample teacher survey). A composite picture of the results of the teachers surveyed in our previous studies in Boston, Brooklyn, Corpus Christi, Honolulu, Providence, and Washington indicated that no serious threat existed for about 50 percent of the teachers, while salary was a serious threat for between 25 and 33 percent.

❖ **Attitudes and opinions.** In addition to displaying the mean scores and the percentage of teachers who strongly agree with the items concerning attitudes and opinions (items 46 to 81 on the sample teacher survey), we suggest reporting the average agreement rating for the themes shown in Exhibit 2-18 (see Exhibit 2-19).

Exhibit 2-19. Sample Display for Selected Attitudes of Teachers

Average Agreement by Elementary School Teachers on Selected Issues

Group	Principal Supports Teachers' Discipline	Principal Fairly Assigns Respons	Principal Effective Leader	Principal Encourages My Potential
Religious	3.45	3.50	3.50	3.64
Number	166	167	165	165
Strongly agree	56.6%	56.9%	60.0%	68.5%
SA or agree	89.8%	94.0%	91.5%	95.8%
SD or disagree	1.2%	1.2%	1.2%	.6%
Lay Catholics	3.36	3.30	3.31	3.45
Number	1459	1461	1460	1458
Strongly agree	48.8%	42.6%	45.7%	53.3%
SA or agree	89.7%	89.5%	88.6%	93.6%
SD or disagree	2.9%	2.2%	3.5%	1.5%
Non-Catholics	3.24	3.36	3.35	3.48
Number	55	55	55	54
Strongly agree	43.6%	47.3%	54.5%	61.1%
SA or agree	83.6%	90.9%	85.5%	90.7%
SD or disagree	3.6%	1.8%	5.5%	3.7%
Mean	3.37	3.32	3.33	3.47
Number	1709	1713	1709	1707
Strongly agree	49.7%	44.2%	47.5%	55.1%
SA or agree	89.6%	90.2%	88.9%	93.7%
SD or disagree	2.7%	2.0%	3.3%	1.5%

Exhibit 2-20. Attributions for Student Success (Item numbers are from sample teacher survey)	
Student	**Teacher**
36. Family environment	41. Effective teaching
37. Economic situation	42. Enthusiasm and perseverance
38. Intellectual ability	43. Willingness to give extra help
39. Enthusiasm and perseverance	44. Attention to student's talent/interest
40. Work habits and interests	45. Knowledge of subject matter

Exhibit 2-21. Teacher Instructional Goals (Item numbers are from sample teacher survey)	
Religious	**Academic**
27. Church participation/Catholic doctrine	29. Critical thinking skills
30. Spiritual development	32. Academic/basic skills
34. Moral/religious values	
Personal	**Social**
31. Growth and fulfillment	28. Human relations/understanding
33. Work habits/self-discipline	35. Citizenship

❖ **Attributions for student success.** We suggest a table that shows, for elementary school teachers and for secondary school teachers, the average importance rating given to student factors and teacher factors (see Exhibit 2-20) and the percentage of teachers that rated a factor as most important and as among the three most important reasons for student success (items 36 to 45 on the sample teacher survey).

❖ **Instructional goals.** We suggest tables that show the average ranking for each instructional goal given in Exhibit 2-21 and the percentage of teachers that rated a goal as most important and as among the three most important in their teaching (items 27 to 35 on the sample teacher survey) for the following groups (see Exhibit 2-22):

   ❖ All elementary school teachers with separate

tabulations for religious, lay Catholic, non-Catholic teachers

❖ All high school teachers with separate tabulations for religious, lay Catholic, non-Catholic teachers

❖ High school teachers grouped by major teaching responsibility (religion, English/language, social studies, math/science, other—item 14 on the sample teacher survey)

In our previous studies, the four personal instructional goals ordinarily designated as most important by the greatest number of elementary school teachers were developing moral and religious values, fostering the personal growth and fulfillment of students, developing academic skills, and assisting with the spiritual development of the students. The four goals ordinarily ranked as most important by the greatest number of high school teachers were fostering personal growth and fulfillment, developing academic skills, developing critical thinking skills, and developing moral and religious values.

Principal Survey

Audience

All principals should be invited to complete a survey, which should be done anonymously.

Content

The principal survey should include demographic information about the principals and their attitudes and opinions concerning their reasons for working in a Catholic school, their style of administration, their satisfaction, the goals for their schools, and the key issues being addressed by the planning study. A sample copy of a principal survey that we have used in previous studies is included in Appendix D.

❖ The **demographic information** from the principals should include at least the following:

- ❖ Employment status, religion, and state in life
- ❖ Race/ethnicity, sex, and age
- ❖ Level of education and educational background in Catholic schools
- ❖ Type of school they administer and their certification status
- ❖ Their tenure in Catholic schools and in other schools
- ❖ Recency of formal graduate coursework and professional updating

Exhibit 2-22. Sample Display of Teacher Rankings of Goals

	Most Important				Among Top Three			
	All	**Rel**	**Lay C**	**Non-C**	**All**	**Rel**	**Lay C**	**Non-C**
Elementary School Teachers								
Moral/Religious Values	30%	43%	29%	18%	64%	79%	63%	53%
Personal Growth	26%	15%	26%	28%	55%	46%	56%	55%
Academic Skills	16%	0%	18%	18%	44%	14%	47%	51%
Self-Discipline	4%	3%	4%	6%	33%	18%	34%	41%
Spiritual Development	7%	21%	6%	8%	33%	70%	30%	24%
Critical Thinking	5%	2%	5%	12%	22%	11%	23%	31%
Catholic Doctrine	9%	16%	8%	4%	26%	46%	24%	24%
Human Relationships	4%	0%	4%	8%	16%	11%	17%	18%
Citizenship	1%	1%	1%	2%	7%	7%	7%	8%
High School Teachers								
Personal Growth	29%	25%	31%	31%	58%	53%	61%	49%
Moral/Religious Values	18%	30%	14%	9%	45%	61%	40%	24%
Critical Thinking	14%	9%	15%	22%	44%	31%	47%	64%
Academic Skills	15%	9%	17%	20%	44%	29%	50%	51%
Self-Discipline	6%	4%	6%	9%	38%	28%	42%	51%
Spiritual Development	9%	15%	8%	7%	32%	55%	24%	16%
Human Relationships	4%	1%	5%	2%	19%	18%	19%	27%
Citizenship	1%	0%	1%	0%	8%	4%	9%	13%
Catholic Doctrine	4%	8%	3%	0%	12%	22%	9%	4%

❖ The principals' **attitudes and opinions** should gauge at least the following:

- ❖ Reasons for working in a Catholic school
- ❖ Satisfaction with their present situation
- ❖ Any serious threats to their remaining in the schools
- ❖ Importance of religion in their lives
- ❖ Relationships between faculty and administrators
- ❖ Goals and priorities of their schools
- ❖ Strengths and weaknesses of their schools
- ❖ Importance placed on various administrative roles
- ❖ Need for and importance of Catholic schools
- ❖ Perceived effectiveness and quality of Catholic schools
- ❖ Financial support of Catholic schools
- ❖ Governance of Catholic schools

Analysis and Report of Results

We suggest that the data be analyzed and reported separately for elementary school principals and secondary school principals. The diocesan planning committee may also want to analyze the data separately for principals from religious congregations and for lay principals.

The basic report should begin with a demographic profile of the principals, followed by sections dealing with (1) the factors that influenced their decisions to work at their schools; (2) their satisfaction with various aspects of their work; (3) the factors that constituted serious threats to their continuing at their schools; (4) their attitudes and opinions concerning various issues pertaining to the study; (5) their administrative priorities; and (6) instructional goals they want to emphasize in their schools.

❖ **Demographic profile.** The planning committee should prepare a table containing the percentage of all principals, elementary school principals, and secondary school principals with regard to the demographic information requested above.

❖ **Reasons for working in a Catholic school.** In this section, it is helpful to classify the principals into three orientation groups based on their identification of the most important reason for working in the school.

❖ A table should show the percentage of lay principals and those from religious congregations in each of three basic orientation groups. The orientation groups are the same

Exhibit 2-23. Primary Orientation Groups for Principals (Item numbers are from sample principal survey)		
Mission-related	**Profession-related**	**Job-related**
1. Commitment to Catholic education	2. Professional qualifications	4. Salary offered
3. Administration ministry	8. Teachers' influence	7. Only administrative position available
5. Faith witness	13. Social environment	10. Gain experience
6. Catholic environment	15. Work with young	12. Schedule compatible with family situation
9. Student spiritual development	16. Interest in administration	14. Benefits
11. Community assignment	20. Personal growth	17. School request
18. Share values	21. School's academic philosophy	22. Close to home
19. God's choice	26. School's size	25. Contribute to household income
23. Catholic school background		27. Alternative to public school
24. School's religious philosophy		

as defined for the teachers (confer Exhibit 2-13) and are defined by item 16 on the sample principal survey as shown in Exhibit 2-23.

❖ **Satisfaction.** We have found it useful to group the satisfaction items for principals into four themes as shown in Exhibit 2-24 and to report

Exhibit 2-24. Satisfaction Themes for Principals

Professional abilities/personal traits

6. Hiring teachers
14. Managing the school
19. Supervising teachers
21. Sense of accomplishment
23. Working with parents
25. Public relations skills
27. Implementing Catholic vision
30. Helping students grow spiritually
31. Self-esteem as administrator
33. Professional preparation
35. Disciplining students
38. Interest in work
40. Work with groups
46. Comfort with religion
49. Helping teachers grow spiritually
50. Financial expertise
51. Ability to get things done
52. Professional qualifications
53. Problem-solving ability

Job characteristics

1. Professional stimulation
8. Challenge of work
9. Recognition of my talents
16. Recognition of my contributed services
18. Creativity possible
29. Autonomy
34. Recognition of my ministerial role
36. Amount of my responsibilities
37. My influence in the parish
41. Time required
42. My influence on the curriculum
43. My influence on school affairs
44. Opportunity for advancement

School structure/characteristics

2. Discipline in the school
4. Relationships with students
5. Students' academic ability
11. Relationships with teachers
12. Size of the classes
15. School's academic philosophy
20. Communication in the school
26. Expertise of the teachers
28. Achievements of the students
45. Attitudes of the students
47. Community among faculty/students
54. School's religious philosophy

External contextual factors

3. My salary
7. Pastor's interest in the school
10. Relationships with parents
13. Relationships with diocesan personnel
17. Diocesan bureaucracy
22. My benefits
24. Paperwork required by diocese
32. Parents' support of the school
39. Services of Catholic school department
48. Parish's support of the school

Exhibit 2-25. Attitude Themes for Principals
(Item numbers are from sample principal survey)

Need for/importance of Catholic schools

33. Essential to Church's educational mission
34. Needed more than 25 years ago

School community

52. Students proud and happy
54. Different backgrounds get along
61. Strong Christian community among faculty and students

Quality/effectiveness of schools

36. School's religious program effective
37. All lay teachers can provide effective Catholic education
39. School has good academic reputation
44. School adequate in recruiting students
46. Public views Catholic schools as among best
62. Local community has positive perception of this school
63. School develops awareness of Church's social teachings
64. School has good public relations program

Goal consensus

57. School's goals/priorities are clear
59. Most faculty share my vision of school's mission
68. Communicated vision of school's mission to faculty
69. Parents understand school's mission and philosophy

Principal's self-esteem

45. Satisfied with current position
47. Feel respected in society
53. Still would choose education as career

Financial issues

35. Make personal contributions to support school
38. Diocese establish endowment fund
48. Paid as much as school can afford
51. Cannot afford to work in Catholic schools much longer
67. Salary adequate in light of school's circumstances
70. Increase teacher salaries, even if tuition increases significantly

Principal's role

40. Important role in students' spiritual development
43. Support teachers in discipline
49. Effective administrator
55. Fair assigning responsibilities
56. Effective leader
65. Important job: promote school's philosophy, vision, purpose
66. School quality depends primarily on principal's coordination/planning

Governance

41. Teachers have adequate voice
42. Parents should have more voice

Teacher morale

50. Teacher morale is high
58. Teachers continually learn and seek new ideas

Exhibit 2-26. Principal's Administrative Priorities	
Manager	**Instructional leader**
18. Managing the school on a daily basis 22. Managing the school's resources	21. Providing staff development opportunities 23. Supervising the instructional program 25. Developing the curriculum
Community builder	**Promoter**
19. Building community among staff and students 20. Motivating the staff to excel	24. Working with parents 26. Promoting school in parish and community

the percentage of elementary school principals and secondary school principals who indicated they were satisfied or very satisfied with each item, as well as their average satisfaction scores for each item and for each theme. The diocesan planning committee may find it helpful also to analyze the responses of lay principals and those from religious communities separately.

❖ **Serious threats.** We suggest a table showing the factors that the different groups of principals identified as serious threats to their continued employment at the school (item 28 on the sample principal survey).

❖ **Attitudes and opinions.** In addition to displaying the mean scores and the percentage of principals who strongly agree with each of the items concerning attitudes and opinions (items 33 to 70 on the sample principal survey), we suggest reporting the average agreement rating for each of the themes shown in Exhibit 2-25.

❖ **Administrative priorities.** We suggest a table showing the percentage of principals from various groups (elementary-secondary; religious-lay; boys-girls-coed schools; private-diocesan schools) that rated an activity as most important, as well as the average ranking for each activity. Exhibit 2-26 shows a classification scheme for the activities, which may be helpful in making comparisons between groups of principals.

❖ **Instructional goals.** We suggest tables that show the average ranking for each goal and the percentage of principals that rated a goal as most important and as among the three most important for the students in their schools for the following groups:

- ❖ All elementary school principals, with separate tabulations for religious principals and lay principals
- ❖ All high school principals, with separate tabulations for
  - ❖ Religious principals and lay principals
  - ❖ Boys' schools, girls' schools, and coed schools
  - ❖ Privately owned schools and diocesan-owned schools

Gathering Other Resources

In addition to compiling statistics about the schools, the diocesan planning committee and study team should review long-range planning efforts of other dioceses, practices of other dioceses that might be helpful, and research on the effectiveness of Catholic schools.

The experiences of other dioceses regarding their policies for schools can provide very useful information for the diocesan planning committee. For example, at the time of the Washington elementary school study, the Archdiocese of Baltimore was conducting a study of school financing. Baltimore's experiences were helpful in planning the study for Washington. In addition, examination of practices in Philadelphia, Cleveland, Arlington, and

Youngstown provided helpful information. Furthermore, our experience in working with the Dioceses of Baltimore, Boston, Brooklyn, Corpus Christi, Honolulu, Providence, and Washington has indicated that, despite differences in size, location, and tradition, strikingly similar issues confronted the schools in these dioceses. Chapters 4 and 6 contain more information on these similarities.

Another source of invaluable information for the diocesan planning committee and study team is the research and popular literature on effective schools in general and on Catholic schools in particular. A well-designed strategic planning study should provide for the review and synthesis of, at a minimum, the research on Catholic schools recently completed under the auspices of the National Catholic Educational Association, the federal government, and other sources. Exhibits 2-27, 2-28, and 2-29 list some references that may be helpful.

Exhibit 2-27. Recommended Reviews of Research

Convey, J. J. 1989. "Catholic Schools, Research On." In *The New Catholic Encyclopedia*, Vol. 18, ed. B. Marthaler, 73-78. Palatine, Ill.: Jack Heraty and Associates.

Convey, J. J. 1991. "Catholic Schools in a Changing Society: Past Accomplishments and Future Challenges." In *The Catholic School and Society*. Washington, D.C.: National Catholic Educational Association.

Convey, J. J. 1992. *Catholic Schools Make a Difference: Twenty-Five Years of Research*. Washington, D.C.: National Catholic Educational Association.

Greeley, A. M. 1989. "My Research on Catholic Schools." *Chicago Studies* 28:245-263.

Exhibit 2-28. Research Studies from NCEA

Benson, P. L., R. J. Yeager, P. K. Wood, M. J. Guerra., and B. V. Manno. 1986. *Catholic High Schools: Their Impact on Low-Income Students*. Washington, D.C.: National Catholic Educational Association.

Benson, P. L., and M. J. Guerra. 1985. *Sharing the Faith: The Beliefs and Values of Catholic High School Teachers*. Washington, D.C.: National Catholic Educational Association.

Bryk, A. S., P. B. Holland, V. E. Lee, and R. A. Carriedo. 1984. *Effective Catholic Schools: An Exploration*. Washington, D.C.: National Catholic Educational Association.

Guerra, M. J., M. J. Donahue, and P. Benson. 1990. *The Heart of the Matter: Effects of Catholic High Schools on Student Values, Beliefs and Behaviors*. Washington, D.C.: National Catholic Educational Association.

Harkins, W. 1993. *Introducing the Catholic Elementary School Principal: What Principals Say About Themselves, Their Values, Their Schools*. Washington, D.C.: National Catholic Educational Association.

Kushner, R., and M. Helbling. 1995. *The People Who Work There: The Report of the Catholic Elementary School Teacher Survey*. Washington, D.C.: National Catholic Educational Association.

O'Brien, J. S. 1987. *Mixed Messages: What Bishops and Priests Say About Catholic Schools*. Washington, D.C.: National Catholic Educational Association.

Sebring, P. A., and E. M. Camburn. 1992. *A Profile of Eighth Graders in Catholic Schools*. Washington, D.C.: National Catholic Educational Association.

Yeager, R. J., P. L. Benson, M. J. Guerra, and B. V. Manno. 1985. *The Catholic High School: A National Portrait*. Washington, D.C.: National Catholic Educational Association.

Summary

In this chapter we have described five types of data we believe are necessary for good planning: enrollment data, demographic data and projections, financial data, staffing data, and attitude and opinion data. The close study of these data and their appropriate displays will help all involved in the study gain insight into the type of recommendations needed to ensure the future stability of the schools. In addition, the gathering of data concerning attitudes and opinions enables parents, priests, principals, and teachers to participate more fully in the study and, it is hoped, to develop a greater commitment to the recommendations ultimately adopted by the bishop.

The next chapter describes two major meetings, the problem element meeting and solution element meeting, which also produce essential data.

Exhibit 2-29. Selected Other Primary Research Studies

Bryk, A. S., V. E. Lee, and P. B. Holland. 1993. *Catholic Schools and the Common Good.* Cambridge, Mass.: Harvard University Press.

Chubb, J. E., and T. M. Moe. 1988. "Politics, Markets, and the Organization of Schools." *American Political Science Review* 82:1055-1087.

Cibulka, J. G., T. J. O'Brien, and D. Zewe. 1982. *Inner-City Private Elementary Schools.* Milwaukee: Marquette University Press.

Coleman, J. S., T. Hoffer, and S. Kilgore. 1982. *High School Achievement: Public, Catholic, amd Private Schools Compared.* New York: Basic Books.

Coleman, J. S., and T. Hoffer. 1987. *Public and Private High Schools: The Impact of Communities.* New York: Basic Books.

Flynn, M. 1993. *The Culture of Catholic Schools.* Homebush, New South Wales: St. Paul Publications.

Greeley, A. M. 1982. *Catholic High Schools and Minority Students.* New Brunswick: Transaction Books.

Riordan, C. 1990. *Girls and Boys in School: Together or Separate?* New York: Teachers College Press.

Tarr, H. C., M. J. Ciriello, and J. J. Convey. 1993. "Commitment and Satisfaction Among Parochial School Teachers: Findings from Catholic Education." *Journal of Research on Christian Education* 2:41-63.

Vitullo-Martin, T. 1979. *Catholic Inner-City Schools: The Future.* Washington, D.C.: United States Catholic Conference.

CHAPTER 3
Problem and Solution Elements

Chapter Objectives

In this chapter you will learn the following:

1. What a problem element meeting and a solution element meeting are and why they are important

2. What the nominal group process is and how to conduct it

3. How to prepare for the problem element meeting and the solution element meeting, including a description of the specific materials you will need

4. How to conduct the problem element meeting and the solution element meeting, including guidelines for forming the groups and for training the facilitators needed for the groups

5. How to analyze and use the data from the problem element meeting and the solution element meeting, including how to prepare taxonomies that summarize the results from each meeting

Introduction

Once the preliminary data are assembled, the diocesan planning committee gathers qualitative data from stakeholders and encourages vital involvement from them in the study. To accomplish these objectives, the diocesan planning committee conducts the study's two major input meetings: the problem element meeting and the solution element meeting. This chapter details these meetings, the preparation for them, types of participants, the processes used, and the treatment of the qualitative data collected.

The objectives of this problem-solution element phase of the planning study are as follows:

❖ To inform and build interest in the study by inviting key individuals from all parishes and schools in the diocese

❖ To assist in the definition of the issues to be examined

❖ To determine the perceived problems and difficulties facing the schools

❖ To obtain suggested solutions to identified problems

To accomplish these objectives, the diocesan planning committee arranges two special all-day meetings. The first meeting, the problem element meeting, focuses on issues, concerns, and problems facing Catholic education in the diocese. The second meeting, the solution element meeting, concentrates on surfacing potential answers, responses, and solutions to the identified problems. Instrumental to the success of these meetings is a highly structured agenda that includes large and small group work. Within the small groups, the nominal group process fosters a creative dynamic to generate ideas.

General Preparation

The problem element and solution element meetings require extensive preparation because of the number of participants, the nature of the group work, and the tight agendas. In addition to deciding upon the site or sites and making arrangements for food at the meeting, the diocesan planning committee identifies the participants and places them into groups, arranges for facilitators, and prepares the materials needed at the meeting. Exhibit 3-1 provides an overview of the activities that must be accomplished before the meetings. Generally, the project director handles these details.

Participants

The problem element meeting and the solution element meeting each gather representatives from the entire diocese. In particular, the diocesan planning committee ensures that every parish has representation. Specifically, the committee or project director informs every pastor about the meetings and invites him to attend with at least one representative of his parish who has an interest in Catholic schools. This person often is a parent with children in Catholic school or a member of the education committee of the parish. The committee invites the principals of the schools of the diocese and one teacher from each school. It may also decide to invite representatives of various diocesan organizations, representatives of religious congregations, task force chairpersons and members, and prominent area educators. See Exhibit 3-2 for a suggested process for inviting participants.

Before the meeting, the project director groups the attendees into relevant constituency groups. Usually, there are at least three groups: (1) clergy, (2) educators (sometimes principals and teachers are identified separately), and (3) lay representatives (perhaps parents, board members, and parish representatives). Sometimes other groups—representing a specific subgroup, such as religious education administrators, religious community representatives, or diocesan personnel/officials—are treated as a separate constituency. The project director prepares a color-coded name card designating the appropriate constituency group for each person coming to the meeting.

The project director asks all participants to pre-register. Prior to the meeting, the project director prearranges small groups (ideally about ten in number) to encourage persons to talk across constituencies and among parishes. The following principles govern the formation of groups:

❖ Balance group membership with a proportionate number of clergy, educators, and parish representatives.

❖ Place persons from the same parish in different groups. If possible, avoid having two individuals from the same parish in a group.

❖ Plan for group sizes ranging from eight to twelve participants. No group should have more than twelve participants.

❖ If for some reason a group has six or fewer participants, absorb it into other groups.

❖ If there is more than one site, keep the process for each site separate and intact.

Exhibit 3-1. Arrangements for the Problem Element Meeting

❖ Decide on site(s)
  ❖ Decide on the room assignment for the small group sessions

❖ Order food for the meeting
  ❖ Coffee and donuts at registration
  ❖ Lunch
  ❖ Optional: afternoon break
  ❖ Optional: facilitator refreshments (in appreciation)

❖ Send letters inviting participants
  ❖ Arrange for small group facilitators
  ❖ Recruit persons (one for every ten participants)
  ❖ Send a letter to begin orientation

❖ Prepare supplies for small group process

❖ Prepare the composition of the small groups

❖ Prepare materials needed by participants at the meeting

❖ Arrange to have all materials transported to site(s)

Exhibit 3-2. Process for Inviting Parish Participants

❖ Send a letter to every pastor and every principal of a school that is not attached to a parish to notify them of the purpose, date, time, and place of the meeting and ask them to respond with the names of the persons who will be attending the meeting

  ❖ Ask pastors with a school to attend with his school principal, a teacher from the school, and a lay representative from the parish. This representative may be a member of the parish planning committee.

  ❖ Ask each pastor without a school to attend with two lay representatives from the parish.

  ❖ Ask each principal of a school not attached to a parish to attend with a teacher and a parent from the school. The parent might be a board member, officer of the parent organization, or a member of the school planning committee.

❖ Include a response card that will include spaces for the names of those persons who will be attending.

<u>Sample Reply Card</u>   Please reply by _____.

Participants for the Problem Element Meeting
(Date) (Time)

Name of Parish or School _____

(If applicable) We will attend the meeting at _____(site)

Pastor_____

Principal_____

Teacher _____

Lay Representative_____

Lay Representative_____

❖ Request reply return at least three weeks before the meeting so you have adequate time to arrange the groups.

Exhibit 3-3 contains a specific procedure for placing participants into groups.

Nominal Group Process

The group process technique suggested is the nominal group process, which was developed by Andre Delbecq and Andrew Van de Ven of the School of Business at the University of Wisconsin (Delbecq and Van de Ven, 1971; Delbecq, Van de Ven, and Gustafson, 1975; Van de Ven and Delbecq, 1971, 1975). The technique involves individual silent effort in a group setting of from eight to twelve individuals, rather than spontaneous group discussion.

The nominal group process is useful for fact-finding, idea-generating, problem definition, goal-setting, solution-finding situations when searching for information from a group of people. The nominal group process has six steps:

❖ Silent general listing of ideas in writing

❖ Round-robin recording of ideas on a chart

❖ Clarification of ideas on the chart

❖ Preliminary vote to prioritize items on the chart

❖ Discussion of results of the preliminary vote

❖ Final independent vote on priorities

Research shows that nominal groups are superior to brainstorming, interacting groups on three criteria: (1) average number of total ideas produced, (2) average number of unique ideas produced, and (3) quality of ideas produced. "Interacting groups often contain inhibitory influences which are not easily dissipated. These influences often result in decreased quality of ideas generated, in terms of creativity, originality, and practicality" (Van de Ven and Delbecq, 1971).

Several reasons exist for the success of nominal groups:

❖ Individual commitment to the search process is enhanced by the presence of others, the silence, and the evidence of activity.

❖ Evaluation or elaboration is avoided while problem dimensions are being generated.

❖ Individuals have time and opportunity to engage in reflection and are required to record their thoughts.

❖ The dominance of strong personality types is avoided.

❖ Premature closure to alternatives is prevented.

Exhibit 3-3. Suggested Process for Group Assignment

❖ Take several sheets of paper—one for each anticipated group. (If you expect 45 people at a site, plan on five groups; 163 people, plan on sixteen groups, and so forth.) Number each paper one to ten.

❖ According to the order of the names on reply cards, fill in all groups simultaneously (add the second-named persons to groups before adding the third-named persons, etc.). This will facilitate keeping the numbers and the distribution of parishes and constituencies even.

  ❖ Assign all clergy first:
    ❖ Write the name of the priest and his parish on the first line of each group list in turn.
    ❖ As you place the person in the group, put the assigned group number *on the registration reply card* beside the person's name.
    ❖ Prepare an appropriately colored name card with the name, parish, and the assigned group number on it.

  ❖ Using the same process, go back through all reply cards a second time to assign all educators, trying to ensure that the educator is in a different group than the pastor of his or her parish. (The number you wrote on the reply card will help you.)

  ❖ Go through the cards a third time to assign all parish representatives, repeating the above procedures and watching that no persons from the same parish are in the same group.

  ❖ If necessary, after all reply cards are assigned, go through and fill in groups by randomly assigning planning committee members and any others who are coming to the meeting but not as part of a particular parish/school contingent or a specific constituency.

❖ After completing group assignments and precoding name cards, type separate lists (in triplicate) of the persons assigned to each small group.
  ❖ Copy 1 is for your records.
  ❖ Copy 2 is for the on-site coordinator to help with directions and in case someone must be located in an emergency.
  ❖ Copy 3 is for the small group leader to take attendance.

❖ Label the top of each small group list with
  ❖ Group number
  ❖ Meeting room number
  ❖ Site (if applicable)

- All participants share in the opportunity to influence group decisions.

- The generation of minority opinions and ideas is encouraged; consequently, these are more likely to be voiced.

- Conflicting and incompatible ideas are tolerated since all ideas are recorded.

- The process induces a sense of responsibility in the members to achieve group success.

- The process imposes a burden upon all participants to work and produce their share.

- Because all ideas are recorded rather than just spoken, a greater feeling of commitment and permanence results.

Meeting Preparations

Facilitators

Critical to the success of both meetings is the recruitment of an adequate number of facilitators who conduct the small group sessions. Since each facilitator is responsible for one group, approximately one facilitator will be needed for every ten participants. Project directors can often recruit facilitators from among the faculties of diocesan elementary and/or secondary schools or parish staff personnel. Depending on the location, local college and university students may also be possible recruits. Appendix E contains a sample letter that may be used to recruit facilitators.

The basic task of a facilitator is to lead the group through the nominal group process. The facilitators do not enter into the process by offering ideas themselves; rather they moderate the generation of ideas in the group. The process at the problem element meeting is deliberately paced so that the participants can become familiar and comfortable with the process. The solution element meeting is more demanding because the participants are required to address several issues in a more rapid fashion. The major responsibilities of a facilitator in a nominal group process are to

- Keep the group on task and on schedule

- Record group-generated ideas

- Report group priorities to the final large group session

For the process to be implemented effectively, the facilitators must be trained before each meeting. We suggest that the diocesan planning committee or project director arrange that the facilitators

- Receive a copy of the appropriate small group facilitator guide for either the problem element meeting (Appendix F) or the solution element meeting (Appendix G) at least one week before the meeting

- Attend a brief training session on the morning of the meeting day

Ordinarily, a thirty- to forty-five-minute session before the formal registration time on the meeting day is sufficient to inform the leaders about the purpose and steps of the process. The project director also provides all instructions in writing. During the training session it is important to caution the facilitators to resist the pressure from the group to combine items. This is an important point because the quality of data depends on the members of the groups making distinctions between equally desirable ideas. Groups frequently try to circumvent the making of clear choices by combining several loosely connected ideas. It is not appropriate for a facilitator to have any other responsibility (e.g., registration, greeter) because the responsibility of the small group is very demanding and often the training session is held concurrently with registration.

Site Arrangements

An ideal size for these group meetings is around two hundred participants at one site. Such a number allows for about twenty small groups. Therefore, depending on the number of people invited and the capacity of the meeting places, one or several sites might be necessary. Washington, Corpus Christi, and Baltimore required one site; Providence had two sites. Because of the size of each diocese, four meetings were held simultaneously in Boston and Brooklyn. Four meetings were held in the Diocese of Honolulu because of the unique geography of Hawaii.

The project director chooses a facility that can accommodate a large group meeting and enough small group areas, usually separate classrooms, to allow each small group a private place to work. This is usually a high school or a large grade school with auditorium and/or cafeteria space for the large group gatherings, as well as several classrooms (one for every ten to twelve people).

Since these meetings are scheduled to last several hours, the project director provides for snacks and lunch. Depending on local custom, coffee and rolls are usually provided at the time of registration.

Exhibit 3-4. Supplies Needed for Meetings

General

❖ *Name cards:* Two for each participant per meeting. Decide on the colors to be used by each group: clergy, red; educator, blue; lay representative, yellow; other participants (group leaders, observers, bishop, steering committee), a fourth color.

❖ *Index cards:*
  ❖ 5"x8" cards in separate colors to match name cards. Allow ten to fifteen per participant in the appropriate color.
  ❖ 5"x8" white cards for group summaries. Allow eight per leader.
  ❖ 3"x5" white cards. Allow at least five per participant.

Group Leader Supplies (Eight to Twelve to a Group)

❖ *Problem element meeting:* For each group, assemble the following supplies:

  ❖ Ten flip chart/newsprint sheets rolled and fastened with a rubber band.
  ❖ In a plastic bag (such as a zip lock freezer bag or baggie), the following supplies:
    ❖ Wide nib magic marker in black
    ❖ Wide nib marker in red
    ❖ Roll of masking tape
    ❖ Pencils (three to four per group in case someone comes without one)
    ❖ Rubber bands (five or six)
    ❖ Counted-out index cards:
      ❖ Twelve 3"x5" white cards (one per participant)
      ❖ Ten 5"x8" cards in each of the three colors (thirty colored cards total; this allows for at least two cards per person in the appropriate color)
      ❖ Two white 5"x8" cards for the leader's summary

❖ *Solution element meeting:* For each group, assemble the following supplies:

  ❖ Forty flip chart/newsprint sheets rolled and fastened with a rubber band
  ❖ In a plastic bag (such as a zip lock freezer bag or baggie), the following supplies:
    ❖ Wide nib magic marker in black
    ❖ Wide nib marker in red
    ❖ Roll of masking tape
    ❖ Pencils
    ❖ Rubber bands (five or six)
    ❖ Index cards:
      ❖ Thirty-six 3"x5" white cards (one per participant per topic); this allows for a group of twelve addressing three topics
      ❖ Thirty-six 5"x8" cards in each of the three colors
      ❖ Six white 5"x8" cards for the leader's summary

Provision for a simple lunch that can be served to the entire group in fifteen to twenty minutes is adequate. Some dioceses contract the cafeteria services of the site school; others have engaged caterers who provide buffet-style serving or box lunches.

Two other arrangements are optional and have varied with location. Some dioceses have made snacks available during the breaks and have provided, at the end of the day, light refreshments to acknowledge the valuable services of the volunteer facilitators.

Materials

The large group meeting and small group process require specific materials. At registration, the project director provides each person with the following:

- A pre-coded name card
- An agenda
- A map of the building
- A packet of data containing important information about the status of the schools in the diocese

The small group process requires the following:

- Colored 5"x8" index cards
- White 3"x5" index cards
- Large charts of newsprint
- Magic markers and masking tape

See Exhibit 3-4 for a detailed description of the supplies needed for the meetings.

The Day of the Meetings

A staff member from the Catholic school office acts as the on-site coordinator to ensure that all personnel and materials are delivered and in place for that day. One coordinator is needed for each site. Exhibit 3-5 shows the activities that the coordinator should oversee. Appendix H contains a checklist for use by the on-site coordinator.

The Problem Element Meeting

The problem element meeting has four major objectives:

- To inform the participants about the long-range planning study

- To review with them the relevant data about the schools
- To determine their understanding of the problems and difficulties that face the schools now and in the future
- To identify the most important problems and concerns that face the schools.

Exhibit 3-6 provides a typical agenda for the problem element meeting.

Format

The problem element meeting, which lasts approximately five hours, begins with a large group meeting in which a formal presentation is made that includes a description of the design of the study and a presentation of the preliminary data that the diocesan planning committee has gathered. The presentation team emphasizes data on enrollment, finances, staffing, population demographics, and projections and results of any surveys that have been administered up to this point. Ordinarily, the project director provides each participant with a handout that contains tables of enrollment and financial data for each school, graphs depicting enrollment trends, demographic projections, and other relevant data.

After data are presented, the presentation team explains how the nominal group process will proceed in the small groups. This explanation stresses two important points:

- The process was designed to surface many varied ideas from different perspectives, rather than achieving consensus or convincing others of a particular viewpoint.

- No idea written legibly on a card will be lost. All ideas will become part of the analysis report. Therefore, a spirit of cooperation and communication rather than competition is appropriate within the group.

The participants then go to their assigned groups of between eight and twelve individuals, which normally meet in separate rooms in the facility at which the meeting is held. The groups proceed in the following manner:

- A trained facilitator in each group begins the nominal group process by asking each participant to think about and write responses to the focus question: *What problems, concerns, or issues need to be addressed in the course of this planning study for the Catholic schools of the diocese?*

❖ The facilitator distributes to each member of the group a color-coded index card that corresponds to the name card color of the constituency: clergy, educators, parents/parish representatives, board members, others. These colored index cards differentiate the opinions of the individuals from a specific constituency, which enables analysis of their comments. The

---

Exhibit 3-5. On-Site Meeting Arrangements

1. *Registration set up*

   ❖ Arrange and label areas [tables?] for
     ❖ Clergy
     ❖ Educators
     ❖ Parish lay representatives
     ❖ Group leaders
     ❖ If necessary, the bishop, planning committee, task forces, and others

   ❖ Arrange name cards in alphabetical order by separate groups

   ❖ Provide, for each participant, at the registration table
     ❖ A prenumbered, color-coded name card
     ❖ The agenda for the meeting
     ❖ The map of the school on the opposite side of the agenda (Ensure the small group areas are clearly designated on the map.)
     ❖ The preliminary data assembled by the diocesan planning committee

2. *Training site for group facilitators*

   ❖ Arrange for a designated area that is quiet and private
   ❖ Have the folder and supplies available
   ❖ Prepare a folder to include
     ❖ A list of the persons assigned to the small group, labeled by area, group number, and meeting room number
     ❖ Agenda with map
     ❖ Direction sheets for group facilitator process

3. *Large group area*

   ❖ Overhead projector/screen (if needed)
   ❖ Microphone
   ❖ Water for the speaker

4. *Signs*

   ❖ Small group areas
   ❖ Restrooms, cafeteria
   ❖ General directions

5. *Food arrangements*

   ❖ Near registration area
   ❖ Lunch time
   ❖ Optional: at breaks
   ❖ Optional: for facilitators

---

facilitator then reiterates the guidelines of the nominal group process:

- ❖ Work silently and independently
- ❖ List ideas in short phrases, not long paragraphs
- ❖ Push oneself to be creative; early finishers should think harder
- ❖ Resist the temptation to talk to others at this point

❖ After fifteen or twenty minutes, the facilitator solicits in a round-robin style one idea from each individual and writes it in numbered sequence on newsprint in full view. Participants are asked to read the idea from the card without comment. The solicitation continues until all unique ideas have surfaced. On average, each group typically produces forty to sixty ideas.

❖ After all ideas are listed on the newsprint, the facilitator allows a short time, about five minutes, for the participants to ask for clarification of any statement. No discussion is permitted about the merit of an idea at this stage. The facilitator permits only questions of clarification, such as the meaning of terminology.

❖ The groups then break for lunch, at which time the participants usually mingle. It is not unusual for the participants to discuss among themselves what surfaced in each of their groups. This type of discussion is not only permitted, but encouraged, for it can help to stimulate new ideas that the participants may want to share when they return to the small group setting.

❖ After lunch the small groups reconvene to continue the nominal group process. The facilitator asks if anyone from the group would like to add another idea to those listed on the newsprint. Once the list is complete, the facilitator asks each member in the group to list, on a 3"x5" index card, the numbers of the five items he or

---

Exhibit 3-6. Agenda for the Problem Element Meeting

Problem Element Meeting

Diocese of _____ Long-Range Planning Study

[day and date]

AGENDA

9:00 Coffee and registration (pick up materials)

9:20 Large group meeting: Opening prayer, welcome, introductions, housekeeping items

9:45 Introduction of major presenter, overview, purpose of the study, brief presentation of background data, explanation of small group work—nominal group process

10:45 Break

11:00 Small groups—focus question:

What problems, concerns, or issues need to be addressed in the course of this planning study for the Catholic schools of the diocese?

12:15 Lunch

1:15 Return to small group work: Addition of ideas that arose through lunch discussion, establishing priorities, discussion, voting

2:00 Break

2:15 Large group assembly: Small group reports on priorities, description of next phases of study, closing remarks

3:00 Closing prayer

---

she feels are so important that they must be addressed by the study. The facilitator collects these cards and records the votes on the newsprint by placing a tally mark by the statement for each vote that it receives.

❖ The facilitator then allows ten to fifteen minutes for discussion. At this point the participants can interact at a level that has been denied by the process up to this point. Participants are encouraged to lobby for the problems they consider most important and to point out problems that received no votes or just a few votes. But participants are reminded that the purpose of the meeting is to develop an idea bank. Therefore, it is not necessary to come to a consensus on issues or to try to "convert" others to a personal way of thinking.

❖ After the discussion is ended, the facilitator again asks the members of the group to vote for the five statements that each considers the most important. Individuals may vote for the same statements that they voted for on the preliminary vote or they may change their votes. It is important that the facilitator remind the group that votes may be cast for all listed statements, even those with no preliminary votes.

❖ After the final vote is recorded, the facilitator writes on a separate white 5"x8" card the five statements that received the most votes from the group. These more-frequently chosen items become the priority statements for the group,

and they are reported by the facilitator when all groups reassemble.

❖ The facilitator collects all color-coded index cards. All participants then assemble in the large group area. A summary of the work of the individual groups is presented by the small group facilitators who read, in turn and without comment, the results of the final small group vote.

Problem Themes

Two types of data are produced within the small groups:

❖ **Group priority statements,** which identify the five most important problems or concerns that surfaced in each of the groups

❖ **Individual problems and concerns,** listed on the colored cards, which identify all the issues identified by each of the participants at the meeting

After the problem element meeting, the project director or diocesan planning committee classifies the group priority statements into problem themes. In past studies, we have grouped the problem themes according to the types of task forces that typically are needed. Exhibit 3-7 provides an example of the distribution of priority statements for the Diocese of Providence.

The following taxonomy represents a composite of the themes identified by participants at the problem element meetings held in the following

Exhibit 3-7. Distribution of Priority Statements in Providence

Topic	Number	Percent
Catholic identity	20	11%
Finance	56	32%
Governance	24	13%
Curriculum	27	15%
Public relations/marketing	34	19%
Parents/students	17	10%
TOTAL	**178**	**100%**

dioceses: Boston, Brooklyn, Corpus Christi, Honolulu, Providence, and Washington. The themes are presented without regard to the priority accorded to them in each diocese or the frequency with which each was listed by the participants.

A. Catholic identity
Maintenance of Catholic identity
Philosophy/vision/mission
Value of Catholic schools
Religious education/religious formation
Evangelization
Non-Catholic students

B. Financial
Teacher salaries and benefits
Tuition concerns: affordability and burden, impact on enrollment, access to the "poor"
Low financial resources of families
Need for tuition assistance
Need for long-range financial planning
Best use of parish funds
Distribution of diocesan subsidy
Need for active development programs
Renovation/maintenance/capital improvements of facilities
Alternative sources of funding needed
Creative financing lacking
Government assistance

C. School programs
Quality: academic programs/religious education
Curriculum coordination/update/upgrade
Need for enrichment programs
Meeting special needs
Program evaluation and monitoring of quality
Lack of special services
Concern about racism
Concern about safety
More pre-K, K, before- and after-school care programs
Need for better resources
Transportation needs

D. Students
Enrollment concerns
Changing demographics
Inability to serve less-able and special students
Post-school religious behavior/involvement with the Church
Cultural diversity
Non-Catholic students
Service of minority students
Lack of discipline

E. Teachers/administrators
Recruitment of quality staff
Concerns about qualifications: academic and spiritual
Turnover/retention
Morale needs: lack of recognition
Need for uniform salary scale
Staff development and formation needs
Diminished presence of religious
Lack of professionalism
Better teacher/principal evaluation needed
Commitment of teachers to Catholic faith and values
Multicultural awareness and sensitivity
Concerns about job security
Contracts and due process policies

F. Parental involvement
Lack of involvement in school activities
Need to clarify role of parents
Poor religious commitment of parents; need for evangelization
Need for more consultation of parents
Better communication between schools and parents
Reasons for enrolling: safety or evangelization
Special needs of parents who are single, working, non-English speaking
Need to organize for political action
Dysfunctional families

G. Public relations/marketing/development
Lack of good public relations programs
Need to market Catholic schools
Need to develop/utilize methods of communication
Need to update image of Catholic schools
Messages: make all aware of value of Catholic schools
Need greater stress on Christian principles and values
Lack of well-organized development programs
School-to-school relationships
Lack of positive interchange/support with public schools

Lack of awareness of importance of Catholic schools to the community/businesses

H. Governance

Lack of interparish cooperation and sharing

Lack of understanding of different governance models

Understanding parish schools, interparish schools, and regional schools

Need to pool resources at regional level

Role definition: superintendent, pastor, principal, school board

Need to consider possible restructuring of schools/consolidation

Need for collaborative decision-making by stakeholders

Need for strategic planning

Advisory boards for the schools

Distinction between parish, interparish, and regional school boards

I. Parish/pastor

Attitudes of some clergy toward schools

Lack of involvement of some pastors

Relationship between pastor and principal

Pastor/parish commitment to Catholic schools

Parish-school relationships

J. Central office/diocese

Leadership/vision role

Lack of personnel for development and fund raising

Need for long-range planning

Efforts to secure state services/increased political activity

Decision-making in this long-range study

Need for centralized services

K. Secondary schools

Transition from elementary schools to secondary schools

Collaboration versus competition

Need for better communication between elementary schools and high schools

Adding middle schools/junior high grades to high schools

Gender composition

Lack of non-college-prep programs

Lack of student involvement in parish life

Content Analysis of Individual Statements

During the weeks following the problem element meeting, the diocesan planning committee arranges for the identified problems and concerns to be analyzed and classified into relevant categories. The analysis proceeds in the following manner:

1. The problem framework developed from the priority statements forms the framework for the content analysis.

2. The cards from the individuals are sorted into the relevant constituency groups.

3. Each statement on each card is coded according to the major dimension of the problem framework that is used for the particular diocese. Typically, the major dimensions are finance, governance, Catholic identity, curriculum, and marketing and public relations. In some dioceses, other dimensions emerge, such as parental involvement and parish-school relationships.

4. The number of times a particular problem appears is tallied. If the problem is essentially the same as one of the priority statements in the problem framework, the count is recorded after that statement according to constituency group (e.g., clergy-6, educators-23, and so forth). Site information is also provided if multiple sites were used for the meeting. When a problem statement does not match a priority statement in the problem framework, a new entry is made at the most logical placement and the count is recorded as above. Exhibit 3-8 shows the distribution of problem areas from the Diocese of Brooklyn planning study.

5. The committee reports the results of the content analysis in two stages:

❖ A separate problem framework with the appropriate counts for each constituency group. These documents help draw conclusions concerning the emphasis on problem areas within each constituency group and how this emphasis varies across the diocese.

❖ A combined framework with the counts reported by constituency group, but not by site. This document sheds light on the emphasis on problem areas among different groups. Exhibit 3-9 shows a portion of a framework for Providence.

The diocesan planning committee then arranges for the preparation of a booklet of the problem statements for later reference by its members and the task forces. Appendix I contains a complete problem framework for the Diocese of Providence.

The Solution Element Meeting

The solution element meeting brings together the same participants who attended the problem element meeting to review the problems and concerns identified and to suggest possible solutions. The term "solution element" is used to describe the meeting since it is recognized that solutions to complex problems are elusive. Thus, in this meeting, participants are expected to generate ideas and suggestions concerning possible solutions; these ideas and suggestions are later analyzed and synthesized by the task forces and the diocesan planning committee and developed into full-scale plans.

Preparation

All previously noted preparations for the problem element meeting apply to the solution element meeting. A site must be engaged, food must be arranged, the registration must be confirmed, and so forth. It is particularly important to get a firm response from those who plan to attend. The project director must again form small groups. Group membership may be the same as in the problem element meeting. However, registration for the solution element meeting is typically smaller and includes several persons who did not attend the first meeting. This necessitates a reconfiguration of the composition of the groups. Likewise, the project director needs to confirm the availability of facilitators. As many as a fourth of the facilitators may not be able to attend both meetings.

Aside from the organizational concerns of the meeting, the diocesan planning committee and the project director must pay particular attention to the type and quantity of data to be collected. Ordinarily, four to seven themes emerge from the problem data. Time constraints make it impossible for every group to address every theme in detail. Therefore, the project director arranges a system of topic rotation so that a sufficient pool of ideas is generated for each theme. The rotation is accomplished by systematically assigning specific topics to particular groups. Because people often have more energy for the process earlier in the day, it is also a good idea to rotate the sequence in which the topics will be addressed. Exhibit 3-10 illustrates a partial schema used to assign topics and sequences to groups in several sites in Brooklyn. For example, four groups at Xaverian High School, five

Exhibit 3-8. Diocese of Brooklyn Problem Distribution

Diocese of Brooklyn Planning Study
Problem Element Meeting
February 1, 1992
Problem Elements: Composite

	Clergy	Educators	Parents	Relig/Ed	Total	%
Catholic identity	24%	9%	11%	9%	821	11%
Finance	39%	38%	32%	33%	2564	36%
Governance	13%	15%	8%	14%	919	13%
Curriculum	15%	24%	32%	27%	1870	26%
Marketing/PR	4%	5%	7%	4%	384	5%
Parents	4%	7%	9%	5%	494	7%
Parish CCD	1%	1%	1%	8%	147	2%
Total comments	909	2839	2071	1380	7199	100%

groups at Bishop Ford High School, and four groups at St. John's Prep addressed the three topics in Set 1: finance, curriculum, and parent issues, in that order. Other groups at those sites addressed a different set of topics as indicated in Exhibit 3-10.

Format

Exhibit 3-11 shows a sample agenda for the solution element meeting. The meeting begins with a large group meeting at which the findings of the problem element meeting are summarized by themes. As the presentation team summarizes the major problems and concerns, the participants are encouraged to think about their task for the day, which is to address the following question: *What suggestions do you have that would contribute to a plan to alleviate these problems and concerns or would improve the vitality of the schools?*

At this point in the solution element meeting, if time permits, it is helpful to review studies that other dioceses have conducted, present information about practices in other dioceses, and summarize the findings of recent research on the effectiveness of Catholic schools.

At the end of the large group session, the participants assemble in their small groups. Each group employs the same nominal group technique used to identify problem elements to surface solution elements for the themes assigned to it. Generally, the groups can complete an entire prioritization process for three different problem themes.

At the end of the day the participants gather in a large group session to hear the priority solutions generated by selected groups about the range of themes. Closing remarks often apprise the participants of the next phases of the study.

Exhibit 3-9. Portion of a Problem Element Report

Problem Element Statements
Diocese of Providence
January 9, 1993
(C=Clergy; P=Parents/Parish Representatives; E=Educators)
(B= School Board; O=Others)

Catholic Identity

A. Philosophy/mission lacking for Catholic schools as a whole (C-5, P-1)
   1. What are the priorities for parents, teachers, students, and administrators regarding academics, religion, discipline? (C-4, P-2, E-1, O-1)
   2. What is Catholic schools' mission to poor, minorities, and immigrants? (P-2, E-1, O-2)
   3. Church's mission is to teach: what happens if schools close? (P-2)
   4. Future of schools depends upon future of the Church (B-1)
   5. Perception of "escape" to Catholic schools (C-3, P-3)
   6. Lack of harmony between perceptions of parents and students/school and Church as to purpose of Catholic schools (C-1, P-1)
   7. Lack of *vision* common to all schools (C-1, P-4, E-1, O-1)
   8. Lack of mission statement (E-3, B-3)
   9. Other than academics, what does Catholic school offer parents? (B-1)

B. Identity
   1. Are we maintaining our Catholic identity? (C-13, P-23, E-3, B-13, O-5)
   2. Are Catholic values being passed on effectively? (C-2, P-4, E-6, O-2)
   3. Religious instruction must be for all students (P-1, E-1)
   4. Perception that "catholicity" of faculty, parents, students is weak (C-1)
   5. Few religious present in the schools (C-4, P-2, E-6, B-13, O-2)
   6. How to overcome the materialistic, amoral society that we are up against (P-5, E-1)
   7. Parish not involved in Catholic identity of school (B-1)

Exhibit 3-10. Group Topic Assignments

Diocese of Brooklyn Solution Element Meeting
March 16, 1992

Topic/theme sequence		Group assigned by site	
Set 1:	Finance	Set 1:	Xaverian 1-6-11-16
	Curriculum		Bishop Ford 3-8-13-18-22
	Parent Issues		St. John 7-12-17-20
Set 2:	Public Relations	Set 2:	Xaverian 2-7-12-17
	Governance		Bishop Ford 4-9-14-19
	Catholic Identity		St. John 1-5-8-13-18
Set 3:	Curriculum	Set 3:	Xaverian 3-8-13-18
	Public Relations		Bishop Ford 5-10-15-20
	Finance		St. John 2-6-9-14-19
Set 4:	Catholic Identity	Set 4:	Xaverian 4-9-14-19
	Parent Issues		Bishop Ford 1-6-11-16-22
	Governance		St. John 3-10-15-22

Exhibit 3-11. Agenda for the Solution Element Meeting

Solution Element Meeting
Diocese of _____
[day and date]

AGENDA

9:00 Coffee and registration
9:20 Opening prayer, presentation of data summary from the problem element meeting
10:00 Small group work addressing specified topics
12:00 Lunch
1:00 Finish small group work
2:30 Total assembly for closing summary statements

TOPICS

Catholic Identity Finance Curriculum Governance
Parent Issues Public Relations/Marketing

FOCUS QUESTION

Given the problems and concerns identified at the problem element meeting in the area of (*specific topic assigned to the group*), what suggestions do you have that would contribute to a plan

(1) to address and alleviate these problems and concerns, or

(2) to increase the vitality of the schools in the light of these problems and concerns?

Collectively, the groups will generate hundreds of solution elements. In the Washington elementary school study, for example, the following reflect the strongest concurrence among the participants:

❖ The need for strong, widely communicated public statements of philosophy, goals, and values

❖ Support of long-range planning for the continuation of the schools, with strong support for the merger and/or regionalization of schools, if needed and planned for

❖ A clarion call for centralized services, interaction, supervision, and evaluation

❖ The improvement of the quality of education and excellence in the curriculum, especially in the teaching of religion

❖ The need to improve the salaries and benefits for teachers

❖ The institution of comprehensive programs for development and fund raising

❖ The affirmation of parent responsibility and involvement in the schools

As with the data from the problem element meeting, the study team arranges for the classification of the solution elements along thematic lines and the preparation of a report of the content analysis in the form of a booklet for the diocesan planning committee and the task forces. Appendix J contains the complete solution element framework from the Diocese of Providence planning study.

Practical Issues

❖ Both meetings require precise preparation in order for the participants to feel a sense of purposeful participation and to complete the intended agenda.

❖ Although preparation is labor intensive, much of it is mechanical and can be accomplished by a person with a good sense of organization.

❖ Supplies must be ordered well in advance and adequate provision made for the duplication of materials.

❖ The most successful meetings have had virtually all participants preregistered. However, parishes are often slow in responding and may need to be contacted by phone.

❖ A pressing concern is to begin recruiting persons who will be group facilitators well in advance of the meeting. It is not easy to get a firm commitment from people who are volunteering their time on a weekend.

❖ Emergencies often arise, resulting in the inability of one or several facilitators to appear the day of the meeting. Therefore, provisions should be made for substitutes.

❖ In virtually every study, recruiting an adequate number of small group facilitators has been a challenge.

Summary

The problem element meeting and the solution element meeting gather representatives from parishes and schools around the diocese. Both meetings use a nominal group process to gather extensive data from the participants. The problem element meeting serves to inform the participants about the strategic planning study and about the state of the schools. In turn, the participants help to identify the problems facing the schools now and those that will face the schools in the future. At the solution element meeting, the participants identify "elements of solutions" for the various problems identified.

The diocesan planning committee arranges for a content analysis of the data from these two meetings and the production of a booklet containing the problem element statements and one containing the solution element statements. These booklets provide a core set of data for the work of the task forces.

CHAPTER 4
Task Forces

Chapter Objectives

In this chapter you will learn the following:

1. What role task forces play in the strategic planning study and how many task forces are required

2. What specific responsibilities should be assigned to each task force, including the types of questions that each task force might address

3. Who should be recruited to serve on specific task forces

4. How each task force is organized, including a sample charter that outlines the task force's purpose, methodology, and anticipated products

Introduction

The primary purpose of a task force is to develop detailed recommendations for use by the diocesan planning committee in developing the recommendations for the planning study. The task forces are essential to the success of the study. Unlike the diocesan planning committee which must attend to every issue, task forces concentrate on specific areas. Furthermore, while the diocesan planning committee is ordinarily composed of individuals of diverse backgrounds and with varying degrees of knowledge, task force members are chosen for their expertise in the area that they will address.

The work of the task force can last from six to nine months. If the planning study starts during the fall of the year and the problem element meeting is held before February of the following year, a typical schedule would have the task forces forming in February, presenting a preliminary report to the diocesan planning committee in June, and presenting its final report in October.

Each task force accomplishes four tasks:

❖ Studies the data from the problem element meeting and the solution element meeting and defines the major issues that it will address.

❖ Studies a variety of solution possibilities for each major issue, including

  ❖ Proposed solution elements from the solution element meeting

❖ Current practices in the diocese and in other dioceses

❖ Innovative strategies being tested anywhere in the United States or in other countries (including those used by other religious denominations)

❖ Current state-of-the-art thinking about the issue in the scholarly or popular literature

❖ Develops possible solutions for each issue, assessing their strengths and weaknesses, their feasibility for implementation, and their costs and benefits.

❖ Develops recommendations for each major issue and provides a rationale for each recommendation.

Membership

The diocesan planning committee normally compiles an extensive list of potential members to serve on the task forces. Individuals to be considered for particular task forces should have expertise and experience in a specified area and should be interested in the future of Catholic schools. To provide balance and ensure multiple perspectives, the diocesan planning committee should also consider gender, state in life (lay/religious/clerical), race and ethnic background, and residential area of the diocese when choosing individuals for task forces.

A task force typically has five to fifteen members. Members are asked to serve by a member of the study team first through a phone call and then through a follow-up letter from the bishop, the vicar for education, or the superintendent of schools.

The most effective task forces have chairpersons of high standing in the diocese, with reputations for effective leadership and expertise in the specified areas. These persons must be willing and able to devote considerable time to completing the work of the task force. Chairpersons are usually nominated by the diocesan planning committee. The designated chairperson is then invited personally by the bishop to serve in this leadership position.

Orientation

The diocesan planning committee should conduct a special orientation meeting for the task forces. Ideally, this meeting occurs close to the date of the problem element meeting so that members have ample time to get organized and become familiar with the data collected. In past studies, we have often invited the task force members to the problem element meeting and have held the orientation at a convenient time during the meeting.

At the orientation meeting, representatives from the diocesan planning committee explain the design of the planning study and the purpose of the task force. In addition, the diocesan planning committee should brief each task force separately regarding its specific task.

At the orientation meeting, each task force receives a charter that includes

* A detailed explanation of its purpose and scope of responsibility
* A description of the expected format and content of the final report
* A description of the types of progress reports expected
* A listing of the chairperson's responsibilities
* Suggestions to facilitate the work
* Guidelines concerning the confidentiality of the work

A sample task force charter appears in Appendix K.

Organization and Content

The issues addressed by the planning study and the results of the problem element meeting will normally determine which task forces are required. In our experience, a full diocesan planning study may require task forces in the following eight areas: Catholic identity, central office, curriculum, finance, governance, marketing and public relations, parental involvement, and secondary schools. Occasionally, the problem element meeting surfaces other areas that call for additional task forces. For example, in the Diocese of Corpus Christi, two public relations task forces were formed: one to deal with marketing and public image and one to examine school-to-school and school-to-parish relationships. In some cases, fewer than eight task forces may be needed. For example, the Washington elementary school study had four task forces: curriculum, governance, finance, and central office.

The following are brief descriptions of the areas that ordinarily come under the purview of each task force. The final determination of the issues, however, is made after topics have surfaced at the problem element meeting.

* The **Catholic identity** task force makes recommendations about the school's religious identity and philosophy; the qualifications of administrators and teachers, particularly those who teach religion; the religion curriculum; and Catholic identity issues that may relate to parents and to students.

* The **finance** task force makes recommendations about tuition policies, including plans for tuition assistance; use of parish and diocesan funds to support the schools; salaries and benefits of teachers and administrators; diocesan and local development efforts; and long-range financial planning and budgeting.

* The **governance** task force makes recommendations about possible governance models for the schools, which may include parish-sponsored schools, inter-parish schools, regional schools, diocesan schools, and private schools; and the formation of diocesan, regional, and local school boards and the nature of their jurisdiction.

- The **curriculum** task force makes recommendations about the quality and scope of the curriculum, evaluation strategies, staff development, the qualifications of administrators and teachers, enrichment programs, and services to children with special needs.

- The **marketing and public relations** task force makes recommendations about diocesan and local public-relations efforts for schools, including ways to increase attendance at Catholic schools, to improve knowledge about Catholic schools, and to garner more support for Catholic schools from the Catholic community and the general public.

- The **parental involvement** task force makes recommendations regarding ways to increase the level of parental support of their children's spiritual and academic development, their attendance at school functions, and their involvement in actively pursuing state and federal support for Catholic schools.

- The **central office** task force makes recommendations about the structure and staffing of the Catholic school office, the duties of its members, and its role regarding mission, policies, and communication.

- The **secondary school** task force makes recommendations about policies that affect the high schools of the diocese, and, in some cases, the number of high schools needed to serve the future needs of the diocese.

The questions listed below represent those addressed by the task forces in previous diocesan studies.

Catholic Identity

Mission and Philosophy
- What identifies a Catholic school and makes it unique?
- What is the essential mission of a Catholic school?
- How does a school maintain its Catholic identity when parent and student backgrounds are diverse and frequently not Catholic?
- What should be the policy regarding the participation of non-Catholic students in religious instruction and in the liturgical life of the school?

- How is the academic and religious mission of the school kept in balance?
- How can the faith community of the Catholic school be strengthened?
- To what extent does the school's curriculum assist students to understand how the person of faith views the content of the instruction?

Religion Program
- How can the quality of the religious instructional program be maintained or improved?
- What are the certification requirements for religion teachers?
- What role should the pastor and other priests have in the school's religion program?
- What should be the relationship between the school's religion program and the parish's religious education program?

Finance

Tuition
- How can Catholic schools arrive at a tuition that is within reach of most families and yet will support the school program?
- How can Catholic schools stabilize the cost of tuition?
- Is it feasible for schools in defined areas of the diocese to have a standard tuition?
- Should non-parishioners be charged the same tuition as parishioners in a parish school?
- How much should schools depend on fund raising to keep tuition down?
- How much of the cost per student should tuition cover?
- Should tuition be discounted for a second child and additional children from the same family who attend the school?

Financial Assistance
- Should Catholic schools be available to any Catholic family regardless of its financial circumstances?
- What criteria should be used to determine the eligibility of families to receive financial assistance and the amount they should receive?
- Should financial assistance be distributed by the schools, the parishes, or the diocese?
- What are the sources of funds for financial assistance?

Salaries and Benefits
- What are just wages and benefits for Catholic school teachers?
- Are present salaries and benefits adequate for the teachers?

Parish Funds
- Should the support of Catholic schools be the responsibility just of the parents with children in the schools or of all Catholics in every parish?
- Given the parish's responsibilities, what is a reasonable parish subsidy to the school?
- What should be the financial obligations of parishes that support interparish or regional schools?
- What is the responsibility of a non-school parish to its families who want their children in Catholic schools?
- How much of a parish's income should be used to support Catholic schools?
- Should a tax be imposed upon parishes for the support of Catholic schools?
- Should the parishes establish endowment funds for Catholic schools?

Diocesan Funds
- What responsibility does the diocese have for the support of Catholic schools that serve low-income students?
- What is the best use of the diocesan funds that are available for the support of Catholic schools?

Development
- Should the diocese embark upon a major fund-raising campaign for Catholic schools?
- Should a separate diocesan development office be established for the support of Catholic schools?
- Should individual schools begin their own development programs?
- What support can the diocese give to individual schools starting their own development programs?

School Budgets and Financial Planning
- What kind of financial planning is needed to secure the future of the schools?
- Does a standard procedure exist for school budgets and accounting practices, and do parishes and schools adhere to it?

Governance

Diocesan Governance
- What priority does the diocese place on its Catholic schools?
- What is the role of diocesan leadership in promoting Catholic education?
- To what extent does a priest's interest in supporting Catholic schools enter into the assignment of pastors to parishes with schools?
- How should a diocesan board of education be structured and what are its responsibilities?

School Structures
- How committed is the diocese to the concept of parish elementary schools?
- Are there regions of the diocese where interparish or regional schools would be appropriate?
- What are the advantages and disadvantages of every parish supporting its own school?
- Should the diocese establish separate middle schools in strategic locations?
- Are there too many Catholic schools in certain parts of the diocese?
- Are there areas in the diocese where additional Catholic schools may be required?

School Governance
- Should each school have a school board?
- How should a parish school board be structured, and what responsibilities should its members have?
- What is the relationship between the pastor, the principal, and the board with regard to the governance of a parish school?
- How should the board of an interparish or regional school be structured and what are its responsibilities?
- What are the responsibilities of the sponsoring or cooperating parishes regarding the governance and financial support of an interparish or regional school?

Curriculum

Programs and Services
- Does each school challenge its students to excel by setting high standards?
- Does each school maintain a comprehensive curriculum that satisfies the requirements and

standards of quality established by the state, the diocese, and appropriate accrediting agencies?

❖ How does each school regularly evaluate its curriculum?

❖ Does the curriculum provide for an integration of faith and knowledge?

❖ How do the schools compare with the public schools in quality and resources?

❖ How can the schools improve their offerings, especially in math, science and technology?

❖ Should there be guidelines regarding the maximum number of students in a class?

Administrators and Teachers

❖ What are the essential personal characteristics and professional qualifications of Catholic school administrators and teachers?

❖ What is the role of the principal in providing for the instructional leadership in the school and in ensuring its Catholic identity?

❖ Who is responsible for developing and implementing a program of spiritual formation for teachers and administrators?

❖ Is there an adequate in-service program to upgrade the skills of the teachers and administrators?

❖ To what extent do the diocese, the parishes, and the schools publicly recognize the professional excellence, length of service, and commitment to the Church of Catholic school administrators and teachers?

Special Services

❖ To what extent are the schools meeting the needs of all the students who attend?

❖ What are the present and future needs of the children who come from diverse family circumstances?

❖ How can the schools within an area cooperate to provide programs for learning disabled, gifted and talented, and other children with special needs?

Public Relations/Marketing

Public Image

❖ What should be the role of the diocese in school public relations?

❖ Is the diocese aggressive enough in publicly promoting Catholic schools?

❖ Should there be a diocesan public relations office for Catholic schools?

❖ What is the message that should be conveyed about Catholic schools and how is that message best communicated?

❖ How can we foster a positive image about the benefits of Catholic education?

❖ How can schools become better prepared in public relations techniques?

❖ What are the affordable media to spread the message about the schools?

Marketing

❖ How can the marketing program in each school be improved?

❖ What are effective methods of increasing enrollment?

❖ Should each school have a recruitment brochure?

❖ How can schools in a specific region of the diocese cooperate in their marketing efforts?

Relationship Between Parish and School

❖ To what extent does each parish publicly proclaim its commitment to Catholic schools?

❖ How does the parish publicize the positive achievements of students in Catholic schools?

❖ How are parishioners made aware of the contributions that the school makes to the parish?

Parents

Involvement in Religious Formation

❖ What can each school do to enhance the involvement of parents in their children's religious formation?

❖ What can parishes do to promote the involvement of families in the life of the parish?

Involvement in the School

❖ How can the schools increase the involvement of parents?

❖ How can parent organizations be strengthened?

❖ Do the schools provide parents with an understanding of the school's philosophy, let parents know what is expected of them, and give parents an opportunity to express their concerns and expectations?

❖ Does each school have a handbook for parents?

❖ To what extent do the schools have guidelines regarding how parents can help with homework, discipline, fund raising, volunteering, transportation, and the like?

- Are parents invited to attend activities held during the school day?

Political Action
- How does the diocese plan to organize parents to monitor legislation that affects Catholic schools and to join other groups to lobby federal and state legislatures to secure tax-supported financial assistance for the education of their children?

Central Office

Structure
- What should be the optimal administrative structure of the Catholic schools office?
- Are there sufficient personnel to carry out the normal functions of the office?
- What changes in the number, type, and responsibilities of the staff may be necessary to implement the recommendations of this strategic planning study?

Services
- What are the essential services of the Catholic schools office?
- Are services being offered by the Catholic schools office that could be decentralized?
- Are there essential services that should be coordinated by the Catholic schools office, such as purchasing of supplies?
- What additional services could the office offer to the schools?
- To what extent does the office provide adequate service in its areas of responsibility?

Secondary Schools

Number and Type of Schools
- Is there a sufficient number of high schools in each part of the diocese?
- Is there an appropriate number of single-sex and coed high schools in the diocese?
- Should a new high school be proposed for any section of the diocese?
- Should any high school be closed?
- Under what conditions should a high school be encouraged or permitted to add middle-school or junior-high grades?

Programs and Services
- Are students of varying abilities adequately served by the high schools?
- How can cooperation rather than competition be fostered among the high schools?
- In what areas would the high schools benefit from mutual cooperation?
- How can the dialogue between high schools and elementary schools be improved?
- Should any high school be asked to consider changing its curriculum or the composition of its student body to serve the diocese better?
- What can be done to increase the amount of tuition assistance available to high school students in the diocese?
- Are the high schools adequately publicized? What can be done to increase the public relations and marketing efforts of the high schools?
- How can the faith community in each of the high schools be nurtured?

Process

The task forces, which meet independently, study the preliminary data collected by the diocesan planning committee, along with the information from the problem element and solution element meetings. The task is formidable because the data, particularly those from the problem element meeting, will yield many more questions and issues than can be reasonably addressed in the course of the work. One of the responsibilities of the task force, then, is to narrow and prioritize the focus of its work. Some indication of the more pressing issues will be indicated in the priority statements generated by each group at the problem element meeting. Likewise, the sheer number of solution ideas proffered for any one issue at the solution element meeting make it necessary for the task force to sort and rank ideas in terms of appropriateness, feasibility, and desirability of final effects. Solutions that are frequently repeated give the task force some evidence of the prevalent thinking in the diocese and perhaps how easily certain changes might be embraced. In compiling its final report, a task force has the right to accept solutions proposed at the solution element meeting, modify them, or develop different ways to address the issues.

After three or four months of work, the task forces are asked to meet with the diocesan planning committee to give a preliminary progress report. The chairperson, who is often accompanied by additional task force members, presents a brief oral report that summarizes the major recommendations of the task force. At this time, a preliminary draft of the report is also provided for the diocesan planning committee members to review. The report should indicate the major issues being considered, along with the actions being recommended. The report often includes the guiding principles under which the task force operated, along with the rationale for the direction being taken.

Following the report, members of the diocesan planning committee and task force discuss the various issues. The diocesan planning committee may react in any or all of the following ways to the report: affirm the direction of the report, direct the task force to pursue additional aspects of its charge, or refer certain aspects to other task forces. For example, the role of the pastor and principal in the parish school may be addressed from different perspectives by the governance, Catholic identity, and finance task force groups. The diocesan planning committee has the responsibility to coordinate the direction of the task forces so that undue duplication of effort is minimized.

The task force presents its final report to the diocesan planning committee about three months later. The format for the final presentation is similar to the interim presentation. After the presentation, a discussion period is provided in the event that clarification of any recommendation is required. At this point, the diocesan planning committee ordinarily accepts the report and does not request the task force to do additional work.

Summary

Task forces play an important role in the diocesan planning model described in this book. Task forces consist of individuals who have expertise in the areas they are asked to study. Normally, task forces are needed in at least six areas: Catholic identity, finance, governance, public relations and marketing, curriculum, and parental involvement. In some studies, task forces will be needed for secondary schools, the central office, or particular issues that arise from the problem element meeting.

The work of the task forces, which can last from six to nine months, is used by the diocesan planning committee to help it formulate the major recommendations of the study. In this chapter, we have provided a list of some of the issues that the task forces in our diocesan studies have frequently encountered.

The next chapter provides a description of the parish planning process, which normally occurs at the same time as the work of the task forces.

Chapter Objectives

In this chapter you will learn the following:

❖ What the parish planning process is and its role in the strategic planning study

❖ How to form a parish planning committee, what responsibilities its members have, and what its relationship to the diocesan planning committee is

❖ How to conduct a consultation of the parishioners, including recommended resources, surveys, and agendas for meetings

❖ How the diocesan planning committee can provide an orientation for members of parish planning committees

Introduction

The parish planning process provides an opportunity for a parish to (1) gain perspective about its resources in the light of its needs, (2) develop a plan to meet its obligations, and (3) participate in the formation of a diocesan plan for Catholic schools. During the parish planning process, a parish

❖ Establishes a parish planning committee

❖ Consults its parishioners and, if it has a school, the families who enroll their children

❖ Formulates a parish plan that contains recommendations concerning the parish's role in supporting its own school, if it has one, and/or the Catholic schools of the diocese

❖ Submits this plan to the diocesan planning committee before that committee develops the diocesan proposals and area plans

❖ Helps to shape the final recommendations of the planning study by reacting to the preliminary diocesan proposals and area plans

This chapter contains a description of the purpose, membership, and responsibilities of the parish planning committee; the levels of informal and formal consultation recommended; the nature and format of the parish plan; and some practical suggestions about how to complete the parish planning process.

The Parish Planning Committee

The parish planning committee (PPC) is an ad hoc group that the parish forms to better understand its own circumstances and to assist the diocesan planning committee in planning for the future of the schools in the diocese. After examining the school situation in its parish and in its area of the diocese, and in light of its parish's total educational mission, the PPC develops a series of recommendations regarding the parish's role in meeting the needs of Catholic schools in its section of the diocese. The diocesan planning committee then uses these recommendations to develop a five- to ten-year diocesan strategic plan for the schools.

The PPC plays a vital role in planning for schools. Not only does it formulate recommendations concerning the future of the Catholic schools and the policies that affect them, but, more importantly, it conducts formal consultations with parishioners regarding the parish's recommendations to the diocesan planning committee and the preliminary proposals that it receives from the diocesan planning committee. These consultations help raise the parish's consciousness regarding the planning study, build support for its final recommendations, and encourage the parish to explore ways to enhance its participation in the education of children. Because the PPC has a critical role in the planning study, each parish in the diocese must form a PPC, whether or not it has a school.

Members

The pastor is ordinarily responsible for forming the PPC, which should have broad representation from the parish community. Our experience indicates that a committee of six to eleven members is sufficient. The PPC needs to be large enough to allow diverse input and to accomplish its specific tasks, but small enough to be manageable and efficient. The recommended members of the PPC are

❖ The pastor
❖ A parochial vicar (associate pastor)
❖ The principal of the parish school (if applicable)
❖ The director of religious education for the parish
❖ A teacher in the parish school (if applicable)
❖ A teacher in the parish religious education program
❖ A representative from the school board or the home and school association (if applicable)
❖ A representative from the parish's pastoral council or finance council
❖ A parent who has a child currently enrolled in a Catholic school (the parish's school, if applicable)
❖ A parent who has a child currently enrolled in a public or other private school
❖ An at-large member of the parish

Collectively, the PPC should represent those who have an interest in the proposed parish plan. The recommendations made by the PPC should have the support and acceptance of those who will be affected by their implementation.

The responsibilities of a member of the PPC are to

❖ Attend meetings of the PPC and any subgroups formed for special assignments
❖ Study the materials provided and become knowledgeable about the parish's school situation
❖ Participate in the consultation process conducted within the parish
❖ Learn and then represent the views of others in the parish and/or the school
❖ Exercise personal judgment about what is best for the parish
❖ Have full and equal voice and participate with other committee members in formulating recommendations and making decisions

Chairperson

The chairperson of the PPC must be familiar with the issues involving the schools, possess good organizational skills, and have the time to devote to the activities of the PPC. In most cases, the pastor appoints the chairperson; however, the chairperson may be elected by the members. Ordinarily, the pastor should not be chairperson because of his other responsibilities in the parish.

The chairperson has the responsibility to provide leadership to the PPC, including

Exhibit 5-1. Parish Planning Committee Activities and Timeline	
1. Pastor appoints members of the PPC	Month 0
2. PPC reviews data and plans consultation of parishioners	Month 1
3. PPC analyzes parish questionnaire data and conducts parish hearing	Month 2
4. PPC drafts parish plan and obtains feedback from parishioners	Month 3
5. PPC submits parish plan to the planning committee	Month 4
6. PPC reviews area plan received from the planning committee	Month 10
7. PPC sends the planning committee a written reaction to the area plan	Month 11
8. Representatives attend area/deanery/regional meetings	Month 12

- Communicating with the diocesan planning committee
- Ensuring that the parish pastoral council and the parish finance committee are consulted and kept apprised of the PPC's activities and discussions
- Arranging for cooperative endeavors with PPCs from neighboring parishes, if appropriate
- Managing the meetings of the PPC
- Ensuring that someone records actions of the PPC
- Arranging for the appropriate materials to be present at the meetings of the PPC
- Appointing individuals (or asking for volunteers) to carry out PPC assignments
- Ensuring that the PPC meets its deadlines

Timeline

Ordinarily, the PPC exists about one year. The PPC will need three to four months to complete the first phase of its work, the development of the parish plan. More time will be needed if the planning period includes the Christmas holidays or the summer. A typical schedule would be to get the PPCs started soon after the problem element meeting, that is, by mid-February, and ask for a complete parish plan by mid-to late-June.

After submitting its parish plan, the PPC waits until the diocesan planning committee is ready to conduct the consultation on its preliminary diocesan proposals and area plans, which usually is four to six months later. Exhibit 5-1 contains a listing of the PPC activities and an approximate timeline.

Consultation

The PPC consults with the parishioners of the parish and, if the parish has a school or cooperates in the sponsorship of a school, with the users of the school who are not parishioners, at the following times: (1) before formulating the parish plan; (2) after developing a preliminary parish plan; and (3) after receiving the preliminary diocesan proposals and the area plan from the diocesan planning committee.

Stakeholders

Who should be consulted concerning the development of the parish's recommendations? The stakeholders are of two general types: (1) the parishioners of the parish, and (2) the users of the parish school, if one exists, who are not parishioners of the parish. Each of these groups can be divided into subgroups, which might be expected to have different levels of interest in, and support for, Catholic schools. Nevertheless, each of these subgroups is entitled to have some voice in the development of the parish's recommendations.

The parishioners of the parish can be divided as follows:

- Those who do not have children
- Those who have children beyond school age
- Those with children of elementary-school age or younger who do, or would like to, send their children to a Catholic school
- Those with children of elementary-school age or younger who elect not to send their children to a Catholic school and do not intend to do so in the future

Non-parishioners who are users of the parish school can be divided into (1) Catholics who are members of another parish and (2) non-Catholics. Catholics who are members of another parish will be able to participate in the parish process in their own parish; however, the PPC should consider inviting them to participate also in the parish process where their children attend school.

The Process

Both informal and formal consultation are necessary to develop an adequate sense of how different stakeholders feel about the role of the parish in meeting the needs of Catholic schools in its region of the diocese.

Informal Consultation

Each member of the PPC should continually look for opportunities to solicit the views of the various stakeholders. In addition to normal social interaction, some suggestions for increasing input are (1) placing a suggestion box in the church or at school, and (2) soliciting comments and suggestions about schools (and perhaps about other aspects of the parish religious education program) through announcements in the parish bulletin, the parish newsletter, or posters in the church or school. Each PPC is encouraged to think of additional ways to increase the level of informal consultation.

Formal Consultation

While informal consultation continually occurs, the formal consultation will ordinarily occur in three stages.

❖ The first stage, which has three parts, consists of (a) informing the parish about its role in the study; (b) obtaining oral and written feedback concerning the relevant issues from the parishioners and users of the school, usually by means of a parish questionnaire; and (c) testing tentative proposals and several alternatives at a general meeting of the parish.

❖ The second stage consists of informing the parish about the specific recommendations which the PPC intends to submit to the diocesan planning committee. This is best accomplished through a formal hearing, although the PPC may decide upon some other means of communication.

❖ The third stage consists of informing and seeking input from the parish and users of the school about preliminary proposals developed by the diocesan planning committee.

Stage 1a: Informing the Parish. The PPC should inform the parish about the purpose and activities of the study and invite parishioners to participate fully in the consultation process.

We suggest that the pastor or his designee talk at all the Masses on a designated weekend to inform the parishioners about the study and speak about Catholic education in general and Catholic schools in particular. We urge that particulars about finances be omitted from this announcement. Finances and other relevant data should be included in the cover letter that should accompany the parish questionnaire. Specifically, the talk should

❖ Inform the parishioners about the study, its design, and the parish's involvement

❖ Summarize the history and achievements of Catholic schools, including the research concerning their effectiveness (see Exhibit 5-2)

Exhibit 5-2. Selected Resources for History and Achievement of Catholic Schools

Bryk, A., V. Lee, and P. Holland. (1993). *Catholic Schools and the Common Good*. Cambridge, Mass.: Harvard University Press.

Buetow, H. A. (1988). *The Catholic School: Its Roots, Identity, and Future*. New York: The Crossroad Publishing Company.

Convey, J. J. (1991). "Catholic Schools in a Changing Society: Past Accomplishments and Future Challenges." In *The Catholic School and Society*. Washington, D.C.: National Catholic Educational Association.

Convey, J. J. (1992). *Catholic Schools Make a Difference: Twenty-Five Years of Research*. Washington, D.C.: National Catholic Educational Association.

Exhibit 5-3. Selected Church Documents

The following are the key documents from the Sacred Congregation of Catholic Education: *The Catholic School* (1977), *Lay Catholics in Schools: Witnesses to the Faith* (1982), and *The Religious Dimension of Education in a Catholic School* (1988).

The bishops of the United States expressed their support for Catholic schools and the preeminence of Catholic schools in the educational mission of the Church in their 1972 pastoral message on Catholic education, *To Teach as Jesus Did*, in the 1979 *National Catechetical Directory*, and in their 1990 *Statement of the United States Bishops in Support of Catholic Elementary and Secondary Schools*.

❖ Speak about why the Church supports Catholic schools, citing papal documents, pastoral letters, and other documents from the United States bishops, as well as statements of philosophy of Catholic schools from individual schools (see Exhibit 5-3)

Stage 1b: The Parish Questionnaire. Survey data can provide the PPC with a sense of how the parishioners and users of the school view the relevant issues. The brief questionnaire in Appendix L will assist the PPC in obtaining some initial feedback about the feelings of the stakeholders concerning the issues in the study. The questionnaire requests (1) demographic information, (2) attitudes and opinions, and (3) advice concerning some options. The PPC may want to modify the questionnaire to accommodate local circumstances. Some PPCs may develop a more open-ended survey in which the stakeholders are asked the same questions which the PPC has been requested to address. Open-ended surveys may provide more detailed information to the PPC; however, such surveys require more time for analysis than do surveys with constructed responses.

Cover Letter. Each PPC should prepare a cover letter for the parish questionnaire explaining its purpose and how the PPC intends to use the information. For parishes with schools, we strongly recommend that the cover letter include a brief statement of the philosophy of the school (use school documents, accreditation reports, or diocesan documents). Also, the letter should contain some facts about the school, such as

❖ The cost of educating each pupil
❖ The percent of this cost contributed by the parish
❖ The percent of total parish revenues used to support its school
❖ The enrollment this past year and the trend in the last five years (also prospects for future trends based on available demographic data)
❖ The tuition for registered parishioners, Catholics who are not parishioners, and non-Catholics
❖ The funds received from special fund-raising activities
❖ The average salary paid to the lay teachers in the school (possibly adding the lowest and highest salaries)

We have found that most parishioners are not aware of the cost of maintaining a Catholic school. We believe that more informed parishioners are potentially more supportive parishioners. In any event, we feel that pastors have a responsibility to provide parishioners with a reasonable amount of information about how parish funds are spent.

Administration of the Parish Questionnaire. Each parish should develop its own procedures for administering the parish questionnaire. Time, cost, and likelihood of response are factors to consider in determining when and how to distribute the questionnaire. In past studies, some parishes have provided time during weekend Masses for parishioners to complete questionnaires. Other parishes have included the questionnaire as part of the parish bulletin or have sent it to each parishioner through regular parish mailings. The leadership of the pastor, the other clergy in the parish, and prominent members of the laity, along with careful planning by the PPC, will increase the percentage of returned parish questionnaires.

In a parish with a school, the PPC may want to plan for two administrations of the questionnaire. One administration would be for parishioners and the other for users of the school who are not parishioners. These parishes may decide to distribute the questionnaire first to the parents of all the children in the school, followed a week or two later by the rest of the parish.

Analysis of the Parish Questionnaire. The PPC is responsible for analyzing the results of the parish questionnaire. Basically, what is needed is the tallying of the responses for each question. An efficient way to accomplish this is to divide the completed questionnaires among PPC members and have each member compile a tally for each question. These can then be combined into a final tally.

Most PPCs will have access to a computer that could be used to assist with analysis. If the number of questionnaires returned is large, however, data entry can be very time-consuming. On the other hand, the establishment of a comprehensive data base of parishioner views and their associated demographic characteristics is a valuable resource for the PPC during the study and for the parish after the study ends.

If the PPC wishes, more complex analyses can be performed with the questionnaire data. Some of the questions in the section Demographic Information can be used to form groups and examine how responses from these groups differ. For example, in parishes that have schools, users of the parish school could be compared with non-users. Or parishioners with higher levels of family income could be compared with those with lower levels. However, it is not necessary to form groups. While it is possible to perform these analyses manually, the use of a computer facilitates the calculations.

Stage 1c: Stakeholders Hearing. After analyzing the parish questionnaire and other available data, the PPC should formulate preliminary recommendations. Then the PPC should hold an open meeting (stakeholders hearing) to which all parishioners, and, if the parish has a school, all non-parishioners who are users of the school are invited. At this meeting, the PPC will report on

❖ The needs of Catholic schools from a parish perspective, from a regional perspective, and from a diocesan perspective, as indicated by the data
❖ Some viable means of responding to these needs
❖ Some advantages and disadvantages of each possible way of responding

The PPC will then invite the attendees to comment on its analysis of the issues. We recommend that the PPC use a structured format with groups of eight to twelve persons, which is similar to the nominal group process used at the problem element meeting and the solution element meeting. Exhibit 5-4 contains a suggested format and agenda for the stakeholder hearing.

Stage 2: Consultation on Initial Parish Recommendations. After the PPC drafts preliminary recommendations for the diocesan planning committee, these recommendations should be made available to the various stakeholders for their comments before the PPC forwards its parish plan to the diocesan planning committee.

Exhibit 5-4. Format for Stakeholder Hearing

1. Opening prayer; welcome; introduction of the PPC members; reason for the hearing; agenda; next steps following the hearing.

2. The PPC's assessment of (a) the needs of Catholic schools; (b) several means to respond to each need; and (c) advantages and disadvantages of each way of responding.

3. General questions for clarification only, to clear up misunderstandings or confusion. (It is not appropriate at this point to discuss or suggest alternatives. Do that in small groups.)

4. Small group process. (Groups should be no larger than twelve and include members from different constituencies. The small groups should meet for twenty to forty minutes to discuss ways the PPC has suggested for meeting the identified needs.) Each group should
   ❖ Identify what it likes and does not like about each way of responding to the needs
   ❖ Select a recorder to write down likes and dislikes
   ❖ Select a spokesperson to report back to the PPC in a large-group setting

5. Reports from the small groups. The chairperson of the PPC reiterates the ground rules:
   ❖ No decisions will be made tonight, so there is no need to agree with each other; differences are acceptable.
   ❖ The PPC wants to hear your ideas; members will ask questions if they need a clarification on some issue. If PPC members understand, they need not respond or make comments.
   ❖ Debate or discussion of specific points is not appropriate at this time.

   PPC members should listen to the reports carefully and take notes. (PPC members may ask questions for clarification but should not debate or argue with the constituents' ideas.)

6. Next steps; thanks to participants. Collect the notes from the recorders of each small group.

7. Closing prayer

This consultation may be done in a formal meeting like the stakeholders hearing in Stage 1c. However, most parishes may find it more efficient, due to impending deadlines, to use the parish bulletin or newsletter, the school newsletter, a special mailing, or a posting in the back of the church to invite written comments about the parish's recommendations.

Stage 3: Consultation on Area Plans and Preliminary Diocesan Proposals. After reviewing the parish plans from each parish in a region, the diocesan planning committee will develop the diocesan proposals and an area plan and send these to each PPC for review and comment. In most cases, the diocesan planning committee will incorporate the exact recommendations from each parish plan into the area plan for the parish. In some cases, however, some modifications of the recommendations may be necessary because of information received from other parishes or because of diocesan recommendations from the task forces.

After receiving the preliminary diocesan proposals and the area plan from the diocesan planning committee, the PPC should study them carefully. Depending on the nature of the area plan, the PPC may choose one of the following steps:

❖ If the preliminary diocesan proposals and the area plan contain basically the same suggestions made by the PPC in its parish plan or deviate just slightly from them, the PPC can circulate the preliminary proposals and area plan to its parishioners for their review and final comments.

❖ If either the preliminary diocesan proposals or the area plan deviates significantly from the suggestions made by the PPC in its parish plan or if the area plan contains potentially controversial proposals, the PPC may wish to hold a second stakeholders hearing.

The format of this second stakeholders hearing can be similar to that of the original stakeholders hearing. For example:

❖ Introduction; review area plan

❖ Ask small groups to discuss what they like and do not like about the preliminary diocesan proposals and area plan

❖ Report back to the PPC

The PPC would then review the stakeholders' responses and formulate a parish response to the diocesan planning committee regarding the preliminary diocesan proposals and the area plan.

In the event that major differences still exist between the views of the PPCs in the region and the views of the diocesan planning committee, regional meetings may be necessary until as much agreement as possible is reached on an area plan.

The Parish Plan

The vehicle that the PPC uses to forward the parish's recommendations to the diocesan planning committee is called a parish plan. After developing its preliminary recommendations and consulting with its parishioners, the PPC produces a parish plan that describes the parish's views regarding

❖ The future of its parish school or, if applicable, the interparish or regional school that it sponsors

❖ Any substantial modification in the structure, policies, or operations of its school

❖ The possibility of establishing a parish school, if it does not have a school

❖ Its willingness to cooperate with other parishes to support an interparish or a regional school

❖ Any formal or informal arrangements regarding the use of other parish schools by its parishioners, including the financial details of any arrangement

❖ Diocesan policies concerning the Catholic identity, curriculum, staffing, financing, governance, and marketing of the Catholic schools in the diocese

The PPC should consider the availability of schools nearby, data collected as part of the long-range planning study, and its own data when formulating its plans. In addition to consulting formally with the parishioners regarding its plans, the PPC is urged to discuss its plans with PPCs in neighboring parishes.

To facilitate the review of each parish plan, we suggest that each PPC use a standard format. Based on our experience, we recommend that the parish plan include (1) a cover sheet, (2) the body of the report, and (3) an appendix analyzing results of the parish questionnaire (the parish questionnaire is described later in this chapter).

Cover Sheet

The cover sheet for the parish plan enables the diocesan planning committee to quickly classify the type of action recommended by the PPC. This is particularly important in large dioceses, where the diocesan planning committee may have hundreds of parish plans to review.

Exhibit 5-5 shows an example of a cover sheet used in our diocesan studies. A parish with a school completes Section I, which provides information concerning the parish's proposals concerning the future of its school, as well as proposed changes in the school's operation. A parish without a school completes Section II, in which it can indicate whether it will (1) continue its present practice regarding Catholic schools, (2) plan to open its own parish school, (3) assist in the sponsorship of an interparish school, or (4) financially assist parishioners to attend a Catholic school.

Body of the Parish Plan

The body of the parish plan should consist of four sections:

- ❖ An introduction, briefly describing the parish's school situation

- ❖ A description of the issues (needs) considered by the PPC. Some salient issues are

  - ❖ The identified needs of the parish or its associated school

---

Exhibit 5-5. Parish Plan Cover Sheet

**Planning Study of Catholic Schools
Parish Plan Cover Sheet**

Parish _____ Location _____

Date _____ Deanery _____

Section I: Parishes with Schools

Future of school (check one)

_____ Continue to operate school

_____ Consolidate with another school

_____ Close parish school

Proposed modifications (check those that apply)

_____ No substantial modifications
_____ Admission policy
_____ Curriculum
_____ Grade structure
_____ Governance structure
_____ Teacher salaries
_____ Tuition policy
_____ Other

Section II: Parishes Without Schools

_____ No change in present status
_____ Establish own parish school
_____ Assist in sponsoring an interparish school
_____ Financially assist parishioners who wish to use existing parochial schools

---

- The appropriate number of Catholic schools for the area of the diocese—particularly whether the existing number of schools is sufficient
- Parish contributions to providing a Catholic education to its parishioners
- Ways the parish facilitates parishioner attendance at a Catholic school

- The PPC's recommendations to meet the needs or deal with any of the issues identified

- The recommendations for the bishop, along with a rationale for each recommendation

Appendix

Finally, the PPC should prepare an appendix to its parish plan, which shows the results of the parish questionnaire. The appendix should include the following:

- A copy of the parish questionnaire used by the PPC

- A brief description of recipients and the response rate (number and percent)

- A summary of the results of the parish questionnaire. We suggest reporting the percentage of respondents who picked each option for each question. Some PPCs, however, may wish to analyze the questionnaire more extensively.

Practical Issues

Orientation for PPCs

The proper orientation of a PPC is essential. The diocesan planning committee should conduct well-planned orientation meetings that explain the PPC's role in the study, perhaps using a copy of this book or handouts based on the material in this chapter and its associated appendices.

We suggest that two or three members of the PPC be invited to the general diocesan orientation meeting. Normally, one of these members will be the PPC chairperson. It is also helpful for the pastor of each parish to attend the orientation meeting.

The number of orientation meetings will depend on the size of the diocese. We suggest that meeting planners consider the geography of the diocese and schedule meetings within a week of each other.

At the orientation meetings, the diocesan planning committee will want to

- Describe/review the design of the planning study
- Discuss the nature and purpose of the PPC
- Describe the tasks required of the PPC, especially the phases of the consultation
- Discuss the format of the parish plan
- Establish a series of deadlines for the PPC
- Answer questions

Getting Started

As soon as possible after the orientation meeting, the parish chairperson gathers the materials needed for the first organizational meeting of the PPC. Copies of the following materials will be useful in helping members get started:

- The outline of the tasks and procedures for the PPC
- Materials describing the design of the study and the nature of the consultation
- All relevant parish and school data, especially any data presented at the problem element meeting
- Themes from the problem element meeting
- Priority statements from the solution element meeting
- Copy of the sample parish questionnaire

In addition, the chairperson should schedule the first meeting of the PPC and advise the PPC members to bring their calendars to schedule future meetings.

See Exhibits 5-6 to 5-11 at the end of this chapter for sample PPC meeting agendas. Each PPC should determine the actual number of meetings that would be required to accomplish its tasks.

Anticipated Participation

Ordinarily, not all parishes in the diocese will submit a parish plan, despite the request to do so from the diocesan planning committee or even the bishop. We have found that the number of parishes that return a plan varies. Dioceses that have experienced large enrollment declines or those concerned about Catholic schools will generally have a high percentage of returns. A parish with a school or associated with a school is more likely to submit a parish plan than a parish not associated with a school. The most critical factor regarding whether a parish submits a parish plan, however, appears to be the leadership and interest of the pastor.

In addition, the parish plans submitted will have varying degrees of completeness. Most parishes will submit a full plan as requested; however, some parishes may send the cover page only, the questionnaire results accompanied by a brief commentary, or simply a letter stating the parish's or, perhaps, the pastor's position.

The number of parishes that returned a parish plan in previous studies has varied considerably from diocese to diocese: 111 (70 percent) in Baltimore; 251 (63 percent) in Boston; 180 (82 percent) in Brooklyn; 44 (54 percent) in Corpus Christi; 27 (42 percent) in Honolulu; 110 (70 percent) in Providence; and 114 (88 percent) in Washington. Every plan submitted and every letter received are valuable tools for the diocesan planning committee.

Summary

The parish planning committee is the essential agent for the parish planning process. The diocesan planning committee asks each parish to form a PPC consisting of six to eleven members. The PPC then consults with its parishioners and develops a parish plan, which contains recommendations from the parish about its own school, if it has one, and/or about Catholic schools in the diocese. After receiving the preliminary diocesan proposals and area plan from the diocesan planning committee, the PPC again consults its parishioners and submits a written reaction to the diocesan planning committee.

The parish planning process provides an opportunity for all parishioners in a diocese to participate in planning for the future of the Catholic schools. As such, the parish planning process is a powerful tool in the strategic planning study since it has the potential of focusing the attention of the entire diocese on a single issue. It involves the stakeholders in the planning process and builds ownership for the recommendations that are ultimately adopted by the diocese.

The next chapter describes how the diocesan planning committee (a) develops the preliminary diocesan proposals and area plans, (b) conducts a consultation on these preliminary proposals and area plans, and (c) arrives at the final recommendations that it will present to the bishop.

Exhibit 5-6. Sample Agenda for the First Meeting of the PPC

Objective: Orientation

1. Opening prayer, welcome.

2. Introductions. Ask members to give name and role in the parish and/or the school.

3. Review and discuss the task of the PPC. Refer to the information in Chapter 5 and to the chart describing the overall design of the study. Discuss until all members are clear about the task of the PPC. If necessary, redefine the task and the process in your own terms.

4. Appoint (or ask for a volunteer or elect) a secretary to record the actions of the PPC.

5. Distribute the themes from the problem element meeting and, if available, the priority statements from the solution element meeting. Explain what the material is and how it is organized and ask members to read it by the next meeting, identifying areas that are relevant to the parish's school situation.

6. Distribute the sample parish questionnaire and any materials providing guidelines for the consultation. Review both briefly. Ask members to study them for the next meeting and come to the next meeting prepared to adopt the questionnaire, modify it, or decide to use an open-ended questionnaire.

7. Describe the data that are already available to the PPC. Discuss any additional information the PPC would like to have, Identify relevant parish and school (if applicable) data and assign individuals to gather the information.

8. Establish a meeting schedule. Set the next meeting within two weeks so that the questionnaire can be finalized and the procedures for distributing it worked out. Review the schedule of deadlines for the study and set meeting dates in order to meet these deadlines.

Exhibit 5-7. Sample Agenda for the Second Meeting of the PPC

Objective: Planning for parish consultation

Materials Needed:
* Sample parish questionnaire
* Parish or school data gathered by PPC
* Problem element themes

1. Opening prayer

2. Distribute additional data to study for the next meeting. Quickly review what is in each report and how it is organized.

3. Discuss the problem element themes. Identify problem elements that are relevant to the parish and that should be addressed in the parish plan.

4. Discuss whether the parish questionnaire should be used as is or modified. Discuss whether an alternative questionnaire consisting of open-ended questions would be more appropriate.

5. Discuss what procedures and timetable should be established to ensure that the PPC will get the information needed.

6. Develop detailed plans and dates for the administration of the parish questionnaire.

7. Set aside time and identify specific individuals who will assist with the analysis of the data from the questionnaire.

8. Decide on the format for the stakeholders hearing and appoint a subcommittee to begin planning for it. Have this subcommittee report on these plans at the next meeting of the PPC. Decide on a date and location for the hearing and how to publicize it.

9. Schedule next meeting.

Exhibit 5-8. Sample Agenda for the Third Meeting of the PPC

Objective: Final report on the analysis of parish questionnaire and preparation for the stakeholders hearing

Materials Needed:
   * Solution element priorities

1. Opening prayer

2. Report on the data analysis of the parish questionnaire. Discuss and clarify its major themes and patterns.

3. *Needs assessment.* Discuss and reach agreement on this question: *Given the overall educational mission of the parish, what do the data tell us about the needs of Catholic education in this parish and this section of the diocese for the next ten to fifteen years?*

4. *Solution formulation.* Discuss and reach agreement on the following: *What are three viable ways that this parish can meet or respond to these needs?* Each way must be realistic and viable. Do not yet attempt to narrow options to one . It is important to keep an open mind and permit parishioners to consider several options before recommending one. Review priorities from the solution element meeting.

5. For each of the three ways identified by the PPC, develop a list of major advantages and disadvantages. Aim for four or five advantages and disadvantages for each solution. This will help deepen people's thinking about the viability of each method or approach.

6. Decide on a method to present the possible courses of action at the stakeholders hearing. For example, PPC members could make a presentation with overhead slides or charts; copies of the materials could be distributed at the hearing; and so forth.

7. Report from the hearing preparation subcommittee. Develop detailed plans for hearing publicity and invitees, refreshments (if any), location, discussion leaders, recorders, and so forth. Are last minute details finalized?

Exhibit 5-9. Sample Agenda for the Fourth Meeting of the PPC

Objective: Modify possible courses of action in light of the stakeholder hearing. Develop recommendations to include in the parish plan for the diocesan planning committee.

1. Opening prayer

2. Review the likes and dislikes from stakeholders hearing. Discuss impressions from the hearing.

3. Discuss what modifications are needed to improve the recommendations.

4. Combine the best features and eliminate the worst features of the three approaches to each of the major issues. Select an approach which, in the opinion of the PPC, is the best for meeting the needs associated with each major issue.

5. Develop the specifics of the selected recommendations and draft them into the recommended format.

6. Plan to circulate a copy of the parish plan to the various stakeholders of the parish and, if applicable, the school.

Exhibit 5-10. Sample Agenda for the Fifth Meeting of the PPC

Objective: Review feedback from the parish concerning the draft of the parish plan and prepare the final version of the plan.

1. Opening prayer

2. Review and discuss feedback from parishioners concerning the draft of the parish plan.

3. Develop the final version of the parish plan.

4. Send the completed parish plan, in proper format, to the diocesan planning committee.

Exhibit 5-11. Sample Agenda for the Sixth Meeting of the PPC

Objective: Review the preliminary diocesan proposals and area plan from the diocesan planning committee. Decide upon additional parish consultations.

Before the Meeting:
* Circulate the area plan and the preliminary diocesan proposals to each member of the PPC.

1. Opening prayer

2. Discuss the area plan and preliminary diocesan proposals in light of the PPC's original recommendations. Identify similarities and differences.

3. If substantial differences exist regarding either the area plan or the preliminary diocesan proposals, discuss the PPC's position.

4. If necessary, plan for another stakeholder hearing so that the parish can be informed of the differences and its input solicited.

5. Select a member of the PPC to represent the parish at any meetings where the preliminary diocesan proposals and/or area plan will be discussed.

6. Draft a reaction to the preliminary diocesan proposals and area plan and send it to the diocesan planning committee.

7. Schedule additional meetings of the PPC if necessary.

CHAPTER 6
Arriving at Final Recommendations

Chapter Objectives

In this chapter you will learn the following:

1. What steps the diocesan planning committee takes to arrive at its final recommendations

2. How to design a diocesan-wide consultation

3. What types of preliminary proposals are helpful, how they are developed, and how they are used during the consultation

4. How area plans are constructed and their importance to the consultation

5. How to structure the final report

Introduction

After receiving the preliminary reports from the task forces and the parish plans from the parishes, the diocesan planning committee begins discussions regarding its final recommendations to the bishop concerning the diocesan policies that affect all parishes and schools, as well as the future of each school in the diocese.

The diocesan planning committee uses the following process to arrive at its final recommendations.

❖ The committee discusses the various alternatives and options that it has received from the task forces and the parish plans. The committee then brings these alternatives into harmony with its own thoughts and decides how to proceed in each of the major policy areas.

❖ The committee produces drafts of the preliminary proposals that it intends to send to the parishes and schools for consultation, discusses the wording of these proposals, and modifies them accordingly.

❖ Once consensus is reached regarding the wording of the preliminary proposals, the committee prepares a consultation document. The committee discusses and revises the consultation document and then sends it to the parishes and schools for their reactions.

❖ During consultations regarding the preliminary proposals, members of the diocesan planning committee may meet with standing diocesan committees, representatives of specific constituencies, and/or parish planning committees to obtain their feedback regarding the preliminary proposals.

❖ After reviewing the written responses to the preliminary proposals from the parishes and schools, the committee decides which proposals to modify and to what extent each should be modified.

❖ The committee drafts and discusses the proposed modifications and arrives at consensus regarding the revised proposals.

❖ The committee decides whether to conduct additional consultations regarding the revised proposals. The desirability of additional consultation depends upon the nature of the revised proposals and the source and extent of the objections to the original preliminary proposals.

❖ The committee develops the final recommendations for the study based on the results of the consultation.

Developing Preliminary Proposals

The diocesan planning committee develops the preliminary proposals for the consultation document from the task force reports, the parish plans, and its own discussions of the issues. The preliminary proposals are of two types:

❖ Diocesan proposals concerning the policy areas that the task forces considered

❖ Proposals about the future of each school in each area of the diocese

The development of the preliminary proposals is time consuming, generally requiring four to five months of biweekly meetings. After reading and discussing the task force reports and parish plans, the diocesan planning committee must prepare and discuss drafts of preliminary proposals. In addition, the diocesan planning committee prepares and discusses a consultation document, which is described later in this chapter. The committee will usually revise the consultation document several times before it can be sent to the parishes and schools for their reactions.

Diocesan Proposals

In most studies, the diocesan planning committee will make hundreds of recommendations to the bishop regarding the major policy areas considered in the study. In the studies that we have completed, the policy areas commonly addressed are Catholic identity, curriculum, finances, governance, marketing and public relations, parental involvement, and secondary schools. In some cases, other policy areas may arise from the problem element meeting and may be included in the recommendations.

Many of the recommendations will be fairly routine and not controversial. Generally, all will agree that these recommendations will serve to improve Catholic education in the diocese. To keep the proposals to a reasonable number, many routine, noncontroversial proposals are not included in the consultation document, but rather are reserved for inclusion as recommendations in the final report of the study.

Some proposals, however, may be contentious to some in the diocese because they

❖ Involve major changes in existing practices (for example, the ways the schools are financed or governed)

❖ Are philosophically unacceptable to a significant number of individuals in the diocese (for example, having parishes without schools provide some funds for schools or placing a school tax on parishes)

❖ Involve a significant expenditure of funds (for example, hiring public relations or development personnel)

As a general rule of thumb, the consultation document should always contain four types of proposals: (1) those that involve the expenditure of money; (2) those that involve a major change in existing policy; (3) those that relate to governance; and (4) those that directly affect a particular school or parish. In addition, the diocesan planning committee should include in the consultation document a representative number of proposals for each of the major policy areas. Such inclusions indicate that the study is multi-faceted rather than concentrated on one or two issues.

Appendix M contains the proposals concerning diocesan policy used in the consultation for the Diocese of Providence planning study.

Suggestions

❖ Since they generally necessitate more discussion than other areas, proposals concerning finance and governance should be discussed before proposals in other areas.

❖ The study team should draft, discuss, and come to consensus on the proposals before presenting them to the entire diocesan planning committee.

❖ After one or two meetings devoted to brainstorming and discussing the viability of different approaches recommended by task forces and parish committees, the study team should agree on the approach it will take regarding the issues. At this point, one or two members of the study team or planning committee should be asked to write specific proposals for discussion at subsequent meetings.

❖ To facilitate the review and discussion by the entire diocesan planning committee of what is likely to be fifty to seventy proposals, the study team should send a draft of these proposals to each member of the diocesan planning committee at least one week before scheduled meetings.

Proposals About Schools

Proposals about the future of each school are developed concurrently with proposals on diocesan policy. The discussion of such proposals begins with the study team but continues in subcommittees of the diocesan planning committee. The subcommittees prepare the drafts of the proposals and present them to the entire diocesan planning committee. The work of these subcommittees occurs at the same time the study team is discussing and finalizing the preliminary diocesan proposals.

The development of the proposals concerning schools occurs in these stages:

❖ The diocesan planning committee divides the diocese into a number of meaningful geographical areas, probably between six and twelve. Often existing deaneries or vicariates are used.

❖ The diocesan planning committee establishes subcommittees, each consisting of three or four members of the diocesan planning committee, with at least one member from the study team. Each subcommittee is responsible for developing initial proposals concerning the schools in one or more of the geographical areas, depending upon the number of areas and the number of subcommittees.

❖ Prior to the work of the subcommittees, the study team reviews each parish plan and extensively discusses those plans that propose a major action in its school situation, such as an opening, closing, or merging, or a substantial modification in the school's operations. The study team attempts to reach some degree of consensus on what major proposals might be considered in each area.

   ❖ Before the study team meets, one or more of its members must assume the responsibility for reading the parish plans and identifying those that propose a major action. This can be accomplished by having each member read those parish plans from the area for which the member's subcommittee is responsible.

❖ Copies of the parish plans that propose a major action should be sent to all members of the study team before the meeting.

❖ A map showing the location of schools and parishes in the diocese should be available for reference at the meetings of the study team.

❖ The subcommittees of the diocesan planning committee then draft the preliminary recommendations for the area plans (see next section). The study team member on each of the subcommittees is responsible for communicating the thoughts of the entire study team to the subcommittee.

❖ The full diocesan planning committee then reviews, discusses, modifies, and ultimately approves the recommendations for each area plan. If at all possible, consensus should be reached on an area plan before sending it to the parishes in the area for their review.

Area Plans

The diocesan planning committee uses the area plan to inform the parishes and schools in an area about the preliminary proposals regarding particular schools. A typical area plan would contain

❖ *Summary statistics about the current school situation in the area.* The statistics would normally include information concerning total enrollment, enrollment of minority students and non-Catholic students, tuition, cost per student, and parish and diocesan contributions to the school. Exhibit 6-1 shows an example of the statistics presented in an area plan in the Diocese of Brooklyn planning study.

❖ *Demographic information and projections, if available.* The demographic information will be constrained by what the diocesan planning committee is able to gather. Census data are always available and will provide an indication of past trends. Most dioceses will be able to obtain some information about future demographics, such as expected growth in the number of school-age children or expected number of new

Parish/ School	Total 1992-93	Total 1991-92	Change 1984-92	Percent Minority 1992-93	Percent Non-Cath 1992-93	Tuition 1992-93	Cost Per Student 92 Budgt	Parish Contrib 92 Budgt	Diocesan Contrib 92 Budgt
Parishes with Schools									
All Saints	122	126	-159	99.2	13.1	$1,540	$3,231	$0	$125,000
St. Anthony/ Alphonsus	328	351	-26	28.0	6.1	$1,450	$1,844	$121,150	
St. Cecilia	461	485	-37	29.7	3.3	$1,500	$1,510	$38,481	
SS Cyril & Methodius	119	130	-103	28.8	4.2	$1,375	$2,859	$170,000	
Most Holy Trinity	226	229	-74	96.0	7.5	$1,425	$1,855	$0	$57,000
Our Lady of Mount Carmel	40			22.5	2.5	$1,800			
SS Peter & Paul	220	224	-89	99.5	6.4	$1,400	$2,423	$0	$170,000
St. Stanislaus Kostka	442	401	-90	1.2	0.2	$1,100	$1,823	$174,344	
Transfiguration	245	269	-239	100.0	1.6	$965		$20,000	$71,000
St. Vincent de Paul	123	128	-133	62.6	9.8	$1,700	$3,282	$0	$60,000
St. Nicholas	180	172	-24	70.9	4.4	$1,650	$2,268	$14,000	$60,000
Summary	2506	2515	-974	60.0	4.4	$1,446	$2,344	$53,798	$543,000

public schools that are planned. Exhibit 6-2 shows the demographic information in area plans from the Diocese of Brooklyn planning study and the Diocese of Honolulu planning study.

❖ *A brief summary of the parish plans from the area.* Exhibit 6-3 shows an example of a summary of parish plans in an area plan for the Diocese of Honolulu planning study.

❖ *Proposals that are common to all schools in the diocese.* Exhibit 6-4 shows the proposals common to all area plans in the Diocese of Brooklyn planning study.

❖ *Proposals concerning specific schools or parishes in the area.* Exhibit 6-5 shows the proposals for specific schools and parishes in one of the area plans from the Archdiocese of Boston planning study.

Consultation on Preliminary Proposals

Parish-Based Consultation

The formal consultation on the preliminary proposals commences when the diocesan planning committee distributes the consultation document to each parish planning committee (PPC). This document can take many forms. In the planning studies that we have conducted, the consultation document consisted of the introduction, the listing of the diocesan proposals, and the appropriate area plan for the parish.

❖ **Introduction:** This section has three parts: (1) a description of the philosophy and methodology of the study; (2) how the proposals were generated and the assumptions that the diocesan planning committee made; and (3) the list of names of the members of the diocesan planning committee. All parishes receive this section.

❖ **Diocesan proposals:** This section lists the proposals that apply to all parishes and schools. All parishes receive this section.

❖ **Area plan:** This section has the proposals for the parishes and schools in one geographical area of the diocese. Each parish receives only the specific area plan that contains proposals for its area of the diocese. Parishes that are located near the boundary separating two of the areas should receive the area plans appropriate for those areas.

❖ **Response sheet:** A response sheet enables the parishes to indicate their support or lack

Exhibit 6-4. Proposals Common to All Area Plans in the Diocese of Brooklyn Study

1. Each school shall continue to operate as long as it can provide a quality academic and religious formation program, as determined by diocesan standards, and its enrollment and financial circumstances permit its continuation.

2. In order to ensure its continued viability, each school shall give priority to
   a. Updating or developing a three-year strategic plan
   b. Planning to incorporate programs that emphasize technology
   c. Implementing strategies associated with effective Catholic schools
   d. Establishing a parish-school educational commission and ensuring the existence of an active home and school association
   e. Developing an aggressive marketing and public relations program, and setting a realistic goal to achieve an increase in enrollment
   f. Cooperating with other schools and parishes in the area with regard to long-range planning and sharing of resources

3. All parishes in this area are encouraged to continue their commitment to Catholic schools by
   a. Helping to promote the schools
   b. Contributing funds for the schools' operating costs
   c. Offering tuition plans for families
   d. Offering tuition assistance to families in financial need
   e. Establishing an endowment for the schools

4. In addition to helping Catholic schools in the ways indicated in proposal 3, all parishes shall sponsor local school fairs and aggressively recruit students, especially from their religious education program, for nearby Catholic schools.

5. Each school should establish a local development effort to reach out to local businesses and alumni to increase available income.

---

of support for each proposal. Exhibit 6-6 contains an example of the response sheet for the diocesan proposals in the Brooklyn study.

The consultation document ordinarily is mailed to the parishes. We suggest that a copy be sent to the pastor, the chairperson of the PPC, and, if the parish has a school, the principal. In some cases, however, it may be advantageous to distribute the consultation document at special meetings for representatives of PPCs, since that facilitates both the distribution and explanation of the proposals.

The diocesan planning committee should request that the parishes send their written reactions to the proposals by a certain date. Ordinarily, six to eight weeks is sufficient for a PPC to consult with its parishioners and formulate a response to the consultation document.

Consultations with Other Stakeholders

In addition to the parishes, the diocesan planning committee should also distribute the consultation document to each school in the diocese and to strategic committees around the diocese. The diocesan planning committee may want to invite each school and committee also to send a written response to the proposals contained in the consultation document. Individuals throughout the diocese should be encouraged to do the same.

Before or during the formal parish-based consultation, the diocesan planning committee may want to organize special meetings with strategic groups around the diocese. These special meetings serve several purposes for the diocesan planning committee.

❖ *Information and communication.* The meetings provide opportunities to inform groups about

Area 6: Concord and Medford Vicariates

This area has thirty-seven parishes and eleven parish elementary schools. In addition, one private elementary school, Armenian Sisters Academy, Lexington, serves the area. A slight gain in school-age population is projected for Chelsea. The remaining towns in this planning area are projected to lose pupil population.

Recommendations

13-27 In Chelsea, at most two schools are needed to serve the area. St. Rose School will continue to serve the area; however, the future of Our Lady of the Assumption School is very precarious because of severe underenrollment. In the light of the demographics of the area and local circumstances, St. Stanislaus Parish should become a cooperating sponsor of Our Lady of the Assumption School. In the event that only one school, St. Rose, remains in Chelsea, St. Stanislaus and Our Lady of the Assumption would be cooperating parishes. All parishes should continue to cooperate to ensure that the school enrollment reflects the multicultural nature of the city.

13-28 In Everett, Our Lady of Grace Parish and Immaculate Conception Parish should form one interparish school at the site of the Immaculate Conception School. St. Anthony Parish should continue to operate its parish school.

13-29 The following cooperating parish arrangements are proposed, in which the parishes involved develop a shared responsibility to provide the necessary financial and moral support to ensure a school's continued viability.

  a. Arlington: The Arlington parishes with St. Agnes School
  b. Everett: St. Joseph and St. Theresa with St. Anthony School and the new interparish school at Immaculate Conception (see recommendation 13-28)
  c. Malden: St. Joseph and St. Peter with Immaculate Conception School and Cheverus (Sacred Hearts) School
  d. Medford: Sacred Heart and St. James with St. Francis of Assisi School, St. Joseph School and St. Raphael School
  e. Belmont: The three parishes in Belmont with schools that their parishioners attend

13-30 In the light of present and anticipated growth in the number of children, a new interparish elementary school is proposed for the following area: Concord-Bedford-Maynard-South Lincoln. The parishes in these towns in conjunction with the Catholic school office will conduct a market analysis to evaluate the feasibility of establishing a new interparish elementary school to meet the needs of area families. The market analysis will also include details regarding the location, cost, financing, and projected opening of the school, along with a mechanism to reevaluate the feasibility in the event of changes in the demographics of the area.

the preliminary proposals and to answer questions about them.

❖ *Assessment.* The committee can assess each group's reaction to the preliminary proposals, including which proposals are generally acceptable and which are more controversial.

❖ *Public relations.* The committee recognizes the importance of strategic groups in the diocese and proactively opens lines of communication with them.

The diocesan presbyteral council or priest senate is one of the most important groups that the diocesan planning committee should con-

Exhibit 6-6. Example of Response Sheet for Diocesan Proposals

Diocese of Brooklyn Catholic Education Planning Project
Diocesan Proposals Response Sheet

Parish/School _____

Location/Area _____

Person Responding _____

Please check your support of (Yes) or opposition to (No) each proposal.

	Yes	No		Yes	No		Yes	No		Yes	No
1	__	__	21	__	__	34	__	__	51a	__	__
2	__	__	22	__	__	35	__	__	51b	__	__
3	__	__	23	__	__	36	__	__	51c	__	__
4	__	__	24a	__	__	37	__	__	51d	__	__
5	__	__	24b	__	__	38	__	__	51e	__	__
6	__	__	24c	__	__	39	__	__	52	__	__
7	__	__	25a	__	__	40	__	__	53	__	__
8	__	__	25b	__	__	41	__	__	54	__	__
9	__	__	25c	__	__	42	__	__	55	__	__
10	__	__	26	__	__	43	__	__	56	__	__
11	__	__	27	__	__	44a	__	__	57	__	__
12	__	__	28	__	__	44b	__	__	58	__	__
13	__	__	28a	__	__	45	__	__	59	__	__
14	__	__	28b	__	__	46	__	__	60	__	__
15	__	__	28c	__	__	47	__	__	61	__	__
16	__	__	29	__	__	48	__	__	62	__	__
17	__	__	30	__	__	49	__	__	63	__	__
18	__	__	31	__	__	50a	__	__	64	__	__
19	__	__	32	__	__	50b	__	__	65	__	__
20	__	__	33	__	__	50c	__	__	66	__	__

Indicate on the reverse side any comments, suggestions, or alternative proposals. Please specify the number of the proposal being addressed. Attach additional sheets as needed.

sult during the study. A consultation with the presbyteral council prior to the public release of the proposals is both a courtesy to the council in recognition of its role in the diocese and an opportunity for the diocesan planning committee to test the reaction to its preliminary proposals. We recommend that the diocesan planning committee arrange a consultation with the presbyteral council immediately before the parish-based consultation on the preliminary proposals.

Other groups that the diocesan planning committee may wish to consult at this time include

- ❖ Diocesan pastoral council
- ❖ Major superiors of religious congregations
- ❖ Sisters and/or brothers senate
- ❖ Heads of diocesan departments
- ❖ Deans or vicars
- ❖ Pastors
- ❖ Principals
- ❖ Boards of trustees

Response Process

The feedback concerning the proposals in the consultation document normally occurs in one or more of the ways described below.

In general:

- Written responses from the parishes and schools to the diocesan proposals and area plans

- Minutes and notes from briefing meetings held with the strategic groups indicated in the previous section

In specific situations:

- Special meetings of pastors, principals, and chairpersons of PPCs may be necessary to discuss alternative proposals or to receive final advice concerning the proposals that the diocesan planning committee intends to present to the bishop as recommendations.

- Parish groups may request a special meeting to discuss the diocesan proposals and/or the area plans. In the Washington elementary school study, for example, five such meeting were held.

  - Three meetings were held with the same group of fifteen parishes and mainly involved discussion of a proposed reorganization of schools in the area. These meetings attracted approximately 50, 100, and 150 individuals, respectively.

  - The fourth meeting concerned the discussion of the need for a new school in an area and proposal to charge tuition at the cost per student. Approximately 150 individuals from five parishes in the area attended.

  - The fifth meeting, which concerned proposals regarding tuition, involved representatives of ten PPCs in one area of the archdiocese.

- Members of the diocesan planning committee may wish to visit the pastors and/or principals of key parishes and schools to obtain their advice concerning the proposals about schools in their area.

- Individuals around the diocese may write directly to the planning committee about one or more of the proposals. In the Washington elementary school study, the diocesan planning committee received over a hundred such letters.

Developing Final Recommendations

After the period of consultation, the diocesan planning committee evaluates the reaction to the preliminary proposals and decides whether to change any of them. In the Washington elementary school study, for example, the consultation demonstrated that the majority of pastors, educators, and parents strongly supported most of the recommendations under consideration. Particularly strong support existed for the proposals concerning the religious identity of the schools, school governance, sponsorship of schools by parishes, advisory boards, and development programs. On the other hand, the consultation produced strong, vociferous, and often very emotional objections to a few important proposals regarding finances and the placement of schools. The Washington planning committee dealt with these objections by modifying some proposals, and by clarifying, but not changing, other proposals. For example, the Washington planning committee took the following actions:

- Substantially modified the proposal to charge tuition at the cost per student. This proposal had received the most widespread, negative, and emotional objections. Subsequent consultation demonstrated that the modified proposal was more acceptable to all concerned.

- Produced additional data to clarify the proposed increases in the salaries of teachers. The objections to the original proposal came mainly from a substantial number of pastors, some of whom may have misunderstood the intent of the proposal.

- Recommended a delay in the implementation of the proposal to reorganize four schools in a rural region of the archdiocese into one junior high school and three primary schools and requested that the parishes involved submit an alternative proposal to the archdiocesan board of education. Most of the objections to the original proposal came from parents.

- Recommended a further in-depth study of a group of parishes to determine if the parents' desire for an additional school in the area was warranted.

The Final Report

After all issues have been resolved to its satisfaction, the diocesan planning committee finalizes the recommendations of the study and prepares a final report for the bishop. At a minimum, the final report should contain a description of the methodology used in the planning study, the results of the consultation, the final recommendations of the study, a rationale for the recommendations, and a plan for the implementation of the recommendations.

The final reports we have done for dioceses were divided into four parts, with each part containing two or more chapters. The parts are organization and philosophy, gathering the data, developing the recommendations, and final recommendations. Exhibit 6-7 shows the table of contents from the final report for the Diocese of Brooklyn planning study. If the study also includes high schools, another chapter is added with recommendations for the high schools of the diocese.

Presentation of Report to the Bishop

The diocesan planning committee ordinarily presents the final report to the bishop at a formal gathering, such as a liturgy, a special dinner, or a meeting arranged specifically for the presentation. In the Diocese of Honolulu study, for example, the chairperson of the diocesan planning committee made a formal presentation of the final report to Bishop Joseph Ferrario at the offertory of the opening Mass for teachers at the beginning of the school year following the completion of the study. In the Diocese of Corpus Christi study, Bishop Rene Gracida received the final report at a dinner honoring the diocesan planning committee and task forces. The final reports for the Baltimore,

---

Exhibit 6-7. Table of Contents for Diocese of Brooklyn Final Report

STRATEGIC PLANNING FOR CATHOLIC SCHOOLS

Brooklyn, Boston and Washington studies were presented to the respective bishops privately by the chairperson of the planning committee, the secretary for education, or the superintendent of schools. The reports were subsequently discussed with the bishops at private meetings.

Aftermath and Implementation

The diocese must give special attention to the type of response that the bishop will make to the diocesan planning committee's report and how to publicize that response, as well as the study's recommendations. After receiving and reading the final report from the diocesan planning committee, the bishop ordinarily prepares a written response to the report. The bishop's response may take the form of an extensive pastoral letter or a briefer statement of his intention to accept specific recommendations. Whatever form the response takes, the occasion of its release presents an ideal opportunity to publicize both it and the schools in a public forum by means of a press release followed by a news conference.

Another area requiring attention is the development of a strategy to monitor the implementation of the study's recommendations. Normally, the Catholic school office assumes responsibility for implementing the study's recommendations. The superintendent of schools with the staff of the Catholic school office should carefully evaluate the office's staffing and their responsibilities to determine if a reordering of responsibilities is required. In addition, it is recommended that the superintendent and staff develop an implementation flowchart that delineates the major actions required, the person responsible for facilitating and monitoring those actions, and the anticipated timeline for completing those actions. The implementation flowchart and the report of the diocesan planning committee form a comprehensive blueprint for action that will assist the Catholic school office in its efforts to implement the study's recommendations and increase the likelihood of a successful and timely implementation.

Summary

This chapter describes how the diocesan planning committee arrives at its preliminary proposals,

consults the diocesan stakeholders regarding these proposals, and decides upon the final recommendation of the study.

After receiving the task force reports and the parish plans, the diocesan planning committee begins its discussions regarding the preliminary proposals. After several months of discussion and refinement, the diocesan planning committee sends to each parish and school a consultation document that contains (a) the preliminary diocesan proposals regarding policies that affect all parishes and schools and (b) an area plan that includes proposals regarding the parishes and schools in each area of the diocese. After receiving the written reactions from the PPCs and others to the proposals contained in the consultation document, the diocesan planning committee decides to what extent it will modify any proposal that has received substantial negative reaction and develops its final proposals. In some cases, the diocesan planning committee may wish to conduct another consultation, especially if the modified proposals contain material that has not been widely discussed earlier in the study.

After the diocesan planning committee is satisfied that consensus has been reached on the proposals or, at least, the differences of opinion that exist concerning them have been thoroughly discussed and evaluated, the committee prepares a final report for the bishop. The bishop's formal response to the planning committee report is often in the form of a pastoral letter. The bishop's response, as well as the recommendations of the study, should be widely proclaimed, preferably in a public forum, such as a press release or news conference. The Catholic school office usually assumes the responsibility for implementing the recommendations that the bishop accepts. The development of an implementation flowchart, along with the detailed recommendations in the planning committee's report, provides the Catholic school office with a detailed blueprint that enables it to proceed through the implementation stage successfully.

This chapter concludes the discussion of the planning model for use by an entire diocese. The model is easily adapted to individual schools and groups of schools. The next chapter describes how the model can be adapted for a strategic planning study of high schools in a diocese.

Chapter Objectives

In this chapter you will learn the following:

1. What general approach to strategic planning for all high schools within the diocese is recommended

2. How to form a planning committee for high schools, as well as the advantages and disadvantages of the different types of committees

3. How to perform a school audit, including the types of information required for the audit

4. How to design and conduct a knowledge exploration meeting, at which problems and potential solutions are developed

Introduction

The strategic planning model presented in the previous chapters utilizes a parish-based consultation, which is appropriate for planning for parish, inter-parish, and regional elementary schools. When planning for the future of the high schools in a diocese, a parish-based model may be inadequate or, in some cases, inappropriate. In many dioceses, some or all of the high schools are privately owned. The religious congregations or boards of trustees that control these schools have a responsibility to make decisions regarding the future welfare of their schools. While the owners of these schools may wish to seek input from the parishes, the primary consultative groups are the high school's constituents. In addition, a public consultation regarding the future of a privately owned school, particularly if there is a question about the continuation of that school, may in itself threaten a school's viability.

In this chapter, we describe several approaches to strategic planning for all the high schools in a diocese. For each approach, we indicate its advantages and disadvantages and provide examples of dioceses that have used it.

Rationale

A diocese engages in strategic planning for its high schools to develop a long-range plan that covers the next five to fifteen years or to address a specific issue involving one or more of the schools, such as potential mergers, openings, or changes in the type of students served.

The questions that a diocese might address in the context of a long-range planning study for high schools include

❖ Do students living in each section of the diocese currently have access to a high school?

❖ Is there an appropriate number of single-sex and coed high schools available in the diocese?

❖ Are children with various abilities and needs adequately served by the current high schools?

❖ Does the diocese have the appropriate number of high schools and are they in the right locations? Should some high schools be closed or consolidated? Should additional high schools be established?

❖ What steps should be taken to ensure the future viability of each high school?

❖ How can the diocese and the individual high schools increase the amount of tuition assistance available to high school students?

❖ Are the high schools adequately publicized? What can be done to increase the public relations and marketing efforts of the schools?

❖ What can the diocese do regarding transportation to improve access to the high schools?

Some specific issues that may precipitate a high school study include

❖ Should a new high school be established in a particular section of the diocese? Are there enough students and are there sufficient financial resources to warrant the building of the school?

❖ Should two neighboring schools that have experienced decline in enrollments merge, should one close, or should both remain open?

❖ Should a particular single-sex school be restructured as a coed school or should a particular co-ed school be restructured as a single-sex school? What impact will a restructuring have on other high schools in the diocese?

❖ Should a high school with grades nine through twelve add a junior high school or middle school component? What impact will adding additional grades have on other high schools and on neighboring parish elementary schools?

High School Planning Committee

In conducting a high school study, the diocese could utilize a participative model, like the diocesan planning model described in Chapter 1, or hire a consultant to do a "top-down" analysis of the schools and present recommendations. Whatever approach to planning is chosen, the diocese will probably establish a special high school planning committee that will be responsible for either (1) making the recommendations about the high schools to the bishop or (2) acting in an advisory capacity to a consultant or to an already established diocesan planning committee. In the first case, the high school committee becomes the planning committee for the study. In the latter case, the high school committee acts as an advisory committee to the consultant or as a task force reporting to the diocesan planning committee. In this section, we offer suggestions regarding the possible makeup of the high school planning committee.

We have experienced different configurations for committees and their relationship to a broader diocesan planning study. On the whole, we believe that a committee composed of the school owners or their representatives that makes recommenda-

tions directly to the bishop is the most desirable structure for planning for high schools.

❖ **A planning committee consisting entirely of the owners of each high school**

Membership
A school owned by a religious congregation is represented by a member of the religious congregation, preferably from the congregation's governing council or leadership team. The chairperson of the board or another officer would represent a high school operated by separately incorporated board of trustees. A diocesan school is represented by a delegate of the bishop, most likely the vicar or secretary of education or the superintendent of schools. A pastor ordinarily represents a parish high school.

Responsibilities
Since the committee functions as the planning committee and not as an advisory committee or task force, it has the responsibility to oversee the conduct of the study and to decide which recommendations are made to the bishop.

Technical Assistance
The planning committee ordinarily is assisted by staff from the Catholic school office and/or by a professional evaluator or planner.

Advantages
Those directly responsible for the ownership of the schools participate in the planning and decision making. These individuals ordinarily are in the best position to make informed decisions concerning the schools. In particular, the leaders from the religious congregations are usually able to view the situation concerning their local school or schools in the light of the priorities and plans of their own congregations and often have a less emotional view of the local situation than local principals.

Disadvantages
Meetings may be difficult to coordinate because of busy schedules. Some religious congregations may be unable or unwilling to commit personnel from their governing councils to participate in the study, especially if the congre-

gation's provincial house is located at some distance from the diocese.

The Archdiocese of Washington high school study (1983-1984) utilized this configuration. The archbishop appointed the committee and it made recommendations directly to him.

❖ **A planning or advisory committee consisting of owners and principals**

Membership
In a diocese with few high schools, a representative of each owner and each principal are members of the committee. In a diocese with many high schools, a subgroup of owners and principals could be elected to the committee as representatives of all owners and principals. The elections could be based on type of ownership (diocesan, parish, private), gender composition (coed, all boys, all girls), or geographic region of the diocese.

Responsibilities
If the committee is established as the planning committee for the study, it has the responsibility to oversee the conduct of the study and to decide which recommendations are made to the bishop. If the committee is advisory to a larger diocesan planning committee or a consultant, it assists the diocesan planning committee or the consultant in the conduct of the study and provides advice about which recommendations are given to the bishop.

Technical Assistance
If established as the planning committee, assistance ordinarily is provided by staff from the Catholic school office and/or by a professional evaluator or planner.

Advantages
Owners and principals often have different perspectives that can enrich the planning study. Electing individuals provides for representation and a sense of participation by all schools, in addition to resulting in a committee of manageable size.

Disadvantages
Elected representatives may, consciously or unconsciously, favor their own school, or may be unwilling to make recommendations about other schools, especially if resolutions involving the possible consolidation of schools appear to be necessary.

The Diocese of Brooklyn high school study (1992-1993) utilized this configuration. The superintendent of education invited all high schools to participate in the study and all accepted. The committee, which consisted of elected representatives of the religious congregations and the principals, as well as one representative appointed by the diocese, acted as the planning committee and made recommendations directly to the bishop.

❖ **An advisory committee or task force consisting of the principals of each high school or their delegates**

Membership
The principal of each high school or a few elected or appointed principals that represent all the principals are members of the committee.

Responsibilities
The committee advises the consultant or planning committee that is responsible for making recommendations to the bishop. If the committee is established as a task force within the framework of a larger planning study, the committee presents its recommendations to the diocesan planning committee, as outlined in Chapter 4.

Technical Assistance
An advisory committee generally does not require extensive technical assistance. A task force could utilize the resources available to the diocesan planning committee. An advisory committee and a task force normally have access to the data that are collected for the overall study.

Advantages
The principals are very knowledgeable about their schools and their schools' traditions and prospects for the future. Furthermore, the principals are the most likely group to be familiar with the problems facing the high schools, the circumstances of other schools, the demographic trends in the area, and possible long-term solutions. The principals can strongly

influence the course of the planning study and yet not be required to make the final decision regarding the high schools.

Disadvantages
Some principals may lack perspective on their own schools because of their inability or unwillingness to view the larger picture or because of their emotional attachment to their schools. In addition, some principals may be uneasy about the prospects of cooperation with present competitors. Finally, the consultant or the diocesan planning committee may not heed the recommendations made by the advisory committee or task force.

The Archdiocese of Baltimore high school study (1988-1989), conducted by Meitler and Associates, and the Diocese of Honolulu planning study (1990-1992) used this configuration. In the Baltimore study, the principals acted as an advisory committee and consultative group to the consultants. In the Hawaii study, the principals formed a task force and made recommendations directly to the diocesan planning committee.

❖ **An advisory committee or task force with a general membership**

Membership
The committee or task force consists of elected or appointed principals, teachers, board members, parents, and individuals from the community.

Responsibilities
The committee is advisory to the consultant or planning committee that is responsible for making recommendations to the bishop. If the committee is established as a task force within the framework of a larger planning study, the committee presents its recommendations to the diocesan planning committee, as outlined in Chapter 4.

Technical Assistance
Ordinarily, an advisory committee and a task force have access to the data that are collected for the overall study and do not require extensive technical assistance.

Advantages
A diverse group brings multiple perspectives to the planning study.

Disadvantages
Some members may feel that they are not competent to advise on weighty decisions that may be facing the schools. As in other configurations in which the committee is advisory, the consultant or the diocesan planning committee may not heed the recommendations made by the advisory committee or task force.

The Archdiocese of Boston planning study (1989-1991) utilized this configuration. The task force consisted of elected principals from the diocesan, parish, and private high schools, teachers, and some members from the diocesan planning committee. The task force made its report directly to the diocesan planning committee.

The Process

Regardless of its structure and purpose, the high school planning committee needs to become familiar with each of the schools, develop a common core of data that all can share, identify the major issues that it will study, and consult with the owners of the schools prior to developing its final recommendations. Three major activities will help the high school planning committee accomplish its tasks.

❖ School audit: Each school collects pertinent information, which will help to produce a common core of data that will help the high school planning committee familiarize itself with all of the schools.

❖ Knowledge exploration meeting: This general meeting assists the high school planning committee in identifying the study's major issues and some possible solutions to them.

❖ Resource controllers meeting: This consultation meeting provides the high school planning committee with the opportunity to confer with the owners and controllers of the schools regarding the future of the high schools in the diocese.

School Audit

To help its administrators, its governing board, and the planning committee understand the high schools better and assist them in identifying the school's strengths and weaknesses, we suggest that each school perform an extensive school audit. The school audit gathers information concerning enrollment indicators, attrition patterns, academic trends, student participation, parent/family circumstances, and finances. Exhibit 7-1 lists the major tables that are suggested for the school audit. Appendix N contains forms that may be helpful to schools in compiling the data for the audit and for their reports.

Chapter 2 contains some information to assist the school in compiling the audit. The enrollment trends for the high schools, as well as those for the elementary schools, and the demographic projections regarding potential future students are particularly useful. The school may also benefit from some of the information obtained from the surveys of parents, clergy, principals, and teachers that also are described in Chapter 2.

Exhibit 7-1. High School Audit Summary

Enrollment Indicators

Recruitment history
Recruitment analysis by zip code and feeder school
Enrollment history
Ethnic/religious composition
Feeder patterns by zip code and school

Attrition Patterns

Attrition rate: three-year history
Parent reasons for withdrawing students
Student reasons for leaving the school
Schools receiving transferred students

Academic Analysis

Student academic profile
Student GPA profile
SAT/ACT five-year history
Five-year graduate profile
Graduates' honors
College attendance patterns
Student participation
Club/sports participation by grade
Participation by gender and ethnic/minority
Student responsibilities

Parents/Family Circumstances

Parents' educational background profile
Family structure profile
Parents' occupational profile
Parent participation in school

Financial

Cost and income profile
Tuition history
Enrollment/staffing averages
Staffing profile and salaries
Salary scale

Enrollment Indicators

Data concerning the school's recruitment program are good indicators of potential student interest in the school. The school should record annually and report for the past four years the number of inquiries, visits, and applications and the percentage of applicants who enrolled. The analysis also should note the zip codes, parishes, and the elementary, middle, or junior high schools of the previous year's inquirers.

The school should compile student enrollment figures by grade, religion, and racial/ethnic composition for the past four years. The report should include the residential patterns and feeder schools for the current year's students, by grade.

Attrition/Retention Patterns

The school should tabulate the number of enrolled students who left the school before graduation during the past three years and report this analysis by grade. In the attrition analysis, the school identifies those who moved, dropped out, were counseled out, or transferred to another school without moving after October 1st. The school also should ascertain and record the reasons given by parents and students for leaving the school. Finally, the schools receiving transfer students should record the school the student last attended and its tuition.

Academic Analysis

The school should compile an academic profile of its students that includes, by grade, the percentage of students who make the honor roll for all grading periods, the percentage with less than a C-cumulative average, the percentage with perfect attendance, the average GPA for each grade, and the cutoff GPAs that identify the highest and lowest 10 percent of the students.

In addition, the school should gather a five-year profile that reports the number of students who took a college entrance test, such as the SAT or the ACT, along with average verbal and quantitative scores. The school should also gather statistics on its graduates for the past five years regarding the percentages that went to college and to work, the honors and scholarships earned, and the colleges most frequently attended.

Student Participation

The school should collect and tabulate information concerning the participation of students in sports, academic clubs, service clubs, and the arts. For each activity, the tabulation should include the number of students in the organization or activity, along with the percentage of females and the percentage of minority students in each one. We also believe that gathering information regarding the work responsibilities of students is helpful.

Parent and Family Circumstances

The school may wish to ascertain and tabulate the level of education and the occupation of each student's parent(s). If possible, the school should gather the data concerning the percentage of families in which both parents work and the percentage of disrupted families (breakup of the child's natural parents by divorce, separation, or death) in each grade. In addition, charting the extent that parents participated in fund raisers, volunteer programs in the school, and other parent-oriented programs during the last year and over the past four years is informative.

Financial

The financial information needed by the school includes a financial profile (cost per student and percentage of income from various sources); a tuition history that includes information regarding the amount of tuition uncollected; and the number of students receiving financial aid and the amount of aid given. Enrollment and staffing patterns related to class size and pupil-teacher ratio should be listed. The school should develop a faculty profile that includes number of full-time and part-time teachers, the salary schedule in place, and an individual profile for each teacher that includes experience, education, and certification.

After completing the school audit, each high school should forward it to its respective board or governing body. Based on the results of the audit, the board or governing body should assess the school's situation from various perspectives and develop recommendations for the school and a plan for its future. The following points of deliberation are helpful. Appendix N contains a form to record the outcomes of each of these deliberations.

- ❖ List the assets and strengths of the school.

- ❖ List the liabilities and weaknesses of the school.

- ❖ Describe the future prognosis for the school.

- ❖ Specify the reasons for the continued need for the school in the area and in the diocese.

- ❖ List the obstacles to the support for the school from the governing board, religious community, parish, or diocese.

- ❖ Specify the recommendations and the plan for the future.

The board or governing body's report of their deliberations will help the high school planning committee or task force develop its recommendations for all of the high schools in the diocese.

Knowledge Exploration Meeting

The knowledge exploration meeting is an all-day gathering of representatives from the high schools and the diocese that unites the identification of major problem areas with suggested solutions. In reality, the knowledge exploration meeting combines the problem element meeting and solution element meeting, which were described in Chapter 3, into one all-day meeting. Exhibit 7-2 contains a typical agenda for the knowledge exploration meeting.

Participants

The knowledge exploration meeting should be held early in the high school study. The preparation for this meeting and its conduct are similar to those for the problem element meeting and solution element meeting, as described in Chapter 3. A major meeting of this nature should have at least fifty participants to allow for some diversity in the group work.

Each high school in the diocese is invited to send at least four representatives: the principal, a teacher, a member of the board, and a parent. If a diocese has parish high schools, the pastor of the parish should be invited to the meeting. In some cases, high schools may ask that one or two active alumni be included in the meeting. The exact number of representatives depends upon the number of high schools in the diocese.

In addition, to include the perspective of those not directly involved in the high schools, we suggest that the high school planning committee invite representatives from some elementary schools and parishes. The representatives could include principals, teachers, parents of school-age children, and interested parishioners.

Exhibit 7-2. Agenda for Knowledge Exploration Meeting	
8:30	Registration, coffee/danish
9:00	Welcome, opening prayer
9:15	Overview, presentation of current data, explanation of group process
9:45	Small groups—identification of problems
11:00	Large group—report of problem priorities
11:30	Small groups—solutions for first problem
12:30	Lunch
1:15	Small groups—solutions for second problem
2:15	Large group—report of solution priorities
2:45	Closing remarks, closing prayer

Like the problem element and solution element meetings, the representatives should be asked to register at least a week before the meeting so that groups of between eight and twelve members can be formed prior to the meeting. The organizers of the meeting should ensure that the groups are heterogeneous with regard to schools and types of individual. Therefore, as far as possible, no individual in a group should be from the same high school, and each group should have approximately the same number of principals, teachers, board members, and parents.

First Session: Data and Process

The knowledge exploration meeting includes both large and small group sessions. The large-group sessions are utilized to explain the format of the meeting, present data, report on problems and concerns, and report on suggested solutions. During the first session of the day, which involves the full group, general enrollment trends and other relevant data are presented. This session is normally very brief. At the end of the session, the procedures for the rest of the meeting and the process for the small groups are explained.

Second Session: Problems and Concerns

At the second session, the participants gather in small groups and use the nominal group process, which is described in Chapter 3, to identify problems and concerns facing the high schools of the diocese. The small groups meet in separate areas for about an hour to address a focus question, such as the following: *As we look to the future of Catholic education, what problems, concerns, or issues need to be addressed concerning the high schools of the diocese?*
The procedure in each small group is as follows:

❖ The participants write their ideas on index cards without discussion.

❖ On large sheets of newsprint, a facilitator lists the ideas as dictated by the participants.

❖ The participants may ask for clarification of ideas.

❖ Each participant chooses five ideas from the newsprint which, in the opinion of the participant, merit special priority.

❖ The facilitator records the priority votes beside the appropriate ideas on the newsprint.

❖ A brief discussion occurs regarding the initial list of priorities.

❖ Each participant again selects five items that merit special priority.

❖ The facilitator records the final votes and copies the priority statements.

Third Session: Reporting of Problems and Concerns

The participants gather in a large-group session to listen to the priority statements chosen by each group. The organizers of the meeting sort the problem statements into categories as each facilitator reports on them. The following categories frequently emerge:

❖ **Identity,** which includes the catholicity of the schools, the particular image of each school, and elitism versus service to the poor

❖ **Finance,** which includes escalating expenses, tuition increases, imbalances in tuition among schools, more financial assistance, teacher salaries and benefits, and attracting and retaining quality teachers

❖ **Cooperation versus competition,** which focuses on ways the schools need to work together and includes problems of competition

❖ **School affairs,** which includes the meeting of student needs, the strengthening of academic programs, general curricular issues, the religion programs and spiritual formation, parental participation, and extracurricular activities

❖ **Public relations,** which includes marketing and recruitment concerns, the need for better coordinated public relations efforts, and increased political action

❖ **Diocesan issues,** which includes leadership, governance, commitment and support, and long-range planning

Fourth Session: Suggested Solutions

At the fourth session, the participants return to their small groups and generate solutions to the problems and concerns identified during the first small-group session. The organizers of the knowledge exploration meeting assign to each small group two problem areas from among those identified by the facilitators at the third session. The organizers should rotate the problem areas among the groups so that all problem areas have approximately equal coverage. The groups then generate solution ideas about the questions assigned to them, one question at a time, by using a focus question such as the following: *What should be done to address the problems and issues in the area of_____ as it affects the high schools?*

Each group then goes through two complete cycles of the nominal group process. If not enough time is available to complete two cycles, the groups should complete one cycle for their first assigned problem area and have the members list their solutions for the second assigned problem area on their index cards.

Fifth Session: Reporting of Suggested Solutions

The participants then return to the final large-group session of the day to hear some of the suggested solutions.

After the knowledge exploration meeting, the high school planning committee should arrange for a complete content analysis of the index cards from each of the two small-group sessions.

Resource Controllers Meeting

The resource controllers meeting brings together those individuals associated with each high school who have the authority, either solely or in conjunction with others, to make decisions concerning the school's future. Depending upon a school's ownership, the resource controllers may include religious superiors and/or members of a religious congregation's governing council, chairpersons and other members of boards of trustees, pastors, and diocesan officials. In addition, each high school may bring to the meeting other individuals, such as the principal, other administrators, teachers, and parents.

The primary purpose of the resource controllers meeting is to examine and prioritize specific models for the future configuration of the high schools in the diocese. The intent of the meeting is to consult with the resource controllers and the others in attendance to determine plausible models that could be implemented in the diocese and to eliminate models that have little or no support. No firm decision, however, is sought at this time concerning which model should be adopted.

The configuration models should reflect considerations regarding the number of high schools needed, the location of the schools, and the type of students they should serve. In addition, attention must be given to the methodology needed to move from the status quo to a future configuration, in the event that the status quo is not possible to maintain.

Rationale

The resource controllers meeting provides for an extensive consultation of those directly responsible for the ownership of the high schools concerning their future over the next five to fifteen years. The meeting also attempts to break down the competitive instincts of the schools and invites cooperation and compromise. In addition, the meeting may also provide the incentive for individual initiatives on the part of each high school, such as a private school making known, either publicly at the meeting or in confidence to the bishop or superintendent of schools after the meeting, its specific plans or its willingness to cooperate formally with another school. An overriding philosophy of such a meeting is that the collective wisdom of the whole will best serve the diocese.

Development of the Models

Prior to the resource controllers meeting, the high school planning committee or a subcommittee develops the configuration models. Generally, no model should represent the status quo, which we feel is not helpful to discuss at the meeting. We recommend that a range of models be considered, having some deviate only slightly from the present configuration of the schools and having others represent more dramatic variation from the status quo. Exhibit 7-3 contains an example of several models developed during the Archdiocese of Boston study.

The planning committee will probably consider many more models than would be feasible to present at the meeting. Part of the success of the meeting depends upon the planning committee constructing feasible models that will challenge the group and elicit a reaction. Only when that happens will the high school planning committee and the participants benefit from the meeting.

In deciding on the configuration models to present, the planning committee should consider

❖ The impact on nearby schools if a single-sex school becomes a coed school

❖ How the relationship among the other high schools changes if a high school closes

❖ The schools most likely to merge if a consolidation is needed in an area

❖ The impact on nearby schools if a new high school is built

❖ How nearby schools can share resources and programs

After the planning committee has decided on the models to present, it needs to prepare a writ-

---

Exhibit 7-3. Some Configuration Models from the Archdiocese of Boston Study

The following models, which are described very concisely, are presented as tentative options for discussion and reaction. In the discussion, it is expected that the advantages and disadvantages of each model will emerge and that other possibilities may be suggested. The characteristics of the thirteen high schools included in this group are as follows:

School	Type	Owner	Students	Tuition
Boston College HS	boys	private	1110	4,100
Don Bosco	boys	private	666	3,400
Mt. Alvernia	girls	private	138	3,675
Mt. St. Joseph	girls	private	253	3,300
St. Columbkille	coed	parish	129	2,020
Trinity	coed	parish	130	2,200
			650	
Catholic Memorial	boys	private	648	3,400
St. Clare	girls	central	211	3,300
Cardinal Cushing	girls	central	210	2,030
Msgr. Ryan	girls	parish	223	2,150
St. Gregory	girls	parish	176	2,500
			820	
Cathedral	coed	central	290	1,825
Mission	coed	parish	249	1,600

Assumptions

1. A model that maintains the status quo will continue to be discussed; however, the status-quo model may not be viable for this area.
2. Boston College High School and Don Bosco do not materially affect any model, unless the possibility arises that either will become coed or add additional grades.
3. At most, two girls' schools are needed to serve the Dorchester/South Boston/Roslindale area.
4. A regional junior high serving the inner city is a possibility.
5. If Catholic Memorial remains as a boys' school, the establishment of a junior high there has a high probability.

ten description of the models, similar to the example provided in Exhibit 7-3.

Organization of the Meeting

Exhibit 7-4 shows a typical agenda for a resource controllers meeting. The meeting begins with a large-group session during which the high school planning committee or consultant explains the process for the day and describes how the models were developed. During this session, the presenter should emphasize the following points:

Exhibit 7-3. Some Configuration Models from the Archdiocese of Boston Study (continued)

Models

Model A: Two girls' schools for Dorchester/South Boston/Roslindale
  1. Cardinal Cushing and St. Gregory
  2. St. Clare and Msgr. Ryan
  3. St. Clare and St. Gregory
  4. Cardinal Cushing and St. Clare
One coed school for the inner city (Cathedral or Mission High)
One coed school for the Allston-Brighton-Newton area (St. Columbkille or Trinity)
Mt. St. Joseph, Mt. Alvernia, Catholic Memorial, BC High, and Don Bosco continue as is.

Model B: Same as Model A, except
Mt. St. Joseph Academy becomes a coed school serving the Allston-Brighton-Newton area.
St. Columbkille and Trinity close.

Model C: Same as Model A, except
Catholic Memorial becomes a coed school and St. Clare closes.
Msgr. Ryan and St. Gregory merge at St. Gregory as an interparish school that serves girls.

Model D: One girls' school serving Dorchester/South Boston area:
  1. An interparish Msgr. Ryan-St. Gregory
  2. Cardinal Cushing

One coed school for the Allston-Brighton-Newton area:
  1. Mt. St. Joseph Academy
  2. St. Columbkille or Trinity

One coed school for West Roxbury/Roslindale at Catholic Memorial

One coed school for the inner city (Cathedral or Mission)

Two boys' schools for the area: BC High and Don Bosco

Exhibit 7-4. Agenda for Resource Controllers Meeting

8:30	Registration, coffee/danish
9:00	Welcome, opening prayer
9:15	Overview of the day: explanation of model development, ground rules for the process
9:45	Groupings for configuration models
12:00	Lunch
1:00	Continue with configuration models
2:30	Large group—description of next steps
3:00	Closing prayer

- The need to develop a comprehensive diocesan strategy regarding the placement of high schools

- The tentativeness of the models that will be discussed

- The legitimacy of difference of opinion at this point

- The desirability of finding ways to overcome objections and to reach compromise

- The need for candor

- The need to recognize the good of the whole, as well as the good of an individual school

- The need for different owners (private, parish, and diocesan) to dialogue

The presenter then explains the ground rules that govern the discussion of the models and the voting:

- The status quo model continues to be considered but is not discussed at the meeting.

- Each school, regardless of the number of individuals present who represent that school, gets one vote on each model.

- Each school designates one spokesperson.

- The possible votes are
  - Favor the model
  - Tolerate the model
  - Cannot tolerate the model

- Each school should vote on each model, regardless of whether the proposed model directly affects the school.

Group Process

After the large-group session, the participants go to their assigned small groups. The number of small groups depends upon the number of high schools in the diocese. In general, we recommend between six and ten schools per group, which are usually organized geographically. In some cases, even when the diocese has more than ten high schools, the high school planning committee may wish to have all the high schools participate in the same group.

Each group has a facilitator who is responsible for presenting the models and guiding the group through the process for the day. The steps in the group process are as follows:

1. The facilitator distributes the models and provides time for the representatives from each school to review and discuss the models among themselves.

2. Each school reports its preference on each model. The facilitator records the preferences on newsprint for all to see.

3. The facilitator selects the model with the fewest "Cannot Tolerate" choices and asks each school voting that way to state its objections to the model. The report of the objections should be brief and factual. The facilitator records the objections on newsprint.

4. The representatives from each school briefly caucus to propose modifications to the model that they think will overcome any objections of the other schools.

5. Each school reports on its proposed modifications. The facilitator records each modification on newsprint.

6. After all the proposed modifications are listed, the facilitator permits questions of clarification but does not permit debate. The facilitator must keep tight control of the meeting at this point. The discussion should flow though the facilitator, who should not permit direct discussion between the schools.

7. The representatives from each school then caucus to decide how to vote on the proposed modifications to the model.

8. Each school votes on the modifications and the facilitator records the vote on newsprint. Any school voting "cannot tolerate" should state its objections, which the facilitator records on the newsprint.

9. Repeat steps 4 to 8 until agreement is reached or until all agree that no further progress is possible on this model.

10. Select another model with the next fewest objections and repeat steps 2 to 9.

11. Continue working until the group has finished with all reasonable models that have at least a chance of being acceptable to most of the schools.

12. Return to the large-group session at the scheduled time to report on what transpired in the small group.

Summary

This chapter presents a planning model for the high schools in a diocese or in a region of a diocese. The model has the same philosophy as the diocesan planning model for elementary schools and follows similar procedures, except for a parish-based consultation.

The selection of the planning committee is probably more critical when planning for high schools than when planning for elementary schools. We believe that a committee consisting entirely of owners offers the best alternative available to a diocese, because these individuals are usually in the best position to make an informed and less emotional decision about the schools than are committees with different membership.

The knowledge exploration meeting held early in the study will assist the planning committee to identify the problems facing the schools, generate possible solutions to these problems, and, perhaps most importantly, build ownership for the problems and solutions among the schools' stakeholders. In addition, the conduct of a comprehensive school audit will help an individual school identify its strengths and weaknesses.

The resource controllers meeting permits the planning committee to consult with the schools' owners, board members, and administrators, as well as with parents, teachers, and community and business leaders, regarding the future of each high school. The results of the discussion of models during this meeting enable the planning committee to identify promising models and eliminate ones that are not feasible.

Chapter Objectives

In this chapter you will learn the following:

1. How an individual school can adapt the diocesan planning model to do strategic planning

2. How to form a planning committee and conduct a needs assessment

3. What data are essential to have and how to gather them

4. How to develop preliminary recommendations and conduct a consultation concerning them

5. How to structure the strategic plan for the school

Introduction

Individual schools can also use the consultative model presented in the previous chapters for strategic planning. Virtually all the issues that are relevant to diocesan planning are also applicable to planning for individual schools. This chapter presents a framework for planning that describes the way in which an elementary school or a high school can adapt the model to its own individual circumstances. The framework presents the elements of a strategic plan and the major issues that it should address.

A Framework for Planning

The responsibility for strategic planning rests jointly with the school board, the school administrators, and, for parish-related elementary schools or high schools, the pastor or pastors of the parishes that have a financial and/or governance responsibility for the school. From its very inception, the planning process should involve the entire school community: administrators, teachers, students, parents, board members, alumni, interested supporters of the school, and, if applicable, parishioners. While respecting each other's roles and responsibilities, those responsible for planning should work together to ensure the success of the planning effort.

Six steps are involved in strategic planning for an individual school:

1. Form a planning committee

2. Gather essential data
3. Conduct a needs assessment
4. Develop preliminary recommendations
5. Write the preliminary plan
6. Consult with constituents and finalize the plan

Step 1: Form a Planning Committee

The planning committee might be the school's governing or advisory board, a committee of the board, or a special ad hoc planning group. Long-range planning is one of the major responsibilities of the school board. Every board should have a long-range planning committee that helps the entire board assess the school's current status and what it hopes to accomplish during the next five years. On the other hand, if a planning study is required because of special circumstances, the school may wish to establish a special ad hoc committee to conduct the study.

The planning committee coordinates the development of the strategic plan by

❖ Involving the school's constituencies actively in the planning process

❖ Identifying the assumptions that will guide the planning process

❖ Developing the goals and objectives that flow from these assumptions

❖ Identifying the specific steps necessary to ensure the timely meeting of the goals and objectives

As the spiritual, educational, and managerial leader of the school, the principal is responsible for working with the school board or special ad hoc planning committee to ensure the successful development and implementation of the long-range plan. Key to the strategic planning process, the principal often is responsible for its daily management, including the mobilization of the school's faculty, communication with parents and other interested constituencies, and coordination of essential planning activities.

Because of the intimate relationship between a parish and a parish school, the pastor must be fully involved in planning for the school's future. In a parish school, the pastor's responsibility in planning goes beyond simply commissioning the long-range plan and receiving it at the end of the planning process. As the canonical administrator of the parish that sponsors the school, the pastor shares with the principal, school board, and school community the responsibility for the school's welfare, not only because the school is an important ministry of the parish, but also because of the financial reality that, in many cases, the school's budget exceeds that of the entire parish.

Step 2: Gather Essential Data

The planning committee needs information to help it understand the school's situation and develop an informed strategic plan. The committee will need data about enrollment, demographic trends and projections, financial aspects, and attitudes and opinions of the school community. High schools should complete the audit described in Chapter 7; elementary schools should collect the data that are described below. Appendix O contains forms to facilitate the collection and display of these data.

Enrollment

❖ Each grade's enrollment for the past five to ten years (see elementary school chart 1 in Appendix O). Chart 1 helps the planning committee examine

  ❖ Changes in total enrollment by year

  ❖ Changes in each grade's enrollment by year, particularly PK, K, and first grade

❖ Grade-to-grade stability of cohorts, e.g., first grade to second grade to third grade, and so forth, for the same group of students

❖ The school's enrollment by zip code for the past five years (see elementary school chart 2 in Appendix O). Chart 2 helps the planning committee determine the communities where students live. With this information, the planning committee can ascertain whether significant shifts in the source of students have occurred. In addition, the data will enable the committee to suggest how the school's marketing and public relations program can be better targeted to recruit strategically from underrepresented areas.

❖ The school's racial/ethnic enrollment for the past five years (see elementary school chart 3 in Appendix O). Chart 3 assists the planning committee in describing changes in the school's racial/ethnic makeup by tracking the enrollment patterns of the major racial/ethnic groups and other groups (e.g., Cambodian, Cape Verdean, Chinese, Cuban, Haitian, Hawaiian, Hmong, Korean, Mexican, Portuguese, Puerto Rican, Russian, Vietnamese, and so forth) that may have a significant number of students enrolled in the school.

❖ The school's non-Catholic enrollment and its enrollment of Catholics according to feeder parishes for the past five years (see elementary school chart 4 in Appendix O). Chart 4 provides the planning committee with details regarding the number of parishes that send children to the school. This information, like that in chart 2, will help the committee suggest strategies for marketing, recruitment, and public relations.

Demographic Data and Projections

❖ Demographic projections from state or local governments or public school systems regarding the number of school-age children anticipated in the next give to ten years.

❖ Population trend data from the Census Bureau, chamber of commerce, or county/state planning agency.

❖ Projections from the local chamber of commerce or appropriate government agency data regarding recent and anticipated building of new homes over the next five to ten years in the area served by the school.

Financial

The planning committee should obtain these financial data for the past five years (see elementary school chart 5 in Appendix O):

* Tuition charged for students in the parish, those out of the parish, and non-Catholics
* Cost per student
* Total operating expenses for the school
* Total salaries and benefits (reported by actual amount and by percentage of total operating expenses)
* Total revenue for the school
* Revenue from tuition (reported by actual amount and by percentage of total income)
* Parish subsidy (reported by actual amount and by percentage of total income)
* Revenue from fund raising (reported by actual amount and by percentage of total income)
* Other revenue (reported by actual amount and by percentage of total income)
* Total tuition assistance provided to students

Surveys: Attitudes and Opinions

The planning committee should develop questionnaires to survey the opinions of the various constituencies that have an interest in the school. These constituencies are listed below, along with a brief description of the most relevant information sought from them. In some cases, interviews in person or by telephone may be more appropriate than written questionnaires. The sample surveys described in Chapter 2 and presented in Appendices A, B, C, D, and L could form the basis for some of these questionnaires.

Parents of current students. Appropriate for elementary schools and high schools

* How parents learned about the school
* Reasons for selecting the school
* Why the school was selected over other schools, if applicable (particularly relevant for high schools)
* Strengths of the school

* Areas in need of improvement or change
* Attitudes and opinions about various issues being considered in the planning study

Teachers in the school. Appropriate for elementary schools and high schools

* Reasons for choosing to teach at the school
* Reasons for remaining at the school
* Satisfaction with various aspects of the school
* Strengths of the school
* Areas in need of improvement or change
* Attitudes and opinions about various issues being considered in the planning study

Current students. Appropriate for elementary schools and high schools

* Satisfaction with various aspects of the school
* Strengths of the school
* Areas in need of improvement or change
* Attitudes and opinions about various issues being considered in the planning study

Clergy from parish and feeder parishes. Appropriate for elementary schools and high schools

* Satisfaction with various aspects of the school
* Strengths of the school
* Areas in need of improvement or change
* Attitudes and opinions about various issues being considered in the planning study
* Comparison of this school with competitors, concerning such areas as
  * Quality of academic program
  * Scope of the curriculum
  * Quality of teachers
  * Gender composition of the school
  * Size of student body
  * Racial/ethnic mix of student body
  * Location of the school
  * Disciplinary standards
  * Tuition and fees
  * Athletic program
  * Extracurricular activities
  * School facilities
  * Transportation

Parishioners. Primarily appropriate for elementary schools

- Perception of the school
- Attitudes and opinions about various issues being considered in the planning study

Personnel from feeder schools. Primarily appropriate for high schools

- Perceived strengths of the school
- How school compares with others attended by their students
- Areas in need of improvement or change
- Attitudes and opinions about various issues being considered in the planning study
- Comparison of this school with competitors, concerning such areas as
  - Quality of academic program
  - Scope of the curriculum
  - Quality of teachers
  - Gender composition of the school
  - Size of student body
  - Racial/ethnic mix of student body
  - Location of the school
  - Disciplinary standards
  - Tuition and fees
  - Athletic program
  - Extracurricular activities
  - School facilities
  - Transportation

Parents of students in feeder schools. Primarily appropriate for high schools

- What parents look for in choosing a school
- Perceived strengths of the school
- How school compares with others considered by their children
- Areas in need of improvement or change
- Attitudes and opinions about various issues being considered in the planning study
- Comparison of this school with competitors, concerning such areas as
  - Quality of academic program
  - Scope of the curriculum
  - Quality of teachers
  - Gender composition of the school
  - Size of student body
  - Racial/ethnic mix of student body
  - Location of the school
  - Disciplinary standards
  - Tuition and fees
  - Athletic program

- Extracurricular activities
- School facilities
- Transportation

Parents of non-enrolling or transfer students. Appropriate for elementary schools and high schools

- Reasons for choosing the school that their child(ren) attends
- Reasons for not selecting this school
- Perceived strength of this school
- Comparison of this school with competitors, concerning such areas as
- Quality of academic program
- Scope of the curriculum
- Quality of teachers
- Gender composition of the school
- Size of student body
- Racial/ethnic mix of student body
- Location of the school
- Disciplinary standards
- Tuition and fees
- Athletic program
- Extracurricular activities
- School facilities
- Transportation

Step 3: Conduct a Needs Assessment

A needs assessment is a process that helps the planning committee evaluate the progress a school has made towards satisfying its goals and objectives. A needs assessment consists basically of four phases:

- Assessing the school's progress relative to its stated goals and objectives

- Determining the discrepancies (needs) between what should be and what is

- Placing the needs in priority order

- Determining which of the priorities that school should concentrate on during a specific time period

School Stakeholders Meeting

In addition to other means that the planning committee may use to gather data for the needs assessment, we suggest that a school stakeholders meeting, which is similar to the knowledge exploration meeting that combines the activities of a problem element meeting and a solution element meeting as described in Chapter 7, be held early in the planning study. Alternatively, the planning committee could have a meeting for identifying problems and one for identifying solutions on two different evenings. Some general considerations for the school stakeholders meeting or series of meetings are participants, formation of groups, nominal group process, and schedule.

Participants. The participants should include the school's stakeholders: parents, teachers, priests and parishioners of the parish, members of the school board, students, and interested business and professional leaders. The planning committee should decide upon the number of participants to invite to the meeting, which primarily is a function of the size of the available facilities. However, like the knowledge exploration meeting, the school stakeholders meeting should have at least fifty participants to permit some diversity in the group work.

Formation of Groups. Similar to the problem element meeting, solution element meeting, and knowledge exploration meeting, the participants in the school stakeholders meeting should be identified at least a week before the meeting so that groups can be formed beforehand. The groups should consist of six to eight members, a number that is more effective with smaller assemblies than the eight to twelve members normally suggested for the nominal group process. The organizers of the meeting should ensure that the groups are heterogeneous with regard to the types of individuals. Since many participants will likely be parents and/or parishioners, in addition to the constituency each represents, the heterogeneity of groups could be based on gender, grade child attends, length of time in the parish, and so forth.

Nominal group process. The participants in each group, under the guidance of a facilitator, will use the nominal group process to generate their ideas and suggestions. The procedure in each small group is as follows:

❖ The participants write their ideas on index cards without discussion.

❖ A facilitator lists on large sheets of newsprint the ideas as dictated by the participants.

❖ The participants may ask for clarification of ideas.

❖ Each participant chooses five ideas from the newsprint, which in his or her opinion merit special priority.

❖ The facilitator records the priority votes beside the appropriate ideas on the newsprint.

❖ A brief discussion occurs regarding the initial list of priorities.

❖ Each participant again select five items that merit special priority.

❖ The facilitator records these final votes and writes out the list of priority statements.

Schedule. The participants at the meeting will identify problems and produce possible solutions. Thus, the schedule of the school stakeholders meeting is similar to that of the knowledge exploration meeting in Chapter 7.

❖ A large group session is utilized to explain the format of the meeting and present any relevant data (ten to fifteen minutes).

❖ The participants gather in small groups and use the nominal group process to identify problems and concerns facing the school (forty-five minutes).

❖ The participants come together in a large group to hear the priority statements from each of the small groups (fifteen minutes).

❖ The participants return to their small groups and generate possible solutions to the problems and concerns identified during the first small-group session. Each group goes through two complete cycles, time permitting. If time is short, the groups can simply write their solutions on cards and the group process can end at this point (twenty-five to ninety minutes).

❖ The participants then return to the large group to hear some of the suggested solutions (ten to fifteen minutes).

Focus Groups[1]

In addition to or in place of a school stakeholders meeting, the planning committee may wish to use focus group interviews to assist in the needs assessment. A focus group usually consists of eight to twelve individuals who have a common status, such as parents, students, business executives, teachers, administrators, pastors, and so forth. The membership of a focus group differs from the membership of a nominal group. Normally, the focus group is homogeneous with regard to characteristics, while the nominal group is heterogeneous. The participants provide qualitative data concerning a particular issue during an interactive group interview that typically lasts from one and a half to two and a half hours. Each focus group is led by a moderator who attempts to keep the discussion centered on the issues of interest and who encourages the participants to react to each other's views.

Popham (1993) describes these steps in planning and conducting focus groups.

Step 1: Formulating the focus group's data-gathering purpose. The planning committee should identify the issues that the focus groups will examine, based on the issues that are part of the strategic planning study and/or the information needs of the planning committee. The number of focus groups needed depends upon the complexity of the issues to be considered and the number of different constituencies that should be involved in the needs assessment.

Step 2: Identifying and recruiting participants. Each focus group should be homogeneous in its composition. Variables that could be used to determine the composition of a particular focus group include age, educational level, race/ethnicity, gender, state in life (clergy, religious, lay), occupation (educator, pastor, researcher, business executive), relation to the school (parent, school board, teacher, parishioner), and so forth. Popham offers these steps once a set of potential participants has been identified:

❖ Establish convenient meeting times and places.
❖ Invite potential participants at least two weeks before the session.

1. The material in this section draws heavily from Chapter Nine, "Focus Groups: A Potent Qualitative Data-Gathering Procedure," in W. J. Popham (1993). *Educational Evaluation* (3rd edition). Boston: Allyn and Bacon.

❖ Establish appropriate incentives, including emphasizing the contribution that the invitee can make to the group discussion.
❖ Send a follow-up letter one week before the scheduled session.
❖ Call each potential participant a day or two before the session.

Step 3: Developing the interview guide. The interview guide contains the questions that the moderator uses to help maintain the group's focus. The interview guide usually consists of ten to fifteen questions that the moderator will attempt to cover during the session. Because of the interactive nature of the focus group, the moderator may not have the opportunity to explore all questions in the guide, and new questions may occur in light of the focus group's discussion. Thus, all truly significant questions must be asked early during the focus group session. Popham offers these suggestions concerning the nature of the questions:

❖ Use open-ended questions so that they serve as stimuli for group discussion rather than evoking discussion-suppressing factual or yes/no responses.
❖ Avoid lengthy, complex, or ambiguous questions and those with esoteric vocabulary.

Step 4: Selecting the moderator. Popham recommends the use of a moderator, who leads the discussion, and an assistant moderator, who takes notes and participates in the discussion at strategic times. According to Popham, focus group moderators should be able to

❖ Express themselves clearly
❖ Be good listeners
❖ Quickly comprehend the essence of what participants are communicating via verbal or nonverbal means
❖ Be spontaneous and lively
❖ Be empathetic regarding the way that participants feel about the issue being discussed
❖ Keep the group on task
❖ Be flexible in the face of unanticipated events

Step 5: Preparing for the session. Prior to the session, the moderator should completely master the interview guide and commit it to memory. As the participants arrive, the moderator should engage them in informal conversation before seating them in the focus group in an attempt to identify individuals who are talkative, shy, or seem to consider themselves experts. The moderator should try to arrange the seating so that more reserved individuals are directly in front of the moderator, thus permitting more eye contact with those who are less apt to speak without prompting.

Step 6: Conducting the session. If possible, focus groups should be tape-recorded so that a complete record can be make of the proceedings. The moderator typically begins the session by welcoming the groups, describing the topic and the nature of information sought, and explaining important ground rules. Popham proposes these guidelines for moderators during a session:

- *Adhering to the guide.* Normally, the moderator will wish to follow the order of questions in the interview guide, with some flexibility according to course of the discussion.

- *Probing.* The moderator, from time to time, should request additional information by asking a participant to elaborate or provide an example.

- *Pausing.* A brief pause by the moderator frequently elicits additional points of view from other participants.

- *Neutral responses.* The moderator should strive to maintain a totally neutral posture during the course of the interview. The moderator should never give her or his opinion.

- *Closing.* A moderator will often use the final moments of a session to ask participants if anything has been omitted. This opportunity sometimes elicits worthwhile comments from the participants.

Step 7: Analyzing focus group data. The moderator and assistant moderator should hold a debriefing meeting to prepare a written summary of the session's key findings. Tape-recorded sessions should be transcribed if cost and time permit. The analysis of the written summary of the session and the transcription, if available, should concentrate on one question at a time. A content analysis technique similar to that described in Chapter 3 for the data from the problem element meeting and solution element meeting could be used for the analysis of the focus group data.

Finally, Popham regards the following as advantages and disadvantages of focus groups:

Advantages

- Focus groups are rooted in social interactions, so they lessen participants' inhibitions.
- The collective contributions of focus-group participants often yield synergistic gains.
- The results of focus groups are readily understandable.
- Focus groups can be quickly implemented.
- Focus groups are relatively inexpensive.

Disadvantages

- Focus groups are interactive; therefore, the moderator has less control than in many other data-gathering procedures.
- Focus group data analysis is highly labor intensive.
- The nature of the interaction that takes place in focus group interviews may distort certain participants' contributions to the interview.
- Focus group data permit only inferences with highly limited generalizability.
- Because of the qualitative nature of focus group data, some researchers interpret the data to support predetermined views.

Step 4: Develop Preliminary Recommendations

Just prior to the school stakeholders meeting, the planning committee should form task forces to deal with the key areas that the strategic plan will address. The purpose of the task forces is to assist the planning committee in the development of the strategic plan. Formation of the task forces prior to the school stakeholders meeting permits the members to attend the meeting to hear first hand about the major problems, concerns, and suggested solutions. The task forces could be ad hoc groups, subcommittees of the planning committee, or subcommittees of the school's board.

The scope of the strategic planning study determines the task forces that are needed. While the planning committee may want to add task forces following the school stakeholders meeting to address particular issues raised there that are not appropriate for already formed task forces to address, we suggest the following task forces to ensure adequate scope for the strategic planning study: Catholic identity, finance, governance, curriculum, and marketing and public relations. Each task force studies the data from the school stakeholders meeting, and collects other information concerning the issues it is charged to examine. The planning committee acts as a sounding board and agent of final approval for the work of the task forces.

The following are suggested topics and issues that task forces may wish to address during the planning study. The task forces should also refer to Chapter 4 for additional topics and relevant questions.

Catholic Identity

❖ Review the school's mission statement and philosophy in the light of the diocesan mission statement and Church documents, including

   ❖ *To Teach as Jesus Did*, United States Catholic Conference, November 1972.

   ❖ *The Catholic School*, Sacred Congregation for Catholic Education, March 1977.

   ❖ *Lay Teachers—Witnesses to the Faith*, Sacred Congregation for Catholic Education, October 1982.

   ❖ *The Religious Dimension of Education in the Catholic School*, Sacred Congregation for Catholic Education, June 1988.

❖ Examine the extent to which the school's physical environment reflects its Catholic nature. Are religious symbols prominently displayed? Do the messages contained on the bulletin boards communicate religious values and ideals?

❖ Evaluate the quality of the school's religious instruction program. Have all teachers of religion satisfied or are in the process of satisfying diocesan certification requirements for catechists?

❖ Determine the extent to which Catholic ideals and religious values inform the school curriculum and the students' learning. Does the curriculum provide for an integration of faith and knowledge?

❖ Examine how the teachers contribute to the maintenance of the faith community by modeling Catholic values and sharing their beliefs with the students.

❖ Examine how well the school carries out its evangelization mission.

❖ Examine the extent to which the school's rituals and practices reflect its Catholic nature.

❖ Develop a five-year plan, which includes several objectives regarding the enhancement of the school's Catholic identity that the school will emphasize.

Physical Plant and Facilities

❖ Briefly describe the design, material, and essential features of each building used for the school.

❖ Conduct a complete structural, safety, and maintenance analysis of all physical facilities, school buildings, and grounds.

❖ Describe any construction or modifications of school buildings over the past ten years.

❖ Identify major long-term structural and repair priorities and include an estimated schedule.

❖ List all necessary or desirable repairs and capital improvements, and prioritize the attention that each should receive.

❖ Develop a five-year plan to attend to the repairs and complete the improvements. Include cost estimates.

Marketing and Development

❖ Evaluate the school's past record in fund raising, establishing building endowments, securing financial support from the business community and foundations, and attracting special gifts and bequests from estates.

❖ Identify the fund-raising and development priorities for the next five years.

❖ Prepare a five-year development plan, along with a case statement that will be used to market the school to various publics and to seek their support.

  ❖ The case statement should contain a summary of the school's history, its unique identity, its religious and academic philosophy, and its specific objectives, presented in such a manner to encourage investment in the school's future.

  ❖ The development plan should contain the specific gift opportunities identified by the five-year strategic plan.

Public Relations and Recruitment

❖ Examine how the school promotes itself to the parishes and the general public.

❖ Determine the image of the school in the community and the reasons parents send their children there or why they do not.

❖ Decide upon the message that should be conveyed about the school and the best means to communicate it.

❖ Identify the media available to get the message out about the school and the expenses involved.

❖ Ascertain whether the school should develop a recruitment brochure.

❖ Examine the quality of the relationship between the school and the parish or parishes that sponsor it or with which it is otherwise associated.

❖ Review the efforts the school has made to keep in contact with its alumni and plan to establish an alumni association if the school does not have one already.

❖ Develop a five-year public relations and recruitment plan that contains specific objectives as to how the school will increase its efforts in public relations and how it will maintain or increase its enrollment.

Finance

❖ Review the NCEA publication, Elementary School Finance Manual (Reck & Yeager, 1984).

❖ Examine the school's budgets for the past three years and evaluate any trends in the light of the school's current and projected conditions.

❖ Examine the school's tuition policy and determine whether the proper balance exists between tuition, subsidy, and fund raising. How much of the cost per student should tuition cover?

❖ Review the criteria that are used to determine the eligibility of families to receive tuition assistance at the school and modify them as needed.

❖ Develop a budget based on projected enrollment, staffing, program needs, tuition assistance, and plant and facility requirements. Clearly identify the assumptions on which the budget is based.

❖ Develop a five-year financial plan for the school's income and expenses, with realistic assumptions, concerning tuition; parish and/or diocesan subsidies, if applicable; fund raising; and operating expenses, including salaries.

Demographics/Enrollment

❖ Study the demographic profiles of the students in the school, including race/ethnicity, religion, location of their residence (zip codes), and parish attended. Note any significant changes that have occurred over the past five years.

❖ Study the attrition and retention patterns in the school over the past five years. Identify key grades where attrition is most likely and attempt to identify reasons for the attrition at these and the other grades.

❖ Examine the feasibility of adding K, pre-K, a before-school program, and an after-school program.

❖ Examine the data concerning the size of classes in the school, and determine whether the policy regarding class size should be modified.

- Study the necessity and feasibility of adding classrooms, expanding physical facilities.

Staffing/Personnel

- Prepare an overview of the professional preparation, workload, and responsibilities of current faculty and staff.

- Assess availability, adequacy, and quality of staff development programs.

- Assess the adequacy of current faculty and staff to deliver a program that meets the school's goals and objectives and that is consistent with its philosophy.

- Project staffing needs for the next five years, including the assumptions concerning professional qualifications, responsibilities, salaries, and benefits.

- Evaluate how well the school community (and the parish community) publicly recognizes the school's administrators' and teachers' professional excellence, length of service, and commitment to the Church. Include a strategy in the long-range plan to increase this recognition.

Curriculum/Academic Quality

- Determine whether the school's curriculum satisfies the requirements and standards of quality established by the state, the diocese, and appropriate accrediting agencies.

- Review the school's accreditation status and make appropriate recommendations concerning it.

- Review the curriculum in light of diocesan guidelines and current curricular standards as promoted by the professional education associations and national groups, such as the National Council of Teachers of Mathematics, National Center for Improving Science Education, American Association for the Advancement of Science, National Council of English Teachers, National Science Teachers Association, National Center for History in the Schools, and Modern Language Association.

- Examine the extent to which the curriculum meets the needs of all the students in the school and make appropriate recommendations.

- Evaluate the offerings in specialized areas such as art, computer science, drama, health education, home economics, music, physical education, and remedial programs, and make appropriate recommendations.

- Evaluate the condition and adequacy of current textbooks, workbooks, computers, audiovisual equipment, laboratory equipment, and general supplies, and plan to upgrade or replace, as appropriate.

- Review the non-curricular professional services of the school, such as guidance, counseling, and campus ministry, and modify as appropriate.

- Develop a five-year plan for specific improvements in the curriculum and support areas.

Parental Involvement

- Determine how the school attempts to enhance the involvement of parents in their children's religious formation.

- Evaluate how involved parents are in the school. What can be done to enhance the effectiveness of the parents' organization?

- Ascertain to what extent the parents understand the school's philosophy, what is expected of them, and how they can help the school. Does the school provide parents an opportunity to express their concerns?

- Develop a plan to help organize parents to monitor legislation that affects the school and to lobby federal and state legislatures to secure tax-supported financial assistance for the education of their children.

Governance/Administration

- Review the NCEA publication, *Building Better Boards* (Sheehan, 1990).

- Evaluate the effectiveness and representativeness of the school's governing board.

- Determine whether the responsibilities of the school's governing board are clearly delineated.

- Ascertain the effectiveness of the working relationship between the school's governing board and parish committees, such as the finance committee and the pastoral council.

- Review the USCC publications, *The Principal as Educational Leader* (Ciriello, 1993), *The Principal as Spiritual Leader* (Ciriello, 1994a), and *The Principal as Managerial Leader* (Ciriello, 1994b).

- Determine to what extent the school's principal manifests spiritual leadership, instructional leadership, managerial leadership, and community leadership in the administration of the school.

Step 5: Write the Strategic Plan

The strategic plan should begin with a brief history of the school, followed by a statement of the school's mission and philosophy, the major assumptions on which the plan is based, and any constraints or limitations that affect it. The subsequent sections, each of which would treat a single topic, might be structured according to the following format:

- Overall goal to be achieved
- Specific actions or objectives necessary to achieve the goal
- A timeline for accomplishing each action or objective

Depending upon the specific needs of the school, the following topics may be in the strategic plan:

- Catholic identity	- Spiritual growth
- Religious education	- Academic curriculum
- Programs & activities	- Personnel
- Public relations	- Marketing
- Development	- Plant and facilities

- Finance	- Recruitment
- Governance	- School community
- Parents	

Step 6: Consult with Constituents and Finalize the Plan

The final step in developing the strategic plan is the consultation of the stakeholders, those constituents who have a vested interest in the future of the school. Prior to finalizing the plan and promulgating it, the planning committee should provide interested constituents an opportunity to review a near final draft of the plan and make suggestions concerning it. The planning committee may wish to conduct this consultation via written communication and/or by means of a meeting or a series of meetings.

The consultation with constituents regarding the finalization of the strategic plan has the following advantages:

- Enables constituents to become familiar with the plan
- Permits the constituents to have some input into the final format and wording of the plan
- Builds ownership for the plan by the constituents
- Builds support for the plan's implementation
- Often surfaces volunteers who are willing to work for the plan's implementation

Summary

This chapter includes a brief description of how the diocesan planning model can be adapted for strategic planning by an individual school. Basically, the dynamics involved in planning and its procedures are the same whether one is planning for an individual school or a large number of schools. A planning committee gathers data, conducts a needs assessment with the help of the constituents served by the school, arranges a process that ensures an adequate review of issues and examination of planning alternatives, develops a preliminary plan, and conducts a consultation on that plan with constituents who are stakeholders in the school. This chapter is best used in conjunction with the material in the preceding chapters, rather than solely on its own.

Diocesan Planning Study for Catholic Schools
Parent Survey

Dear Parent/Guardian:

The diocese is conducting a long-range planning study for its schools. Please take a few minutes to complete this survey. Your responses will help the diocesan planning committee develop recommendations for the schools in your area of the diocese. Please return the completed survey to your child's teacher. Thank you for your help.

Part I: Attitudes and Opinions

Using the following scale, circle the code corresponding to how you feel about each statement:

SA=Strongly Agree   A=Agree   D=Disagree   SD=Strongly Disagree   DK=Don't Know

1. Catholic schools are an essential part of the Church's educational mission. — SA A D SD DK

2. Catholic schools are needed more today than twenty-five years ago. — SA A D SD DK

3. Catholic schools are worth what it costs to operate them. — SA A D SD DK

4. Salaries of Catholic school teachers should be increased substantially, even if that results in significant increases in tuition. — SA A D SD DK

5. The religious education program (CCD) of my parish is functioning well. — SA A D SD DK

6. An additional Catholic elementary school is needed in my area of the diocese. — SA A D SD DK

7. An additional Catholic high school is needed in my area of the diocese. — SA A D SD DK

8. Catholic schools can provide an effective Catholic education with all lay teachers. — SA A D SD DK

9. The Catholic schools that I am familiar with have good reputations. — SA A D SD DK

10. The Catholic schools that I am familiar with effectively teach Catholic doctrine. — SA A D SD DK

11. I would increase my weekly contribution to my parish to support Catholic schools. — SA A D SD DK

12. The diocese should establish an endowment fund for Catholic schools. — SA A D SD DK

13. The public views Catholic schools as being among the best schools in the area. — SA A D SD DK

14. The Catholic schools I know have well-prepared and effective principals. — SA A D SD DK

15. The public schools where I live have good academic reputations.   SA   A   D   SD   DK

16. The Catholic schools I know establish a foundation of
moral and ethical values.   SA   A   D   SD   DK

17. The Catholic schools I know have well-prepared and
effective teachers.   SA   A   D   SD   DK

18. Which of the following is or would be more important to
you in selecting a Catholic school? (circle one letter)
   a. Academic program
   b. Religious atmosphere and values
   c. Both of these are equally important

19. Please write the zip code of your residence_____

Part II: Reasons for Sending or Not Sending Children to Catholic Schools

What are the important reasons why you and other parents send or don't send your child(ren) to Catholic schools? In each column, place a 1 before the most important reason, a 2 before the second most important reason, and a 3 before the third most important reason. In addition, check (√) any additional reasons that are important.

Reasons for Choosing a Catholic School

___ Environment (good discipline, safe, caring)

___ Religious (Catholic, religion, values)

___ Academic (good curriculum, good teachers)

___ Facilities/activities (sports, etc.)

___ Family tradition

___ Better alternative than public schools

___ Convenient location

___ Other:

Reasons for Not Choosing a Catholic School

___ Academic (other schools as good or better)

___ Financial (unable to afford tuition)

___ Poor facilities/limited activities

___ Prefer public schools

___ Child has special needs

___ Friends attend other schools

___ Class size (too large)

___ Other:

Part III: Demographic Information

1. How many children under 19 years of age do you have? _____

2. Do you currently have any children in a Catholic elementary school?   ___Yes ___No
   (If yes, please write the name of the school here_____)
   (If yes, circle his/her/their grade levels: PK   K   1   2   3   4   5   6   7   8)
   (If yes, do you plan to send him/her/them to a Catholic high school?   ___Yes ___No ___Unsure)

3. Do you currently have any children in a Catholic high school?   ___Yes ___No
   (If yes, please write the name of the school(s) here_____)
   (If yes, circle his/her/their grade levels: 7   8   9   10   11   12)
   (If yes, did he/she/they attend a Catholic elementary school?   ___Yes ___No)

4. Check your highest educational level: __Elementary __High School __College __Post-Graduate

5. Check the Catholic schools you
   have attended: ___None   ___Elementary   ___Secondary   ___College/University

6. Check your race/ethnicity: ___American Indian/Alaskan Native   ___Asian/Pacific Islander
   ___Black, non-Hispanic   ___Hispanic   ___White, non-Hispanic

7. Arc you a single parent?   ___Yes ___No

8. Check your annual family income:
   ___Under $10,000   ___$10,000-$20,000   ___$20,001-$30,000   ___$30,001-$40,000
   ___$40,001-$50,000   ___$50,001-$75,000   ___$75,001-$100,000   ___Over $100,000

9. Write the name and location of your parish _____
   (If you are not Catholic, please check here ___)

Comments:

Diocesan Planning Study for Schools
Clergy Questionnaire

Directions: Please complete this questionnaire at your earliest convenience. Your responses will provide important data for the diocesan planning committee in planning for the future of the schools in the diocese. Circle the number corresponding to your answer.

1. In which deanery or vicariate is your parish located?_____

2. What is your age? 1. Under 35 2. Between 35 and 49 3. Between 50 and 65 4. Over 65

3. How many years have you been ordained a priest?_____

4. In which category do you belong? 1. Pastor 2. Associate Pastor 3. Other 4. Retired

5. How many years have you been a pastor?_____the pastor of this parish?_____

6. Does your parish have its own parochial school? 1. Yes 2. No

7. Does your parish cooperate in the sponsorship of a regional school? 1. Yes 2. No

8. Check your race/ethnicity: ___American Indian/Alaskan Native ___Asian/Pacific Islander ___Black, non-Hispanic ___Hispanic ___White, non-Hispanic

9. Check the Catholic schools you have attended: ___Elementary ___Secondary ___College/University

Directions: Use the following scale to indicate how you feel about each statement.

4=Agree Strongly   3=Agree   2=Disagree   1=Disagree Strongly   0=Not Applicable

10. Catholic schools are an essential part of the Church's educational mission.	4	3	2	1	0
11. Catholic schools are needed more today than twenty-five years ago.	4	3	2	1	0
12. Catholic schools are worth what it costs to operate them.	4	3	2	1	0
13. The quality of the Catholic schools in my area of the diocese is high.	4	3	2	1	0
14. Catholic schools should play a greater role in educating the disadvantaged.	4	3	2	1	0
15. Catholic schools are an effective use of the Church's resources.	4	3	2	1	0
16. Catholic schools are the best means for the religious education of the young.	4	3	2	1	0
17. Many of the parish's leaders are graduates of Catholic schools.	4	3	2	1	0

18. Catholic schools are excellent sources of religious and priestly vocations.	4	3	2	1	0
19. Catholic schools should be available to all parts of the diocese.	4	3	2	1	0
20. All Catholics have the responsibility of financially supporting the schools.	4	3	2	1	0
21. Every parish should provide some financial support for Catholic schools.	4	3	2	1	0
22. Having a Catholic school should be one of the highest priorities for a parish.	4	3	2	1	0
23. In an area where there is only one Catholic elementary school and several parishes, each of the parishes should financially support the school.	4	3	2	1	0
24. The maintenance of Catholic schools in poor areas of the diocese should be a top priority.	4	3	2	1	0
25. Catholic school teachers should be paid just wages in accordance with their professional duties.	4	3	2	1	0
26. This area of the diocese has too many Catholic elementary schools.	4	3	2	1	0
27. Catholic schools can provide an effective Catholic education with a trained teaching staff consisting entirely of lay people.	4	3	2	1	0
28. Most parents with children in a Catholic school will settle for an average religion program as long as the school has a strong academic program and good discipline.	4	3	2	1	0
29. In considering a Catholic school, most parents place as much or more emphasis on the religious nature of the school as on the school's academic program.	4	3	2	1	0
30. The Catholic schools that I know effectively teach Catholic doctrine.	4	3	2	1	0
31. The Catholic schools that I know have well-prepared and effective teachers.	4	3	2	1	0
32. The Catholic schools that I know have well-prepared and effective principals.	4	3	2	1	0
33. The diocese should establish an endowment fund for Catholic schools.	4	3	2	1	0
34. Parents should have more voice in the governance of Catholic schools.	4	3	2	1	0
35. The public views Catholic schools as being among the best in the area.	4	3	2	1	0
36. The Catholic schools that I know have clear goals and priorities.	4	3	2	1	0
37. Only Catholic teachers should teach religion.	4	3	2	1	0

38. The Catholic schools that I know are strong Christian communities.   4   3   2   1   0

39. The pastor and the principal share the responsibility for the school's
    spiritual leadership.   4   3   2   1   0

40. Where possible, it is best if each parish finances its own school.   4   3   2   1   0

41. The main reason parents do not select Catholic schools for their
    children, when such choices are available, is the inability to afford
    the tuition.   4   3   2   1   0

42. The pastor should leave the daily operation of the school to the principal.   4   3   2   1   0

43. A collection in each parish would be a good way of raising funds
    for schools.   4   3   2   1   0

44. The differences between Catholic and public schools are no longer
    great enough to justify the continuation of Catholic schools.   4   3   2   1   0

45. Where they exist, Catholic schools strengthen the bonds of unity within
    a parish.   4   3   2   1   0

46. A parish without a school should financially assist schools that
    accommodate its students.   4   3   2   1   0

47. Catholic schools drain money from the parish that should be spent
    on other ministries.   4   3   2   1   0

48. Lay teachers in Catholic schools are not paid adequate salaries.   4   3   2   1   0

49. A serious problem with Catholic schools is the lack of sufficient
    teachers from religious communities.   4   3   2   1   0

50. All Catholic schools should have school boards.   4   3   2   1   0

51. When a school serves several parishes, a representative board
    should be responsible for the school's governance.   4   3   2   1   0

52. I enjoy or would enjoy being the pastor of a parish that has a
    Catholic school.   4   3   2   1   0

53. New Catholic schools should be built in areas of the diocese where
    the growth in the population warrants their establishment.   4   3   2   1   0

54. An additional Catholic elementary school is needed in this area
    of the diocese.   4   3   2   1   0

55. An additional Catholic high school is needed in this area of the diocese.   4   3   2   1   0

56. The Catholic schools that I know establish a foundation of moral
    and ethical values.   4   3   2   1   0

57. Which of the following is the more important purpose of a Catholic school? (circle one letter)
    a. Academic purpose
    b. Religious purpose
    c. Both of these are equally important

Thank you very much for taking the time to complete this questionnaire. Please write any comments that you may have below or on the back of this page. Please return the completed questionnaire to (name and address).

Diocesan Planning Study for Schools
Teacher Survey

Directions: Please complete this questionnaire at your earliest convenience. Your responses will provide important data for the diocesan planning committee in planning for the future of Catholic education in the diocese. Please return the completed questionnaire to your school's office.

1. In what level of school do you teach? 1. Preschool 2. Elementary 3. Secondary

2. In what type of school do you teach? 1. Parish 2. Regional or Interparish 3. Private 4. Diocesan

3. What is your employment status? 1. Full-time 2. Part-time

4. Are you a Catholic? 1. Yes 2. No

5. What is your state in life? 1. Brother 2. Layman 3. Laywoman 4. Priest 5. Sister

6. What is your marital status? 1. Single 2. Married 3. Divorced 4. Separated 5. Widow(er)
   6. Religious

7. How old are you? 1. Under 30 2. 30 to 39 3. 40 to 49 4. 50 to 60 5. Over 60

8. What is your race/ethnicity: ___ 1. American Indian/Alaskan Native   ___ 2. Asian
   ___ 3. Black   ___ 4. Hispanic   ___ 5. White, non-Hispanic

9. Check all Catholic schools you have attended: ___ a. Elementary   ___ b. Secondary
   ___ c. College/University

10. What is your highest academic degree? 1. Bachelor's 2. Master's 3. Professional Diploma
    4. Doctorate

11. Counting this year, write the number of years you have taught in each of the following settings:
    ___ a. This school   ___ c. Private schools other than Catholic
    ___ b. Other Catholic schools   ___ d. Public schools

12. How recently have you taken a graduate course related to your discipline?
    ___1. Currently or within the last year   ___3. Between 5 and 10 years ago   ___5. Never
    ___2. Within the last 5 years   ___4. More than 10 years ago

13. How often do you attend professional development seminars/conferences/workshops?
    ___1. Frequently (at least once a year)   ___3. Seldom (once every 5-10 years)
    ___2. Occasionally (once every 2-3 years)   ___4. Hardly ever or never

14. If you teach in high school or the upper elementary grades, which of the following best describes
    your primary teaching responsibility? (Please circle only one area)
    ___1. Religion   ___3. English/Foreign Language   ___5. Other
    ___2. Social Studies   ___4. Math/Science

15. Do you have state teacher certification?   1. Yes   2. Pending   3. Expired   4. No

16. Use the following scale to indicate how important each of the following factors was in influencing your decision to teach in a Catholic school.

4=Very Important 3=Important 2=Slightly Important 1=Not Important 0=Not Applicable

____ 1. Commitment to Catholic education
____ 2. My professional qualifications
____ 3. View of teaching as my ministry
____ 4. Salary offered by the school
____ 5. Opportunity to witness to my faith
____ 6. Wanted to work in Catholic environment
____ 7. No other teaching jobs available
____ 8. Influence my teachers had on me
____ 9. Opportunity to teach in area of expertise
____ 10. To gain experience for future work
____ 11. Assignment by religious community
____ 12. Schedule compatible with family situation
____ 13. Social environment (discipline, caring, etc.)
____ 14. Benefits package offered (health plan, etc.)

____ 15. Desire to work with young people
____ 16. Love of teaching
____ 17. School requested my assistance
____ 18. Opportunity to share my values
____ 19. God's choice for my life
____ 20. For personal growth and development
____ 21. Academic philosophy of the school
____ 22. Work close to my home
____ 23. My background in Catholic schools
____ 24. Religious philosophy of the school
____ 25. Need to contribute to household income
____ 26. Size of the school
____ 27. Alternative to employment in public schools
____ 28. Other:_____

17. From the preceding question, write the numbers of the three most important factors that influenced your decision to teach at this school.
____ a. Most important   ____ b. Second most important   ____ c. Third most important

18. Use the following scale to indicate how important each of the following factors is in influencing your decision to remain at this school.

4=Very Important 3=Important 2=Slightly Important 1=Not Important 0=Not Applicable

____ 1. Job security
____ 2. Caliber of students
____ 3. Opportunity for advancement
____ 4. Salary
____ 5. General working conditions
____ 6. Helping children develop their faith
____ 7. Personal growth experienced
____ 8. My family situation
____ 9. Satisfaction with my work
____ 10. Opportunity to help others
____ 11. Principal's style and philosophy
____ 12. Relationships with my students
____ 13. Hours, holidays, summers
____ 14. Benefits package (health plan, etc.)
____ 15. Unwillingness to change jobs

____ 16. Regard for my opinion in school matters
____ 17. Working with other committed people
____ 18. Helping create a Christian community
____ 19. The faith community in the school
____ 20. Treatment received from administration
____ 21. Schedule compatible with family situation
____ 22. Proximity of school to my home
____ 23. Lack of bureaucracy in the school
____ 24. Feeling of accomplishment
____ 25. Autonomy enjoyed in my work
____ 26. Satisfaction from students' achievement
____ 27. Teaching subjects I like to teach
____ 28. Well-ordered school environment
____ 29. Relationships with colleagues
____ 30. Other:_____

19. From the preceding question, write the numbers of the three most important factors that would influence your decision to remain at this school.
____ a. Most important   ____ b. Second most important   ____ c. Third most important

20. Use the scale below to indicate your degree of satisfaction with each factor in your present work situation.

4=Very Important 3=Important 2=Slightly Important 1=Not Important 0=Not Applicable

___ 1. Professional stimulation
___ 2. Discipline in the school
___ 3. Salary I receive
___ 4. Relationship with my students
___ 5. Academic ability of the students
___ 6. Religious philosophy of the school
___ 7. Pastor's interest in the school
___ 8. Challenge of my work
___ 9. Recognition of my teaching
___ 10. Discipline in my classes
___ 11. Relationship with other teachers
___ 12. Size of my classes
___ 13. Ability to help my students learn
___ 14. Staff development opportunities
___ 15. Academic philosophy of the school
___ 16. Recognition of my contributed services
___ 17. Amount of bureaucracy in the school
___ 18. Creativity possible in my work
___ 19. My ability to help gifted students
___ 20. Communication in the school
___ 21. My sense of accomplishment
___ 22. Health and other benefits I receive

___ 23. Relationship with my principal
___ 24. Amount of autonomy I have
___ 25. Helping my students grow spiritually
___ 26. My self-esteem as a teacher
___ 27. Support of school by parents
___ 28. My professional qualifications
___ 29. Recognition of my ministerial role
___ 30. Philosophy of my principal
___ 31. Amount of responsibility I have
___ 32. My professional competence
___ 33. My interest in my work
___ 34. Work and family compatibility
___ 35. Ability to teach religion effectively
___ 36. Time required to prepare classes
___ 37. My ability to help slow learners
___ 38. My voice in school affairs
___ 39. Opportunity for advancement
___ 40. The attitudes of the students
___ 41. My comfort with my religion
___ 42. Community among faculty and students
___ 43. Support of school by the parish
___ 44. Teacher evaluation policy
___ 45. Supervision practices of the administration

21. From the preceding question, write the number of any factor that is a serious threat to your continuation at this school. (You may select up to three factors. If no factor is serious enough, write 0 in a.)
___ a. Most serious   ___ b. Second most serious   ___ c. Third most serious

22. Do you anticipate that you will still be working at this school five years from now?
    1. Yes, as far as I know.
    2. No, I will probably be reassigned by my religious community.
    3. No, I will be retired by then.
    4. No, I cannot afford to remain due to salary considerations.
    5 No, I accepted this position only until I can find a better one.
    6. No, I am growing weary of teaching and wish to do something else.
    7. No, I will be moving away from the area.
    8. No, I am just filling in for another teacher.
    9. No, I plan to return to school for an advanced degree.
    10. No, because of my family situation.
    11. No,_____

23. Whether or not you plan to remain at this school, how likely is it that you will devote your professional career to working in Catholic schools?
    1. Very unlikely   2. Unlikely   3. Likely   4. Very likely

24. How often do you attend eucharistic liturgies/worship services?
   1. Frequently (at least once a week)   3. Rarely (once or twice a year)
   2. Occasionally (once or twice a month)   4. Never

25. Other than attending worship services, how active are you in your parish, congregation, or school parish?
   1. Not active   2. Slightly active   3. Very active   4. Extremely active

26. Overall, how important is religion in your life?
   1. Not important   2. Slightly important   3. Very important   4. Extremely important

Directions: If you had to choose from among the nine instructional goals listed below, how would you rank them according to their importance in your teaching? Enter a "1" for the most important goal, a "2" for the next most important goal, and so on, through "9" for the least important goal. Please do not duplicate rankings. (Each of these goals is important. Please try to discriminate among them as best you can.)

27. ___ Fostering participation in the Catholic Church and understanding of Catholic doctrine
28. ___ Fostering understanding of other cultural and ethnic groups (human relations, getting along with others)
29. ___ Developing critical thinking skills
30. ___ Fostering spiritual development
31. ___ Facilitating personal growth and fulfillment (self-esteem, personal efficacy, self-knowledge)
32. ___ Developing academic skills (writing, reading, mathematics, etc.)
33. ___ Fostering good work habits and self-discipline
34. ___ Teaching moral and religious values
35. ___ Developing citizenship (community orientation, service to others)

Directions: Use the following scale to rate how important each of the following factors is in contributing to a student's success in school:

4=Extremely Important   3=Very Important   2=Somewhat Important   1=Not Important

36. Student's family environment	4	3	2	1
37. Student's economic situation	4	3	2	1
38. Student's intellectual ability	4	3	2	1
39. Student's enthusiasm and perseverance	4	3	2	1
40. Student's work habits and interests	4	3	2	1
41. Teacher's effective teaching	4	3	2	1
42. Teacher's enthusiasm and perseverance	4	3	2	1
43. Teacher's willingness to give extra help	4	3	2	1
44. Teacher's attention to student's unique talents and interests	4	3	2	1
45. Teacher's knowledge of subject matter	4	3	2	1

Write the numbers of the **three** most important factors from the above list:
   ___a. Most important   ___b. Second most important   ___c. Third most important

Directions: Use the following scale to indicate how you feel about each statement.

4=Agree Strongly   3=Agree   2=Disagree   1=Disagree Strongly   0=Not Applicable

46. The development of Catholic-educated political, business, and civic leaders is important for the future of our state.   4 3 2 1 0

47. Catholic schools are an essential part of the Church's educational mission.   4 3 2 1 0

48. Catholic schools are needed more today than twenty-five years ago.   4 3 2 1 0

49. Salaries of teachers in Catholic schools should be increased substantially, even if that results in significant increases in tuition.   4 3 2 1 0

50. I would contribute to a fund to provide more support for Catholic schools.   4 3 2 1 0

51. The religious education program in this school is effective.   4 3 2 1 0

52. Catholic schools can provide an effective Catholic education with all lay teachers.   4 3 2 1 0

53. The diocese should establish an endowment fund for Catholic schools.   4 3 2 1 0

54. This school has a good academic reputation.   4 3 2 1 0

55. I have an important role to play in the spiritual development of my students.   4 3 2 1 0

56. Teachers in this school have adequate voice in its governance.   4 3 2 1 0

57. Parents should have more voice in the governance of this school.   4 3 2 1 0

58. My principal supports teachers in disciplinary matters.   4 3 2 1 0

59. My school does an adequate job in recruiting students.   4 3 2 1 0

60. I am satisfied with my current position in the school.   4 3 2 1 0

61. The public views Catholic schools as being among the best in the area.   4 3 2 1 0

62. As a teacher, I feel respected in today's society.   4 3 2 1 0

63. I feel that I am paid as much as the school can afford.   4 3 2 1 0

64. I am an effective teacher.   4 3 2 1 0

65. Teacher morale at this school is high.   4 3 2 1 0

66. I cannot afford financially to teach in Catholic schools much longer.   4 3 2 1 0

67. I believe the students of this school are proud and happy to be here.   4 3 2 1 0

68. If I had another chance, I would still choose teaching as a career.	4	3	2	1	0
69. Students from different ethnic backgrounds get along well at this school.	4	3	2	1	0
70. My principal is fair in assigning responsibilities to the faculty.	4	3	2	1	0
71. My principal is an effective leader.	4	3	2	1	0
72. Goals and priorities for the school are clear.	4	3	2	1	0
73. Teachers in this school are continually learning and seeking new ideas.	4	3	2	1	0
74. Most of my colleagues share my beliefs/values about the school's mission.	4	3	2	1	0
75. Only Catholic teachers should teach religion.	4	3	2	1	0
76. A strong Christian community among faculty and students exists in this school.	4	3	2	1	0
77. The local community has a positive perception of this school.	4	3	2	1	0
78. This school helps its students develop an awareness of and a commitment to the social teachings of the Church.	4	3	2	1	0
79. My principal encourages me to achieve my full potential as a teacher.	4	3	2	1	0
80. I support my principal's vision for the school.	4	3	2	1	0
81. The parents understand the school's mission and philosophy.	4	3	2	1	0

**Thank you very much for taking the time to complete this questionnaire.
Use the space below to make comments.**

Diocesan Planning Study for Catholic Schools
Principal Survey

Directions: Please complete the following questionnaire at your earliest convenience. Your responses will provide important data for the diocesan planning committee in planning for the future of Catholic education in the diocese. Please return the completed questionnaire directly to the Catholic school office.

Circle the number or check the appropriate space corresponding to your answer.

1. In what level of school do you work?   1. Preschool   2. Elementary   3. Secondary

2. In what type of school do you work?   1. Parish   2. Regional or interparish   3. Private   4. Diocesan

3. What is your employment status?   1. Full-time administration   2. Part-time with some teaching

4. Are you a Catholic?   1. Yes   2. No

5. What is your state in life?   1. Brother   2. Layman   3. Laywoman   4. Priest   5. Sister

6. What is your marital status?   1. Single   2. Married   3. Separated   4. Divorced   5. Widow(er)
   6. Religious

7. How old are you?   1. Under 30   2. 30 to 39   3. 40 to 49   4. 50 to 59   5. 60 or older

8. What is your race/ethnicity?
   ___1. American Indian/Alaskan   ___3. Asian   ___5. Black
   ___2. Hispanic   ___4. White, non-Hispanic

9. Check all Catholic schools you have attended: ___ a. Elementary ___ b. Secondary
   ___ c. College/University

10. What is your highest academic degree?   1. Bachelor's   2. Master's   3. Professional Diploma
    4. Doctorate

11. Are you certified as a school administrator in the state?   1. Yes   2. No

12. Counting this year, write the number of years you have worked in each of the following settings:
    ___ a. This school   ___ c. Private schools other than Catholic
    ___ b. Other Catholic schools   ___ d. Public schools

13. Counting this year, write the number of years you have been a principal in each of the following settings:
    ___ a. This school   ___ c. Private schools other than Catholic
    ___ b. Other Catholic schools   ___ d. Public schools

14. How recently have you taken a graduate course related to administration?
    1. Currently or within the last year   3. Between 5 and 10 years ago   5. Never
    2. Within the last 5 years   4. More than 10 years ago

15. How often do you attend professional seminars/conferences/workshops related to your work?
    1. Frequently (at least once a year)   3. Seldom (once every 5-10 years)
    2. Occasionally (once every 2-3 years) 4. Hardly ever

16. Use the following scale to indicate how important each of the following factors was in influencing your decision to work in a Catholic school.

4=Very Important   3=Important   2=Slightly Important   1=Not Important   0=Not Applicable

___ 1. Commitment to Catholic education
___ 2. My professional qualifications
___ 3. View of administration as a ministry
___ 4. Salary offered by the school
___ 5. Opportunity to witness to my faith
___ 6. Wanted to work in Catholic environment
___ 7. No other administrative positions available
___ 8. Influence my teachers had on me
___ 9. To assist in students' spiritual development
___ 10. To gain experience for future work
___ 11. Assignment by religious community
___ 12. Schedule compatible with family situation
___ 13. Social environment (discipline, caring, etc.)
___ 14. Benefits package offered (health plan, etc.)

___ 15. Desire to work with young people
___ 16. Interest in administration
___ 17. School requested my assistance
___ 18. Opportunity to share my values
___ 19. God's choice for my life
___ 20. For personal growth and development
___ 21. Academic philosophy of the school
___ 22. Work close to my home
___ 23. My background in Catholic schools
___ 24. Religious philosophy of the school
___ 25. Need to contribute to household income
___ 26. Size of the school
___ 27. Alternative to employment in public schools
___ 28. Other:_____

17. From the preceding question, write the numbers of the three most important factors that influenced your decision to work in this school.
    ___ a. Most important ___ b. Second most important ___ c. Third most important

Directions: How would you rank the following nine tasks according to the importance you place upon each in your role as the administrator of the school? Enter a "1" for the most important task, a "2" for the next most important task, and so on, through "9" for the least important task. **Please do not duplicate rankings.** (Each of these tasks is important. Please try to discriminate among them as best you can.)

18. _____ Managing the school on a daily basis
19. _____ Building community among the staff and students
20. _____ Motivating the staff to excel
21. _____ Providing staff development opportunities
22. _____ Managing the resources of the school
23. _____ Supervising the instructional program
24. _____ Working with parents
25. _____ Developing curriculum in the school
26. _____ Promoting the school in the parish and in the neighborhood community

27. Use the scale below to indicate your degree of satisfaction with each factor in your present work situation.

4=Very Satisfactory   3=Satisfactory   2=Unsatisfactory   1=Very Unsatisfactory   0=Not Applicable

___ 1. Professional stimulation
___ 2. Discipline in the school
___ 3. Salary I receive
___ 4. Relationships with the students
___ 5. Academic ability of the students
___ 6. My expertise in hiring teachers
___ 7. Pastor's interest in the school
___ 8. Challenge of my work
___ 9. Recognition of my talents
___ 10. Relationships with parents
___ 11. Relationships with the teachers
___ 12. Size of the classes
___ 13. Relationships with diocesan personnel
___ 14. My effectiveness in managing the school
___ 15. Academic philosophy of the school
___ 16. Recognition of my contributed services
___ 17. Amount of bureaucracy in the diocese
___ 18. Creativity possible in my work
___ 19. My skill in supervising teachers
___ 20. Communication in the school
___ 21. My sense of accomplishment
___ 22. Benefits I receive
___ 23. Ability to work effectively with parents
___ 24. Paperwork required by the diocese
___ 25. My public relations skills
___ 26. Expertise of the teachers
___ 27. Implementing vision of Catholic education

___ 28. The achievements of the students
___ 29. Amount of autonomy I have
___ 30. Helping the students grow spiritually
___ 31. My self-esteem as an administrator
___ 32. Support of school by parents
___ 33. My professional preparation
___ 34. Recognition of my ministerial role
___ 35. Ability to discipline students effectively
___ 36. Amount of responsibility I have
___ 37. My influence in the parish
___ 38. My interest in my work
___ 39. Services of the Catholic education office
___ 40. Ability to work effectively with groups
___ 41. Time required to run the school
___ 42. My influence on the curriculum
___ 43. My influence on school affairs
___ 44. Opportunity for advancement
___ 45. The attitudes of the students
___ 46. My comfort with my religion
___ 47. Community among faculty and students
___ 48. Support of school by the parish
___ 49. Helping teachers grow spiritually
___ 50. My financial expertise
___ 51. My ability to get things done
___ 52. My professional qualifications
___ 53. My effectiveness in solving problems
___ 54. Religious philosophy of the school

28. Write the number of any factor from the preceding question that is a **serious threat** to your continuation at this school. (You may select up to three factors. If no factor is serious enough, write 0 in a.)
___ a. Most serious ___ b. Second most serious ___ c. Third most serious

29. Whether or not you plan to remain at this school, how likely is it that you will devote your professional career to working in Catholic schools?
1. Very unlikely   2. Unlikely   3. Likely   4. Very likely

30. How often do you attend eucharistic liturgies/worship services?
1. Frequently (at least once a week)   3. Rarely (once or twice a year)
2. Occasionally (once or twice a month)   4. Never

31. Other than attending worship services, how active are you in your home parish or school parish?
1. Not active   2. Slightly active   3. Very active   4. Extremely active

32. Overall, how important is religion in your life?
1. Not important   2. Slightly important   3. Very important   4. Extremely important

Directions: Use the following scale to indicate how you feel about each statement.

4=Agree Strongly   3=Agree   2=Disagree   1=Disagree Strongly   0=Not Applicable

33. Catholic schools are an essential part of the Church's educational mission.	4	3	2	1	0
34. Catholic schools are needed more today than twenty-five years ago.	4	3	2	1	0
35. I would contribute to a special fund to provide more support for Catholic schools.	4	3	2	1	0
36. The religious education program in this school is effective.	4	3	2	1	0
37. Catholic schools can provide an effective Catholic education with all lay teachers.	4	3	2	1	0
38. The diocese should establish an endowment fund for Catholic schools.	4	3	2	1	0
39. This school has a good academic reputation.	4	3	2	1	0
40. I have an important role to play in the spiritual development of the students.	4	3	2	1	0
41. Teachers in this school have adequate voice in its governance.	4	3	2	1	0
42. Parents should have more voice in the governance of this school.	4	3	2	1	0
43. I support teachers in disciplinary matters.	4	3	2	1	0
44. My school does an adequate job in recruiting students.	4	3	2	1	0
45. I am satisfied with my current position in the school.	4	3	2	1	0
46. The public views Catholic schools as being among the best in the area.	4	3	2	1	0
47. As an educator, I feel respected in today's society.	4	3	2	1	0
48. I feel that I am paid as much as the school can afford.	4	3	2	1	0
49. I am an effective principal.	4	3	2	1	0
50. Teacher morale at this school is high.	4	3	2	1	0
51. I cannot afford financially to work in Catholic schools much longer.	4	3	2	1	0
52. I believe the students of this school are proud and happy to be here.	4	3	2	1	0
53. If I had another chance, I would still choose to be a professional educator.	4	3	2	1	0

4=Agree Strongly   3=Agree   2=Disagree   1=Disagree Strongly   0=Not Applicable

54. Students from different ethnic backgrounds get along well at this school.   4   3   2   1   0

55. I am fair in assigning responsibilities to the faculty.   4   3   2   1   0

56. I am an effective leader.   4   3   2   1   0

57. Goals and priorities for the school are clear.   4   3   2   1   0

58. Teachers in this school are continually learning and seeking new ideas.   4   3   2   1   0

59. Most of the faculty share my beliefs and values about the mission
of the school.   4   3   2   1   0

60. Only Catholic teachers should teach religion.   4   3   2   1   0

61. A strong Christian community among faculty and students
exists in this school.   4   3   2   1   0

62. The local community has a positive perception of this school.   4   3   2   1   0

63. This school helps its students develop an awareness of and
a commitment to the social teachings of the Church.   4   3   2   1   0

64. This school has a good public relations program.   4   3   2   1   0

65. One of my most important jobs as a principal is to promote the school's
philosophy, vision, and purpose.   4   3   2   1   0

66. The quality of the school depends primarily on the coordination
and planning of the principal.   4   3   2   1   0

67. In light of the school's circumstances, I feel that my salary is adequate.   4   3   2   1   0

68. I have communicated to the faculty my beliefs and values about
the school's mission.   4   3   2   1   0

69. Most of the parents understand the school's philosophy.   4   3   2   1   0

70. Salaries of teachers in Catholic schools should be increased substantially,
even if that results in significant increases in tuition.   4   3   2   1   0

Directions: If you had to choose from among the nine goals for students listed below, how would you rank them according to their importance for your school? Enter a "1" for the most important goal, a "2" for the next most important goal, and so on, through "9" for the least important goal. **Please do not duplicate rankings.** (Each of these goals is important. Please try to discriminate among them as best you can.)

71.____Fostering participation in the Catholic Church and understanding of Catholic doctrine

72.___Fostering understanding of other cultural and ethnic groups (human relations, getting along with others)

73.___Developing critical thinking skills

74.___Fostering spiritual development

75.___Facilitating personal growth and fulfillment (self-esteem, personal efficacy, self-knowledge)

76.___Developing academic skills (writing, reading, mathematics, etc.)

77.___Fostering good work habits and self-discipline

78.___Teaching moral and religious values

79.___Developing citizenship (community orientation, service to others)

Thank you very much for taking the time to complete this questionnaire.
Use the space below and the back of this page to make comments.

[Date: (approximately a month before the first scheduled meeting)]

Dear [   ],

You are probably aware that the diocese is embarking on a long-range study of its Catholic schools. The purpose of the study is to discern and develop ways to examine, strengthen, and support Catholic education, so that it will continue to serve the Church in the future. As part of this process, two general meetings will bring together hundreds of people from all parts of the diocese to discuss Catholic education. On [date], an all-day meeting will be held at [site] to address problems and issues facing Catholic education. On [date], the groups will reconvene in an all-day session to propose ideas and ways to resolve these problems. Much of the work of these meetings is done in small groups led by a facilitator.

Your name has been suggested as one who could work effectively as a facilitator with a small group in this process. On the day of the meeting, you will be given specific training concerning the method of facilitating a group of eight to twelve persons. To give you an understanding of the role of a small group leader, some details follow.

You will lead a group of clergy, educators, and parish lay representatives through a process to elicit feelings, concerns, problems, or difficulties that should be considered in planning for the future of Catholic education in the diocese. The major responsibility of a small group facilitator is to record group-generated ideas, keep the group on schedule, and report on the group priorities. Some of you may be familiar with the process employed, called the "nominal group process." At 8:30 a.m. on [meeting date], there will be a training session to familiarize you with the process and what is expected for the day.

For your information, the schedule for the day is as follows [adjust schedule to fit time]:

8:25	Facilitators arrive/collect supplies
8:30	Facilitator training session/small group set up
9:00	Participants arrive
9:20	Large group meeting
11:00	Small group process
12:15	Lunch
1:00	Small group process continued
2:15	Large group report
2:45	Closing remarks
3:00	Conclude

For your information, being a small group facilitator is incompatible with being a group participant. Since you are known to be a capable and interested person supportive of Catholic education, we would not be surprised if you were asked to join the meeting as a participant. However, if that should happen, you will need to make a choice between being a representative or a group facilitator and notify us immediately if you choose not to be a facilitator. This process cannot be carried out effectively without adequate numbers of facilitators, so we will need to make arrangements to have your group covered.

I hope you will agree to participate in this process as a facilitator on both [problem date/solution date]. You will play a vital role in this very important study for the diocese. Please indicate as soon as possible whether you will be able to participate as a facilitator. Thank you for your willing spirit and support of this work.

Sincerely,

P.S. Please return the enclosed reply card by [date].

(Sample reply card)

Please reply as soon as possible but before [date (three weeks prior to meeting)].

Facilitator Name_____

Phone number_____

Check one:

_____ I am willing to be a small group facilitator at [site] on [problem element date] and [solution element date].

_____ I can only come on [problem element date].

_____ I can only come on [solution element date].

_____ Thanks, but I am not able to facilitate either date.

Comment:

Signature: _____

8:25   Arrival

❖ Check in at the registration area to pick up your name card and folder.

❖ Go to the training area to collect supplies:
  ❖ Ten to twelve sheets of newsprint
  ❖ Wide nib magic markers—black and another color
  ❖ Masking tape
  ❖ Pencils
  ❖ White 3"x5" and 5"x8" index cards
  ❖ Rubber bands
  ❖ 5"x8" index cards in four colors

❖ Go to your assigned room and set up for the group.
  ❖ Arrange chairs in a semicircle close to where you will be recording the group responses. (Expect ten to twelve persons.)
  ❖ Arrange supplies.
    ❖ Post chart paper. If there is a firm writing space, tape the individual sheets up consecutively. This will save maneuvering time later.
    ❖ Label each newsprint sheet with your *site, group,* and *room.*
    ❖ Be sure you have a supply of each color card:
      ❖ Clergy—red
      ❖ Educators—blue
      ❖ Parent/parish representatives—yellow
      ❖ School board members—green
      ❖ Others—white

❖ When you are finished, go to the large group meeting area to hear the presentation.

11:00   After Large-Group Session

❖ Return to small group room to greet group.
  ❖ When all are assembled, introduce yourself by giving your name and where you are from and tell participants that you will be the facilitator for that day.
  ❖ Ask each person in the group to give his/her name, parish/school, and reason for attending the meeting. (Check off attendance on your small group list.)

❖ During introductions:
  ❖ Distribute two 5"x8" cards to each member according to the appropriate color: clergy—red; educator—blue; parents/parish representative—yellow; boards—green; others—white.
  ❖ Ask members to *label the top of the card with site and group.*

11:10 Task One: Individual Listing of Ideas (twenty minutes)
[The focus question is listed on agenda sheet]

- ❖ Reiterate the guidelines:
  - ❖ Work independently and silently.
  - ❖ Number and list ideas in short phrases and sentences; avoid long paragraphs.
  - ❖ Push yourself to be creative.
  - ❖ Resist the temptation to talk now; there will be discussion time later.

- ❖ Ask them to begin.
  - ❖ If anyone has a question, respond quietly to the individual; do not hold up the group.
  - ❖ Allow at least twelve to fifteen minutes. Encourage those who finish early to keep on thinking.
  - ❖ Use forceful, direct (but polite) sanctions to those who talk or otherwise are distracting during this time.
  - ❖ When several have finished, but before time is up, you may wish to comment that research shows that often the most creative ideas come in the last five minutes of quiet time, so keep thinking even if you feel finished.
  - ❖ After twenty minutes, call the group to order by reiterating the procedure you will use for listing the ideas.

11:30 Task Two: Listing Ideas on a Chart (thirty minutes)
Request that individuals take turns presenting one idea at a time in "round-robin" fashion. Remind them that this process is used to facilitate the rapid listing of ideas; therefore, comments or discussion is inappropriate at this time.

- ❖ Number consecutively and record each individual idea on the newsprint.
- ❖ Be sure to leave about a five-inch margin on the left-hand side for later tallying.
- ❖ Do not worry about overlap of ideas.
- ❖ Avoid categorizing or redefining items; simply record what you hear verbatim.
- ❖ Avoid discussion of items and interrupting questions or discussions by asking the individual to wait until all the items are listed.
- ❖ Ask the participants not to talk out of turn if that begins to happen.
- ❖ Work for about twenty minutes. Continue around the group at least three times or until you have at least forty ideas. After about the third round, some persons will have exhausted their list; they then may simply say "Pass."
- ❖ Stop at noon even if all the ideas are not out.
- ❖❖ *Reassure the group that all ideas will be considered because all cards will be collected.*

12:00 Task Three: Clarification (five to ten minutes)
Ask for questions of clarification; remind participants that it is not necessary for persons to agree with the items, so there is no need to debate or disagree at this time. However, questions that clarify are important. *Do not permit persons to combine elements.*

12:15 Dismiss the Group for Lunch
Remind them to return promptly to the room for the afternoon session.

1:15 After Lunch
- ❖ Ask if there are any ideas to add to the list and record them on newsprint.
- ❖ Ask if further clarification is needed.

1:20   **Task Four: Preliminary Voting (ten minutes)**

- Distribute one 3"x5" white card to each person.
- Task: Tell group members, "Write down *by item number* the five problem elements that you think should definitely be addressed in this study." "What five items here are most crucial and therefore cannot be ignored?"
- While they are voting, collect all 5"x8" idea cards and separate the colors with rubber bands. Keep blank cards separate from those written on. *Be sure each card is labeled with the group and site.*
- Collect the 3"x5" white cards. Then ask a member of the group to read the numbers aloud while you record by tally marks the votes in the margin before the item.
- Be sure to leave room in the margin for the second vote.

1:30   **Task Five: Discussion (ten to fifteen minutes)**

- When all the preliminary votes have been recorded, open the floor to discussion: "Anyone care to comment on the way the vote turned out?"
- Try to avoid too much discussion on one item.
- Make sure everyone understands the items that received votes, since sometimes terminology is used that is not familiar to everyone.
- Ask the group to notice the items that are *not* showing up as high priorities.
- Resist the group's efforts to try to get you to combine elements.

1:45   **Task Six: Final Vote (five minutes)**

- Distribute the same 3"x5" cards (using the other side; *label* it: "*final* vote").
- Ask the group to vote again by specifying the numbers of the five items that should absolutely be considered as a problem, issue, or concern for this long-range planning study. Participants may vote for any item on the list. They are not restricted to the items nominated earlier.
- Collect the cards and, with a *different color* marker, record the vote as before.

1:55   **Task Seven: Priority List**

- When the group is finished voting, dismiss them for a break. Remind them that the large-group session is at 2:15.
- Record on a white 5"x8" card the five items that received the highest number of final votes. Be sure to head the card with your group, site, and number. If there is a tie for the fifth place, record all items that received votes for that place.

2:15   **Large-Group Reporting Session**

- Take the priority list to the large group area.
- Give a summary of your group's work to the large group. That is, using your 5"x8" card, read *without comment* the items your group chose as the top five priorities.

3:10   **After the Large-Group Session and Dismissal**

- Go back to the small group room
  - Put the chairs back the way you found them
  - Roll together all newsprint sheets containing ideas
  - Label outside by site, group, room
  - Gather all used and unused supplies

- Take everything to the registration area where you picked up your materials.

- ❖ Return
  - ❖ All unused supplies
  - ❖ All cards with ideas on them sorted by color
  - ❖ All general listing (rolled together and labeled) of the ideas recorded
  - ❖ The 5"x8" white summary card

- ❖ Go to the designated facilitator meeting place to celebrate your hard work and to debrief the coordinator of the meeting about your experience.

You are one of ___ facilitators each working with a small group at ____ *simultaneous meetings being held today throughout the diocese.* Without you we could not accomplish this task. Getting the ideas back in an organized fashion is critical to the next phase of the work. *We appreciate your efforts and cooperation.*

Many, many thanks for your participation!

8:30   **Arrival and Orientation**

- Check in at the registration table to pick up your name card and folder.
  - The instructions for facilitators are in this folder.

- Go to the orientation room and collect leader supplies:
  - About 40 pieces of newsprint
  - A roll of masking tape
  - Eight 5"x8" cards in each color for *each participant*
  - Four 3"x5" white cards for *each participant*
  - Eight 5"x8" white cards for the leader to record priority statements
  - One black and one red wide-nib marker
  - A dozen or so rubber bands
  - Three or four pencils

- Stay for the training session to review the process and assign topics.
  - Today you will do the nominal process three complete times.
  - The topics you will address are different for different groups.
  - Your group assignment is on the bottom of this page.

- Go to your assigned room and set up for the group.
  - Arrange chairs in semicircle close to where you will be recording responses. Expect eight to ten persons; some groups may have up to twelve persons.
  - Check your supplies and arrange newsprint sheets.
  - Label each newsprint sheet with your
    - Site name
    - Group number
    - Topic (*this is critical*)

- Very important: The sequence of topics you will address are
  - 10:00   Topic 1 (Here indicate name of topic 1)
  - 11:15   Topic 2 (Here indicate name of topic 2)
  - 12:00   Lunch
  - 1:00   Finish topic 2 (if necessary)
  - 1:30   Topic 3 (Here indicate name of topic 3)

- When you are finished, go to the large-group meeting area.

10:00   After Large-Group Session

❖ Return to your small group room to greet your group.

❖ When all are assembled, introduce yourself by giving your name and where you are from and explain that you will be the facilitator for that day.

❖ Ask each person in the group to give his/her name, parish/school, and reason for attending the meeting. (Check off and/or revise the attendance on your small group list.)

❖ During introductions:

    ❖ Distribute two 5"x8" cards according to the appropriate color to each member: clergy—red; educator—yellow; parent/parish representative—blue; board member—green; others—white.

    ❖ Ask members to label the top of the card with site, group, and topic.

    ❖ Check your direction sheet for your assigned sequence of topics.

The Process

10:10   Topic One: _____

❖ **Task One: Individual Listing of Ideas (fifteen minutes)**
[The focus question is listed on agenda sheet]

    ❖ Reiterate the guidelines:

    ❖ Work independently and silently.

    ❖ Number and list ideas in short phrases and sentences; avoid long paragraphs.

    ❖ Push yourself to be creative.

    ❖ Resist the temptation to talk now; there will be discussion time later.

❖ Tell them to begin.

    ❖ If anyone has a question, respond quietly to the individual. Do not hold up the group.

    ❖ Allow at least ten to twelve minutes for writing ideas; encourage early finishers to keep thinking.

    ❖ Use forceful, direct (but polite) sanctions to those who talk or otherwise are distracting.

    ❖ When several have finished, but before time is up, you may wish to comment that research shows that often the most creative ideas come in the last five minutes of quiet time, so keep thinking even if you feel finished.

    ❖ After fifteen minutes, call the group to order by reiterating the procedure you will use for listing the ideas.

10:25   Task Two: Listing Ideas on the Chart (fifteen minutes)
Request that individuals take turns presenting one idea at a time in "round-robin" fashion. Remind them that the process was chosen to facilitate the rapid listing of ideas. Therefore, discussion is inappropriate at this time.

    ❖ Number consecutively and record each individual idea on the newsprint.

    ❖ Be sure to leave about a five-inch margin on the left-hand side for later tallying.

    ❖ Do not worry about overlap of ideas.

    ❖ Avoid categorizing or redefining items; simply record what you hear verbatim.

    ❖ Avoid discussion of items, interrupting questions, or discussions by asking the individual to wait until all the items are listed.

    ❖ Ask the participants not to talk out of turn, if that begins to happen.

    ❖ Continue around the group at least three times or until you have about thirty-six ideas. After the third round, some persons will have exhausted their list. They then may simply say "Pass."

    ❖ Stop after fifteen minutes even if all the ideas have not been shared.

    ❖ *Reassure the group that all ideas will be considered because all cards will be collected.*

10:40   Task Three: Clarification (five minutes)

Ask for questions of clarification; remind participants that it is not necessary for persons to agree with the items, so there is no need to debate or disagree at this time. However, questions that clarify are important. Do not permit persons to combine elements.

10:45   Task Four: First Vote (five minutes)

❖ Distribute one 3"x5" white card to each person.

❖ Task: Write down *by item number* the five solution elements that you think should definitely be considered in this study. "What five items here are most resourceful and appropriate and therefore should not be ignored?"

    ❖ While participants are voting, collect all 5"x8" idea cards and separate colors using rubber bands.

        ❖ Collect 3"x5" white cards.

        ❖ Ask for a volunteer to read the numbers aloud so you can record them. Tally the votes in the margin before the item.

        ❖ Be sure to leave room in the margin for the second vote.

10:50   Task Five: Discussion (eight to ten minutes)

    ❖ When all the preliminary votes have been recorded, open the floor to discussion: "Anyone care to comment on how the vote came out?"

    ❖ Try to avoid too much discussion on one item.

    ❖ Make sure everyone understands the items that received votes.

    ❖ Ask the group to notice the items that are *not* showing up as high priorities.

    ❖ *Do not allow the group to try to combine elements.* This is very important. When combining takes place, often it is not clear which ideas should be emphasized the most.

11:00   Task Six: Final Vote (five minutes)

    ❖ Distribute the same 3"x5" cards (using the other side). Label it "final vote."

    ❖ Ask the group to vote again by specifying the number of the five items that should absolutely be considered as a solution or idea for this topic in the long-range planning study.

    ❖ Collect the cards and, with a different color marker, record the vote.

11:10   When the Tallying Is Complete, Allow the Group a Short Stand-up Stretch Break (five minutes)

11:15   Topic Two: _____

    ❖ Repeat the same process, taking the group through task one through task six.

    ❖ **Task One: Individual Listing of Ideas**

        ❖ While the group is listing ideas about the second topic

        ❖ Record the priority statements from the first topic on a white card that you have labeled with the site and number.

        ❖ List on a white 5"x8" card the five items that received the most votes.

        ❖ Be sure to head the card with *the topic,* your group, site, and number.

        ❖ If there is a tie for the fifth place, record only the top *four* items.

        ❖ Take down newsprint from the first topic.

        ❖ Put up newsprint for recording the second topic.

        ❖ Label newsprint (now you are ready to list ideas for the second topic).

        ❖ Watch your time.

        ❖ Try to get to at least the first vote before lunch.

11:30   **Task Two: List Second Topic Ideas on Newsprint**

11:45   **Task Three: Clarification**

11:50   **Task Four: First Vote**

12:00   **Dismiss the Group for Lunch; Remind Them to Return at 1:00**

1:00   **Return to the Small Group; Finish the Morning Topic**

1:05   **Task Five: Discussion**

1:15   **Task Six: Final Vote**

1:25   **Topic Three: _____**
- ❖ Tasks one to six. Watch time. Individual listing of ideas.
- ❖ Don't forget to record the priority statements from the second topic. Label the cards with *topic,* site, group.

1:40   **Listing Third Topic on Newsprint**

1:55   **Clarification**

2:00   **First Vote**

2:05   **Discussion**

2:15   **Final Vote**
- ❖ As you collect the white voting cards from topic three, give out one more 5"x8" card. Direct members to label this card "general comments." Participants may then write any other ideas they have about the topics that were not addressed by your group.

2:25   **Dismiss the Group to Go to the Large-Group Meeting**

2:30   **Take the Priority Lists to the Large-Group Meeting**
- ❖ You will be asked to give a summary of the group's work on the first morning topic to the large group. That is, using your 5"x8" card, you will read to the larger assembly the items your group voted as priorities.
- ❖ Do the complete process for the first two topics.
- ❖ If you have time, complete the process for the last topic. However, if you don't have time to complete the process, try to at least get to the first vote on the last topic.

3:10   **After the Large-Group Session and Dismissal**
- ❖ Give the priority cards to the coordinator who conducted the meeting.
- ❖ Go back to the small group room.
  - ❖ Put the chairs back the way you found them.
  - ❖ Roll all the idea sheets together.
  - ❖ Gather all used and unused supplies.

- ❖ Take everything to the facilitator training room where you received supplies.
  Return the following:
  - ❖ All unused supplies
  - ❖ All cards with ideas on them, rubber banded and sorted by *topic* and color
  - ❖ All general lists (rolled together and labeled) of all the ideas recorded
  - ❖ 5"x8" *white* summary cards—one for each topic

- ❖ Spend a few minutes to debrief the site's coordinator about your experience and then get some refreshments.

- ❖ Pat yourself on the back for a job well done! *This was really intensive work.* We are sure that you are tired, but we hope you have a feeling of accomplishment. We could not do this process and gather this much information so quickly without your help. You are truly the "glue" that allows this part of the study to come together. These data are the basis for all future work. You are participating in the future of Catholic education in the diocese. *God bless you, and we thank you!*

Before the Meeting

1. **Large-group area:**
   ___ Is there a lectern and a working microphone?
   ___ Is there a glass of water for the speaker?

2. **Registration area:**
   ___ Is it set up to expedite checking in?
   ___ Are name cards spread out and arranged in alphabetical order—preferably with a sign for each group? (Clergy—red; educators—blue; parents/parish representatives—yellow; board members—green; others—white)
   ___ Are stacks of the agenda, map, and focus sheet for all participants available on each registration table?
   ___ Are the folders (but not the supplies) available on the table for facilitators?
   ___ Is the coffee ready? Where is it?

3. **Facilitator training area:**
   ___ Is the room clearly marked "facilitator training"?
   ___ Are the facilitators' supplies for their groups in the room (in some type of plastic bag)?

4. **Small group rooms:**
   ___ Is each one unlocked and clearly marked with a sign stating the group number?
   ___ If you had time, did you deliver the chart paper to the room for the facilitator? Or is the chart paper in the facilitator training area?

5. **Logistics of the opening session:**
   ___ Did you make arrangements with the host about who would announce the housekeeping details, such as restrooms, lunch procedure, and small group room locations?
   ___ Are you prepared to lead the prayer?

During the Day
   ___ Are the sessions running on schedule?
   ___ Are the group numbers relatively equal in size? The ideal range is between eight and twelve. If groups are smaller than eight or larger than twelve, place individuals in other existing groups.
   ___ Are group members cooperating with the small group facilitators and speaking only in turn? (Occasionally a person will try to change the process or dominate the group. The facilitator may need your help to get the process moving.)
   ___ Does each facilitator have sufficient supplies? Some may need more of the color-coded cards or newsprint.
   ___ Did you help the presenter get the groups to reconvene after lunch according to the schedule?

After the Closing Session
   ___ Did you help the presenter collect the cards, unused supplies, and folders from the facilitators?
   ___ *Did you ensure that all cards have the topic and site listed on the top?* This is critical, since there will be three different topics covered by each group.
   ___ Did you direct the facilitators to the refreshments and talk with them about how the day went in their group?

In case of emergency . . . Recruit small group facilitators at the meeting by approaching persons you know who would be able to fill in and learn the process quickly.

(C=Clergy; P=Parents/Parish Representatives; E=Educators)
(B=School Board; O=Others)

I. Catholic Identity

A. Philosophy/mission lacking for Catholic schools as a whole (C-5, P-1)
   1. What are the priorities for parents, teachers, students, and administrators regarding academics, religion, discipline? (C-4, P-2, E-1, O-1)
   2. What is Catholic schools' mission to poor, minorities, immigrants? (P-2, E-1, O-2)
   3. Church's mission is to teach: what happens if schools close? (P-2)
   4. Future of schools depends upon future of the Church (B-1)
   5. Perception of "escape" to Catholic schools (C-3, P-3)
   6. Lack of harmony between perceptions of parents and students/school and Church as to purpose of Catholic schools (C-1, P-1)
   7. Lack of *vision* common to all schools (C-1, P-4, E-1, O-1)
   8. Lack of mission statement (E-3, B-3)
   9. Other than academics, what does Catholic school offer parents? (B-1)

B. Identity
   1. Are we maintaining our Catholic identity? (C-13, P-23, E-3, B-13, O-5)
   2. Are Catholic values being passed on effectively? (C-2, P-4, E-6, O-2)
   3. Religious instruction must be for *all* students (P-1, E-1)
   4. Perception that "catholicity" of faculty, parents, and students is weak (C-1)
   5. Few religious present in the schools (C-4, P-2, E-6, B-13, O-2)
   6. Overcoming the materialistic, amoral society that we are up against (P-5, E-1)
   7. Parish not involved in Catholic identity of school (B-1)

C. Religion
   1. Lack of religious goals and objectives spelled out for parents and students (C-1, P-2)
   2. Need to teach solid Catholic doctrine in our schools (E-8, B-1)
   3. The person of Jesus should inform all that we do (B-1)
   4. Need to maintain religion as top priority along with excellent academics (E-1, B-1)
   5. Need to relate religious formation to parish life (C-3, P-1, E-1)
   6. Religious/spiritual formation (C-4, E-3)
   7. More students who lack the rudiments of the Catholic faith (P-1)
   8. Student apathy towards religious instruction (P-1)
   9. Problem of action-based living the faith vs. knowledge of the faith (C-3, O-2)
   10. Ineffective passing on of faith commitment (C-2, P-2, E-3, O-1)
   11. Stronger teaching of Catholic values and morals (C-1, P-1, E-3)
   12. Are lay teachers effectively trained to teach Catholic faith/doctrine? (C-5, P-7, E-2)
   13. Lack of religious vocations (C-2, P-1, E-3, B-1)
   14. How to measure success in terms of Mass attendance, social justice, parish involvement (C-2, P-1, E-1)
   15. Is Catholic school "better" than CCD? (B-1, O-1)
   16. Improved CCD teacher training (C-1, E-2)
   17. Need to integrate CCD programs with school religion programs (C-1, P-2, E-3)
   18. Lack of promotion of Catholic schools by CCD coordinators (B-1)
   19. Need to increase availability of CCD (B-2)

20. Need to develop relationship between school students and their CCD peers and people in the parish (C-2)
21. Lack of community service programs in our schools (E-3, B-4)

D. Evangelization vs. catechesis (C-1, P-2, B-1)

II. Finance

A. Parish subsidy
1. Parish subsidies too high; drain on parish funds (C-25, P-8, E-8, B-23, O-2)
2. Need to increase parish subsidy (P-1, E-6)
3. Parish subsidies not given to schools, but to families (C-1, P-1, E-1)
4. Parish subsidy not related to parish revenue (C-1, P-1)
5. Parishes lack sense of "ministry" to schools (C-1, E-1)
6. Parish people not convinced that supporting the schools is important (C-18, P-17, P-8, B-2, O-4)
7. Lack of long-range guidelines for subsidizing inner-city schools (C-1)

B. Parish assessment
1. The need to explain assessments and subsidies to parents whose children are not in Catholic schools (C-3)
2. Is assessment system fair to poor parishes? (P-1)

C. Tuition
1. Rising/affordability, education for the elite (C-12, P-46, E-33, B-19, O-10)
2. Lack of uniform tuition throughout an area or the diocese (Warwick problem) (C-4, P-8, E-3, B-3, O-2)
3. Need to put a cap on/lower tuition (P-2, E-5)
4. Lack of a sliding-scale tuition (P-1, O-1)
5. Need to use cost-based tuition (C-2, E-1)
6. Lack of cost-based tuition commitment from families (C-3, P-2, O-1)
7. Lack of actual cost information given to parents and parishes (C-2, P-2, E-1)
8. Problems of cost-based tuition in poor areas (C-1)
9. The problem of delinquent tuition (C-4, P-3, B-1)
10. Lack of central tuition collection process (C-1)
11. Some schools set tuition at low rates in order to hike up the subsidy (C-1)
12. Lack of negotiated tuition plans (E-2)
13. Lack of family tuition plans (E-3, B-1)
14. Lack of alternate tuition plans (O-1)

D. Tuition assistance
1. Complaints that aid is more available to inner-city non-Catholics than to struggling parishioners (C-1)
2. How to help people who are just above the Warde Fund criteria (C-2, P-5)
3. Inequities in the way the Warde Fund is dispensed (C-2, P-1, E-1)
4. Eliminate the Warde Fund and create a new financial aid system (E-1)
5. Need more (diocesan-funded) subsidies/scholarships (C-5, P-4, E-11, B-1, O-1)
6. Lack of awareness of monies available for tuition assistance (C-1, P-1, E-6, O-1)
7. Need to seek outside sources for tuition assistance (P-4, E-1, B-1)
8. Lack of incentive programs (P-1)
9. Financial aid to minorities (E-3, B-3, O-4)
10. Lack of *full* financial support for low-income families (E-2)

11. Scholarships are not offered according to need, but on academics (E-1)
12. Need to establish program to finance Catholic education like a college education (B-1)

E. Teacher salaries and benefits
1. Need for just wage for teachers (C-19, P-61, E-37, B-21, O-12)
2. Lack of uniform pay scale, standardization of wages (C-5, P-5, E-1, B-1, O-2)
3. High cost of faculty benefits (C-2, P-2, E-1)
4. Lack of benefits that help compensate for low wages (C-2, P-4)
5. Lack of teachers who are religious (C-3, E-4)
6. High teacher turnover (C-2, P-10, E-11, B-2, O-2)
7. No tuition reduction for children of Catholic school teachers (P-2, E-1, B-1)
8. No incentives for long-range commitment to Catholic schools (E-1, O-1)
9. Lack of compensation for extra responsibilities (B-1)
10. No credit for in-service as continuing education (B-1)

F. Costs in general
1. High operating cost of everything (C-7, P-9, E-4, B-1, O-3)
2. Poor economy (C-3, P-2, E-5)
3. Low enrollment (C-5, P-25, E-15, B-11, O-4)
4. Exodus of sixth graders to public schools (C-1, P-1, E-4)
5. Financial instability (P-3)
6. Need to distribute costs among entire Catholic population (P-1)
7. Loss of students to home schooling (P-1, E-2)
8. High cost of needed technology (B-1)

G. Revenues
1. Lack of funds (B-9)
2. Lack of endowments (C-5, P-6, E-3, B-1, O-3)
3. Lack of development programs (C-1, P-5, E-1, B-4, O-1)
4. Lack of development director (B-3)
5. Lack of long-range financial planning (C-4, P-9, E-2, B-3, O-1)
6. "Stopgap" and "survival" funding (C-3, P-1, O-1)
7. Lack of alternate methods of financing (C-7, P-18, E-4, B-1, O-5)
8. Dependence of individual schools on fund raising (C-1, P-3, E-2, B-1, O-1)
9. Lack of equitable distribution of available financial resources (C-1, P-5, E-1)
10. Need for dramatic improvement in fund raising (C-1, P-13, E-7, B-1, O-5)
11. Need contingency fund for future (C-1)
12. Lack of high standards of *financial accountability* for schools (C-2, P-2, E-2)
13. Issue of "gambling" monies for school revenue (C-1)
14. No monies/additional monies needed from central office (P-6, E-6, B-4)
15. Need to restructure finances in order to relieve burdens on parishes, pastors, and parents (C-1, P-1, E-3)
16. Diocese needs to generate more income for the schools (E-5, B-1, O-3)
17. Lack of successful tithing programs (E-2)
18. Strict enforcement by the diocesan office of the 7 percent education tax (E-1)
19. Fewer families attending Mass; therefore less revenue collected (E-1)

H. Government assistance
1. Lack of voucher system or tax credits (C-10, P-13, E-8, B-8, O-3)
2. Need to educate parents/all Catholics to become vocal advocates for school choice (P-6, E-3, B-5, O-3)

3. Need to obtain more, not less government assistance (C-5, P-5, E-2)
4. Possible reduction in state aid (C-3, P-2, B-1)
5. Need to obtain all that we are entitled to (P-3, E-3, B-4, O-1)
6. Need to keep government assistance out of Catholic schools (P-1, E-1)

I. School buildings
1. Run-down buildings and properties in need of regular maintenance/repair (C-5, P-16, E-11, B-2, O-4)
2. Lack of efficient plant budget management (C-1, P-1)
3. Property rich, no cash flow (C-2)
4. Capital expenditures not budgeted (C-3, P-2, E-3, B-4)
5. Lack of diocesan support for building repair and maintenance (C-1, P-1, E-1, O-1)
6. Tenants in buildings don't take care of property (P-1)
7. Need to establish before- and after-school care in unused buildings (P-5, E-1, B-1)
8. No handicapped access (P-3, E-1, O-1)
9. No gyms, cafeterias (P-2, E-1)
10. Need to meet building safety codes (P-2, E-1, B-1, O-1)
11. Best use of plant buildings needs to be determined for each building (P-2, B-1)
12. Insurance costs (E-1)
13. Inferior to public school buildings (E-1)
14. Identify physical environment conducive to learning (B-1)

III. Governance
A. Consolidation issues
1. Need to merge or close schools in some areas (N. Providence, E. Providence/Pawtucket, Woonsocket, W. Warwick, Warren/Bristol, Central Falls) (C-20, P-12, E-8, B-7, O-6)
2. Lack of schools in some areas (C-3, P-1, E-4, O-2)
3. Closing inner-city, poor parish schools leaves education for the elite only (C-3)
4. *Diocesan norms* needed to determine school closings (C-1)
5. Need to *regionalize* part or entire system (C-4, P-5, E-2, B-6, O-1)
6. Avoid too many regional schools (B-1)
7. Parish vs. regional school (B-1, O-1)
8. More dialogue among parishes in regional schools (B-1, O-1)
9. Centralization vs. autonomous schools (C-1, P-4, E-1)
10. Transportation (C-5, P-11, E-14, B-4)
11. Need to pull together to follow through on best solutions (C-1, O-1)
12. Low enrollment in city schools (C-1)
13. The need for seventh- and eighth-grade schools (C-1, P-2, B-4) in West Bay area (P-1)
14. Do we need to emphasize elementary or secondary? (P-2, B-1)
15. Reorganize to maximize strengths (P-1)
16. Shifting demographics (P-3, E-2, B-1)
17. Problem of closing a "too small" but "good" school (P-1)
18. Lack of flexibility in opening/closing schools when demographics change (E-1)
19. What are viable alternatives to Catholic schools if the schools should close? (E-1)
20. Coed vs. gender-specific schools (B-1)

B. Parish issues
1. Need to make all regional parishes live up to financial commitments (C-4, P-3, E-5, B-8)
2. "Parish" school excludes welcome to others (C-1)
3. "Parish" school may be more valued by students and parents than a regional school (C-2, E-1, O-1)

4. Negative reactions if school is thought to be in trouble (C-1)
5. Lack of promotion of schools in non-school parishes (C-1, P-17, E-12, B-1, O-2)
6. Do certain ethnic groups within the parish avoid Catholic schools? (P-1)
7. Need to separate the running of the school from the running of the parish (P-1)
8. Lack of uniformity in the governing structures of parish schools (E-1)
9. Lack of parish support for school activities (E-1, B-1, O-1)
10. Lack of support for schools from members of parish finance committees (B-1)

C. Pastors/priests
1. Are clergy really sold on Catholic education? Lack of support for schools "from the pulpit" (C-5, P-22, E-12, B-8, O-4)
2. Lack of training in how to run a school (C-2, E-1)
3. Poor leadership (C-2, P-3)
4. Problems of assigning to schools pastors and priests who do not support Catholic education (P-3, O-2)
5. Lack of pastor/priest involvement in classrooms (P-9, E-3, O-2)

D. Collaboration vs. competition
1. Need to share resources (C-8, P-6, E-5, B-3, O-1)
2. Need to share what works and what doesn't (C-3, P-1, B-1)
3. Need for collaboration rather than competition in as many ways as possible (C-2, P-15, E-3, B-1, O-1)
4. Competition among schools for the same students (P-3, E-1, B-3)

E. Diocese
1. Greater commitment to Catholic education (C-1, P-7, E-3, O-3)
2. Lack of accountability to an oversight board (B-1)
3. School board should be responsible to parish, not pastor (B-1)
4. Deanery should run schools (B-1)
5. Better leadership in bringing schools together for the common good (O-1)
6. Greater authority in setting policy (C-1, P-1)
7. Lack of "big picture" of Catholic education in R.I. (C-1, E-1, O-1)
8. Central purchasing needed (C-1, P-6, E-1, B-3, O-1)
9. Lack of centralization of schools (C-1, E-1)
10. Centralization of everything to provide better services, benefits, etc. (E-2, B-1)
11. Alternate governance structures needed (C-1, P-1, O-1)
12. Lack of successful governance and policy models to follow (B-1)
13. To what extent should diocese support K-8 schools? (B-1)
14. Our centralized governing body with decentralized control is not working (E-1)
15. Lack of participative style of school management; no input from parents, teachers (E-1)
16. More commitment from National Conference of Catholic Bishops (C-1, P-2)
17. Clear guidelines for proceeding with the results of this study (C-1, E-1)
18. Lack of diocesan training for school boards and principals (P-2, B-1, O-1)
19. Lack of support personnel from the diocese to give assistance to inner-city schools who need help with services to students and families (O-1)
20. Lack of teacher input into diocesan planning boards (P-2)
21. Problem of schools operating as separate businesses (P-1)
22. Problems stemming from separation of a school's governance and financial planning structures (P-1, O-1)
23. Lack of diocesan leadership to urge cohesiveness and support among the schools (P-1, B-1)

24. What problems arise because of *private* vs. diocesan schools? (P-1)
25. Better communication between diocese and individual schools to prevent escalation of problems (E-1)
26. Elementary schools do not operate consistently in areas of tuition, salaries, etc., but as fifty-three separate corporations; no uniformity (E-2, O-1)
27. Too much politics (B-1)
28. Management techniques not used enough in governing schools (B-1)

F. School boards
   1. More lay people than clergy needed to lead school boards (C-1, P-3, B-3, O-1)
   2. Relationships, structure, operations (C-5, P-3, E-1, B-1, O-2)

IV. Curriculum

A. Academic program
   1. Need to maintain/improve strong academic programs (C-5, P-25, E-21, B-3, O-6)
   2. Use same standard tests as public schools to compare results (E-2, B-10)
   3. Need for state accreditation (B-1)
   4. Need to assess our strengths and weaknesses (B-1)
   5. Need for strengthening math, science, language, especially in junior high (C-3, P-7, E-12, B-10, O-1)
   6. Need to make junior high programs more attractive (E-3, B-1, O-1)
   7. Library improvements (C-1, P-2, E-2, B-1)
   8. Problems caused by presence of minority, non-English-speaking children (C-4, P-6)
   9. Textbooks need to be updated (C-1, P-7, E-3, O-1)
  10. Lack of qualified teachers for music and art (C-1, P-7, E-1)
  11. Lack of standardized curriculum program at all levels (P-8, E-3, B-7, O-1)
  12. Lack of regular evaluation of academic programs (P-1)
  13. Lack of innovative programs to attract students (P-2, E-2, B-1, O-1)
  14. Need for approved curricula for education in sexuality, family life, AIDS, justice (O-1)
  15. Class size (P-7, E-6, B-4, O-1)
  16. Poor extracurricular activities (P-9, E-9, B-1, O-2)
  17. Need for teachers to keep abreast of latest educational and technological developments (P-4, E-1, B-1)
  18. Uncertified personnel for assigned position (P-1, E-1)
  19. Flexible curriculum to meet needs of school student population (P-4, E-2, O-2)
  20. Back to basics (P-1, E-1)
  21. Inadequate computer programs (P-3)
  22. Lack of resources to purchase equipment such as computers, musical instruments (P-15, E-16, B-10, O-2)
  23. Lack of programs for non-college-bound (P-2, E-3, B-1)
  24. Lack of fine arts programs (E-3, B-2)
  25. Need more physical education (B-2)
  26. Lack of religious and cultural activities for students (B-1)
  27. Develop a compliance curriculum for each school (B-2)

B. Climate/environment
   1. Is morale high or low among teachers, students, parents? (C-2, P-1)
   2. Lack of sense of community (C-1, P-6)
   3. Lack of "community" among faculty (C-1)

4. Need to build sense of self-worth in a nurturing, caring environment (P-2, E-7, B-6, O-1)
5. Maintaining a safe and disciplined environment (E-2, B-1, O-1)

C. Services
1. Lack of guidance counselors, social workers, resource personnel, testing services (C-3, P-19, E-10, B-2, O-1)
2. Lack of handicapped facilities (C-1, B-2)
3. Special-needs students (C-3, P-2, E-11, B-5, O-10)
4. Lack of resource commitment to special needs (C-3, P-23, E-8)
5. No gifted and talented programs (E-2, B-5, O-3)
6. No pre-K or before- and after-school care (E-6, B-2, O-2)
7. Need to become family-centered rather than child-centered (E-1, O-1)
8. Lack of in-service to teachers in areas of special needs (B-2)
9. Lack of in-service to teachers on legal aspects of child abuse, drug usage, etc. (B-1)

D. Principals
1. Lack of specific training programs and mandatory updates (C-2, P-1)
2. Rotation of principals on a regular basis (C-1)
3. Better teacher/principal evaluation methods (C-3, P-2, B-2)
4. Lack of "professionalism" in our schools (C-1)
5. Poor leadership (C-1, P-3, B-1)
6. Lack of central hiring procedures for principals; should not be hired by pastor (C-1)
7. More school staff needed (P-1, E-5, B-1)
8. Lack of autonomy from pastor and school board (P-1, E-1)
9. Poor communication between principal, faculty, pastor, parents, students (P-2)
10. Ways to recruit more volunteers (E-1, B-1)
11. Principals lack contingency funds (B-1)
12. Poor job descriptions for principals (B-1)
13. Principals must regularly hear teachers' concerns (B-1)

E. Teachers
1. Need to have teachers committed to Catholic faith and values (C-10, P-7, E-6, B-2, O-2)
2. Need to develop a sense of mission (C-1, P-2, E-1)
3. Lack of continued faith development among teachers (C-2, P-10, E-2, O-2)
4. Lack of multicultural awareness and sensitivity (C-1, P-3, E-1)
5. Certification, regular updating of teachers in their fields (C-3, P-1, E-14, B-1, O-1)
6. Need for special programs that prepare personnel for the teaching ministry (C-1, P-3, O-1)
7. Should all teachers be Catholic? (B-1)
8. Need for colleges to help Catholic school teachers further their education (C-1, P-5)
9. Lack of volunteer programs to supplement school staff (C-1, P-6)
10. Teacher recruitment: lack of young teachers willing to devote three to five years to Catholic schools (C-1, P-3)
11. Lack of recruitment program aimed at young teachers for Catholic schools (P-2)
12. Are teachers qualified and certified? (P-6, B-8, O-1)
13. Active recruitment of qualified faculty (E-6, O-1)
14. Stagnant faculty (P-4, E-4, O-1)
15. More teacher input into decision-making (P-4)
16. Teachers spend their own money for supplies (P-2)
17. Lack of facing the fact that our schools of the future will be staffed by lay people (P-1)
18. Lack of in-service programs for teachers (P-8, E-3, B-8, O-2)
19. More interaction with other diocesan teachers (P-1)

20. Low teacher morale (P-1)
21. Need to hire more minority teachers (P-2)
22. Does faculty reflect the racial mix of the school? (P-1)

    F. Students
1. How do we meet the changing needs of our students? (P-1, B-2)
2. Is multicultural diversity viewed as a positive to be capitalized on or a negative to hinder our work? (P-5, E-2, B-2, O-4)
3. Negative attitudes toward learning (C-1, E-1)
4. Lack of discipline (C-1, P-3, E-2)
5. Lack of involvement in parish life (C-1, P-1, E-1, B-1)
6. Lack of vital CYO programs to get students involved in sports and activities (E-1)
7. Lack of faith commitment (C-1)
8. Lack of responsibility for actions (P-1, E-1, O-1)
9. Lack of involvement and pride in the schools (E-1)
10. When students leave, the general response is "they did not belong" (B-1)
11. Many schools have taken students with discipline problems to keep enrollment up (B-1)

V. Parents
A. Parental involvement
1. Lack of involvement in parish life (C-3, P-2, E-3)
2. Lack of involvement; poor attitudes toward schools (C-9, P-22, E-14, B-9, O-4)
3. Lack of programs to get parents involved in the school (C-1, P-6, E-6, B-1)
4. Parents' ideas not solicited or listened to (P-1, E-6, B-1)
5. Lack of parental support programs (P-3)
6. Lack of "ownership" of schools by parents and larger community (O-3)

B. Parental qualities/responsibilities
1. Lack of instruction in the faith (C-3, E-5)
2. Lack of strong family life (C-1, P-6, E-3, B-2)
3. General lack of faith (C-1, B-1, O-1)
4. Lack of parental responsibility in seeing that their children attend Sunday Mass (C-4, P-3, E-1)
5. Parents don't view themselves as primary educators of their children (C-1, P-2, E-1)

C. Parental reasons
1. Using Catholic schools as "escape" from public schools (C-2, P-1)
2. Parents don't see value in Catholic schools—CCD is OK (C-3, P-5, E-5, B-4, O-2)
3. Parents let their children choose which school to go to, usually with their friends (C-1, P-1, E-1)
4. What are the real reasons parents sent their kids to CCD and *not* to Catholic schools? (B-1, O-1)
5. Perception that Catholic schools are just another private school (O-1)
6. Tuition costs higher than quality of Catholic schools (B-1)
7. Fear of a specific school closing once children are there (B-1)

VI. Public Relations
A. Recruitment/marketing
1. Lack of overall marketing strategy by the diocese (C-20, P-33, E-22, B-10, O-13)
2. Need to seek out young families (C-4, P-2, E-1)
3. Need to recruit actively (P-6, E-11, B-3, O-4)

4. Recruitment aimed especially at junior high and senior high prospects (E-3)
5. Need to reach out to minorities and immigrants (C-7, P-19, E-7, O-7); non-Catholics (B-4)
6. Parents who are satisfied with the schools do not "sell" the schools (E-3)
7. No marketing staff (E-3)
8. Use public school crowding to our advantage (B-1)

B. Image
   1. Maximize our strengths; don't apologize (C-5, P-13, E-15, O-1)
   2. Need to publicize our record of success, especially academically (C-6, P-21, E-21, B-8, O-6)
   3. Catholic schools still have their "old" image (C-1, P-5, E-6, O-2)
   4. Public school extracurricular activities seen as superior to Catholic school activities (C-1, P-3)
   5. Negative image that Catholic schools have unqualified teachers (P-4, E-4, O-1)
   6. Public does not see Catholic schools as a single entity (P-1, E-1)
   7. How are we different? What makes us unique? (P-1, E-9, B-7, O-4)

C. Support
   1. Lack of support from the larger community (business, colleges, etc.) (C-1, P-1, E-3, B-3, O-1)
   2. Lack of positive interchange/support with public schools (C-1, P-1, E-2, B-8, O-1)
   3. Lack of alumni involvement (E-5)

VII. High Schools
A. Too much competition for students (P-1, O-1)
B. No affordable high school nearby (P-2)
C. Lack of high school students' involvement in parish life (P-1, E-1, O-1)
D. Lack of involvement in larger community (E-1)
E. More communication between elementary schools and high schools (P-3, E-2, B-1)
F. Lack of non-college-prep programs (P-2)
G. Lack of competitive teacher salaries (P-1)
H. Unfair recruitment practices (P-2)
I. Ways to generate more financial aid at the high school level (E-3)
J. Add junior high schools to existing high schools (E-2)
K. Image of Catholic high school student no different from image of public high school student, so parents choose latter (E-1)
L. Transportation problems (E-2)
M. Need more diverse academic programs (E-1)
N. Regionalize high schools for better offerings or courses and services (E-1)
O. All high schools should be co-ed (E-3)
P. Need high school on Aquidneck Island (E-1)
Q. No high school in Newport County (E-1)

(C=Clergy; E=Educators; P=Parents/Parish Representatives; B=Board Members; O=Others)

Catholic Identity Solutions

I. **Mission/Philosophy**
   A. Mission statement
      1. Published (handbook) for parents, students, parish (C-2, E-8, P-2, B-1)
      2. Keep mission/philosophy statement fresh before our eyes (E-1)
      3. Prioritized and clearly defined goals in worship and service (C-2, E-2, B-1)
      4. Clearly stated and integrated into school daily life (C-2, E-2, P-3, B-1, O-1)
      5. Each school have a mission statement of primary importance (C-2, E-7, B-1, O-2)
      6. Should reflect knowledge of Catholic tradition (C-1, E-2, P-1)
      7. Committed to teaching knowledge, values, and faith (C-1, P-2, B-1)
      8. Conservative position (not ultra-conservative) on faith and morals (C-1, P-2)
      9. Well-formulated *diocesan* statement (C-5, E-4, P-4, B-1, O-1)
      10. *Why* are we operating Catholic schools? (E-1)
      11. Include parents and students in development of mission/philosophy statement (E-2)

   B. Goals
      1. Define what we mean by "Catholic identity"
         a. Make available the NCEA materials on Catholic identity (E-1)
         b. Access documents from Catholic University on what is Catholic identity (C-1)
         c. Do not compromise our Catholic identity for the sake of government funds (P-2, B-1, O-1)
      2. Declare Catholic goals (C-1, E-1, P-1)
      3. Spiritual purposes and aims (C-1, P-1)
      4. "Mission 2000" goal statement (C-1, B-1)
      5. Maintain our traditions but explain and enjoy them (P-1)
      6. To provide Catholic education for
         a. All cultural and social strata (P-3)
         b. Diverse ethnic and cultural groups of Catholics (C-1)
         c. (To seek out) minorities (E-1, P-1)
         d. Catholics/non-Catholics; for those who pay/for all; private ed/subsidized ed (C-1)

   C. Non-Catholic issues
      1. Non-Catholics must participate in all religious activities (C-1, E-4)
      2. Non-Catholics: keep the percentage down (C-1, B-2)
      3. Should not exclude non-Catholics (P-1)
      4. Be clear about what we expect from non-Catholics (E-2)
      5. Non-Catholics must respect our traditions and values (C-1)
      6. Be clear about what we expect from non-Christians (E-2)

   D. Catholic tradition
      1. No apologies for being Catholic (C-3, E-2)
      2. Celebrate our differences (E-4, P-5, B-2, O-1)
      3. Instill pride in our catholicity, Catholic heritage, being Catholic (C-3, E-2)
      4. Clearly identify schools as Catholic (C-1, E-1)

5.   Make sure schools stay "Catholic" and don't become "private" (E-1)
6.   Every Catholic school should have a Catholic name, not a secular or regional name (B-1)
7.   Inner-city schools should not only be "safe" havens, but those students should be evangelized or the schools should close (E-1)

E.   Evaluation
1.   Have only measurable goals and objectives (P-1)
2.   Evaluate, revise, review mission statement/Catholic identity regularly (C-1, E-5, P-1)
3.   Establish minimum requirements influencing Catholic climate of schools (E-2)
4.   Do we accomplish what we say we do? (C-1)
5.   Evaluate students on character development, not on how many Masses they attend (P-1)

F.   Other
1.   Revive old Catholic Teachers College to teach Catholic values and morals to our future teachers (P-1)
2.   Catholic school office highlight Catholic identity issues once in a while (E-1)
3.   When recruiting, stress Christian values and religious teachers present in Catholic schools (C-1, E-2)

II.   **Religious Education in the Schools**
A.   Staff
1.   Pastors/priests/religious presence
   a.   Priests/religious be more present and visible in the schools (C-6, E-18, P-11, B-5, O-3)
   b.   Priests commit to one full day a week (C-1, E-1)
   c.   Assign/commit priests and religious full time to schools (C-1)
   d.   High schools should have priest/chaplain on the faculty (C-2)
   e.   Clergy must be willing to take part in liturgies and para-liturgies (E-1)
   f.   Clergy should not be in the schools (C-1)
   g.   Increase religious presence in the schools (C-3, E-2, P-6, O-1)
      (1) Retired religious on part-time basis (C-2, B-1)
      (2) Religious visit the schools for talks, vocation days (C-1)
      (3) Must have religious teach in the classroom (E-1)
      (4) Diocesan pool of religious to visit the schools (P-1)
      (5) Recruit missionary religious from other countries (P-1, B-1)
      (6) Sisters who teach should have visible sign of their religious life: habit, cross (E-1, P-1)
      (7) Stop lamenting loss of nuns and put our faith and trust in our lay teachers and principals (O-1)
      (8) Involve permanent deacons in the school religion programs (C-1)

2.   Principals/teachers
   a.   Principal and teachers be committed, *practicing* Catholics (C-12, E-6, P-2)
   b.   Principal as spiritual leader must ensure Catholic spirit permeates the school (E-3, P-2)
   c.   Principal and teachers must have mutually supportive faith community (C-1, E-2, P-1, O-1)
   d.   Committed administration and staff (E-1)
   e.   Diocese evaluate principal every three years on practice of Catholic identity (E-2)
   f.   Professional competence as well as religious commitment (C-1, E-1)

3.   Teachers
   a.   Hire teachers specifically trained to teach religion (C-5, E-4, P-2, B-1)
   b.   Hire teachers who are committed to our mission, philosophy, identity (E-3, P-2, B-1)

      c. Require certification *in religion* for religion teachers (E-2, O-2)

      d. Give financial incentives for religious certification (E-1)

      e. Hire only Catholic teachers in our schools (E-2, P-1, B-1)

      f. Board of Review to determine hiring of staff who meet faith requirements (C-1)

      g. Provide in-service workshops in religion and theology for teachers and administrators (C-5, E-17, P-2, B-1, O-2)

          (1)   Opportunities to pray together (retreats, days of recollection) (E-1)

          (2)   Regular times for staff to pray together (C-3)

          (3)   Student/parent/faculty retreats (C-1, O-1)

      h. Encourage faculty to share the faith (E-2, B-2, P-1, O-1)

      i. Look upon teaching as a mission (C-1)

      j. Faculty stance clearly stated on public moral issues (C-1, E-1, P-3)

      k. Non-Catholics must not teach religion (E-1, P-1)

B. Religion program/curriculum

   1. General

      a. Diocesan religion curriculum to ensure authentic Catholic teaching (C-3, E-1, P-2, O-1)

      b. Religious and moral values espoused throughout the curriculum (C-6, E-16, P-5, B-2, O-1)

      c. Catholic Christian atmosphere must permeate the whole school (C-5, E-5)

      d. Review and revise religion curriculum regularly: ACRE test (C-1, E-1, B-1)

      e. Religion taught formally each day (E-1)

      f. Ensure excellent religion program above academics (C-2, E-2, O-1)

      g. Formalize/publicize religion program objectives to inform parents and Catholic community (E-1)

      h. Course offering in Catholic history and development (C-1, E-1)

      i. Standard religion text (P-1)

      j. Modernize texts and teaching methods (E-1)

      k. Capitalize on ability to teach morals, which public schools cannot do (E-2)

      l. Foster Christian community among parents/students/staff (E-3, P-1)

   2. Doctrine

      a. To teach Jesus (C-2, E-3)

      b. *Church* teachings on issues should be taught and not watered down (C-7, E-3, P-3, B-1, O-1)

      c. Teach specific Church doctrine (P-2)

      d. Teaching religion should be more specific, less philosophical, esp. in elem/jr. high (E-1)

      e. Emphasize faith dimension over doctrine (E-1)

      f. Church is one true church (C-1)

      g. Teach *why* we believe what we believe (E-1)

   3. Faith experience: prayer and sacraments

      a. Give students the opportunities to grow in faith (C-1)

      b. Passing on the faith, habits of prayer, etc. (C-1)

      c. Regular daily classroom prayers (C-4, E-5, P-1)

      d. Regular religious practices in the school (E-1)

      e. Frequent Mass (daily/weekly/monthly) (C-2, E-8, P-2, B-1)

      f. Celebration of seasonal liturgies (C-2, E-6)

      g. Make liturgical celebrations central (E-2)

      h. Paraliturgical practices also: stations of the cross, processions, benediction (C-1, E-5, P-1)

      i. Provide a variety of faith experiences (E-1)

j. More teaching on the sacrifice of the Mass (P-1)

k. More Bible study, age appropriate (E-2)

l. Presence of religious symbols throughout the school: crosses, pictures, statues (C-3, E-4, P-1)

m. Work with other Catholic schools on faith-filled experiences (E-3)

n. Prepare list of individuals who might present days of recollection, mini-retreats (C-1)

4. Social action

a. Strong social justice teaching at all levels (C-2, E-6, P-6, O-1)

b. "Projects" and service which flow from Catholic social teaching (C-5, E-17, P-7, B-1, O-2)

c. Sponsor a relationship with area mission/outreach organizations (C-1)

d. Vocation to church ministry as part of the religion curriculum (E-1)

III. Students

A. Publish and enforce a discipline code based on Catholic values (C-2, P-1)

1. Maintain dress code (P-1, O-1)

2. Identify and reward Christian behavior (E-1, P-1)

a. Encourage responsible and disciplined behavior on the part of the students (E-1, P-1)

b. Give students non-liturgical experiences in the parish community (C-1, P-1)

c. Experience personal prayer appropriate to age group so as to know God (C-1, E-3, O-1)

d. Faith practice of students needs to be encouraged and provided for (C-1, E-2, P-2, O-1)

e. Allow students to lead classroom prayers and school liturgies (E-2, O-2)

f. Try to teach non-practicing parents through the faith of their children (E-2, P-2)

g. Focus groups for older students on today's moral issues (E-2, P-1)

h. Encourage students to be counter-cultural (E-1)

i. Workshops/retreats for students (E-2, O-1)

j. Programs that give youth a sense of their own role in the Church (E-1, P-1)

k. Classroom Masses for students (P-1)

l. More opportunity for confession during school hours (E-1)

m. Develop special liturgies for children (E-1)

n. Vocational days for children (C-1, P-2)

o. Educate/train students to be our future leaders in the Church (P-1)

p. Have students write book reports on Catholic literature (P-1)

IV. Parents

A. School's ministry to parents (religious formation) (C-1, E-7, P-2, B-1, O-1)

B. Acceptance in school based on family's practice of the faith (C-2, O-1)

C. Actively model the faith for their children through Mass attendance, prayer, etc. (C-3, E-4, P-1)

D. Outreach to parents alienated from the Church (C-1)

E. Keep church values and social teachings before parents' eyes (C-1)

F. Opportunities in PTO for prayer, teaching, devotions (C-1)

G. Communicate the values of the Gospel (E-1)

H. Administrators and teachers be attuned to the needs of dysfunctional families; incorporate Catholic values when helping them (E-1)

I. Parents must give children the opportunity to practice what is taught in the school (E-1, P-1)

J. Involve parents in school liturgies (E-1, P-1)

K. Schools must not "badger" those who do not practice the faith (E-1)

L. Focus groups for parents on today's moral issues (E-1)

M. Involve parents in ways that allow them to show they support the vision of Catholic schools (E-1, B-1)
N. Parenting classes (B-1)
O. Revive Communion breakfasts (B-1)
P. Have more faith gatherings for families (E-1)

V. **CCD**
A. Greater integration of CCD and religion (C-1)
B. Match religion requirements with CCD requirements (E-1)
C. Move after-school CCD to Sunday with Mass participation (E-1)
D. Catholic school students should not be forced to attend CCD classes (P-1)
E. Better CCD program: make it fun and viable, not a burden and aggravation (P-1)
F. Hire teachers who are qualified (O-1)

VI. **Parish**
A. Establish and define parish ministry to all schools (C-1)
B. Schools must have strong tie-in with parish liturgical, community, social life (C-2, P-2, B-1)
C. Integrate religious and lay teachers into parish life (C-1)
D. Integrate parish and CYO programs into religion curriculum (E-1)
E. Publicize school liturgical and para-liturgical celebrations in school bulletins to emphasize our faith (E-2)
F. Develop ways to link school life to parish life, especially elementary and diocesan/private high schools (C-1, E-2)
G. Students should be visible in parish: wear uniforms, sit together, serve as lectors (E-2)
H. Improve communication between high school and parish to promote student involvement (E-1)
I. School should be part of ongoing Christian community (C-2)

Curriculum Solutions

I. **Curriculum/Instruction Issues**
A. Quality
   1. General academic
      a. Equal/better quality than public schools (C-2, E-3, P-8, B-2, O-1)
      b. Universal standards of Catholic school excellence in religion and academics (E-1)
      c. Cross-curricular opportunities (C-1, O-1)
      d. Programs that stimulate thinking rather than rote memorization (C-1, E-1, P-1)
      e. Should produce a unique product (E-1)
      f. Teach quality *basics* in grades 1-8 (C-1, E-2, P-4, B-2)
      g. Don't compromise basic academic skill curriculum by offering electives (C-1)
      h. Quality rather than quantity (C-1)

   2. Curriculum development
      a. Create/develop (mandated) standardized curriculum for each grade throughout diocese (C-4, E-8, P-6, B-3, O-8)
      b. Flexible curriculum adjusted to the needs of the school population (C-1, E-5, P-2, B-2)
      c. Reflect gospel values as well as state requirements (E-1, O-1)
      d. Based on mission statement (E-1)
      e. Modernize and update secular curriculum (E-2, P-5, B-2, O-1)
      f. Academic program should reflect guidelines of NCTM, NCTE (E-1)
      g. Capitalize on the different Catholic cultures within the school (C-2, E-1, O-2)

h. Emphasize an area that capitalizes on an existing need which the public schools do not fill (C-1)
i. Study curricula of private schools that are attractive to upper middle-class Catholic parents and adjust (C-1)
j. Parental involvement in core curriculum development (C-1, P-2, B-1)
k. Encourage membership in regional accreditation agencies: NEASC, NCEA, RIISA (E-1)
l. Establish quality programs/services in junior high to keep students from going to public schools (E-3, P-1, B-2)
m. Make junior high competitive with good preparation for high school (P-1)
n. State/public schools and Catholic/private schools work together on curriculum (E-3, P-2, O-2)
o. Answer specific needs of students in creative ways: Xavier (C-1)
p. Curriculum that prepares students to deal with modern issues and with the future (C-1, E-6)
q. Enhance curriculum with challenging out-of-school projects (P-1)
r. Direct students to other schools that can meet their needs better than we can (P-1)

3. Curriculum evaluation
   a. Regular evaluation using diocesan and local input (C-4, E-6, P-2, B-1)
   b. Set program goals and evaluate them (E-1)
   c. Use same standardized tests throughout diocese (P-2, B-2)
   d. Use same standardized tests as public schools and compare/publicize results (P-2, O-1)
   e. Parental involvement in curriculum evaluation (P-2)
   f. Allow teachers to weed out the unnecessary stuff (E-1)
   g. Publish handbook for each school which contains curriculum guidelines (E-2, P-2)
   h. Need quality improvement process (P-1)

B. Financial issues
   1. Use major corporations to underwrite science labs, computers (C-2, E-3, P-1, O-1)
   2. Partnerships with business/industry (E-5, P-3, B-2)
   3. Can we realistically afford special services to special kids? (C-1)
   4. Do not get involved in programs we cannot afford (C-1)
   5. Central purchasing of textbooks (E-1, P-1)
   6. Resource sharing (E-6, P-2, O-3)
      a. Networking among teachers (B-2)
      b. Resource teachers/counselors: music, art, P.E., spec. ed, guest speakers (E-11, P-6, B-1)
      c. Ideas (E-2)
      d. Curriculum (E-1)
      e. Central resource center from which to borrow materials (E-1)
      f. Pooling chapter monies for area/cluster video and software libraries (E-1)
   7. Funds to maintain and upgrade equipment (E-3)
   8. Funds for field trips (E-1)
   9. Be honest and open about money needs, future plans, etc. (E-1)
   10. Develop a wish list for what is needed and encourage individuals, parishes, businesses to earmark funds for a specific item of their choice (E-1)

C. Programs
   1. Academic
      a. English/foreign language
         (1) Improve literature program (P-1)
         (2) Summer reading program (P-2)

      (3)   Improve writing program (P-1)
      (4)   Better language arts (P-1)
      (5)   Latin required for all eighth graders (P-1)
      (6)   Better foreign language programs at elem/jr. high levels (C-3, E-5, P-6)
      (7)   Spanish take precedence over French (C-1)
      (8)   Better multi-cultural programs (E-2)
   b. Math/science/technology
      (1)   Improve at all levels (E-3, P-5, B-1)
      (2)   Offer algebra to eighth graders (P-1, B-1)
      (3)   Mandatory computer programs in every school (C-1, E-6, P-8)
      (4)   At least one computer in each class (E-1)
      (5)   Typing courses in all schools (C-1)
   c. Fine arts
      (1)   Improve at all levels (C-2, E-4, P-3, B-1)
      (2)   Eliminate in favor of math/science: encourage use of community programs for these (P-1)
      (3)   Use extended day for fine arts, language, computer programs (O-1)
   d. Special programs
      (1)   Special ed (E-9, P-9, B-5)
      (2)   Do not go into special ed (B-1)
      (3)   Gifted and talented (C-3, E-5, P-6, B-1)
      (4)   Non-college prep (P-2)
      (5)   Devote one school to vocational ed. (E-2, P-2, B-1, O-2)
      (6)   Study skills (P-1)
      (7)   Minorities (C-1)
      (8)   Leadership training (E-1, P-1)
      (9)   Counseling/social services, especially elementary (E-6, P-2)
   e. Extracurricular activities
      (1)   Less important than academics (C-1)
      (2)   Quality activities (E-2, P-4, B-1, O-1)
      (3)   Shared responsibility for programs within areas/clusters (E-1)
   f. Before-/after-school programs
      (1)   Pre-K and day care to attract students to our schools (P-1)
      (2)   Tutoring programs (E-1)
      (3)   Extended day (E-1, B-1, O-1)
      (4)   Reading/writing clinics in each region (E-1)
      (5)   Become a resource for an unfulfilled need and offer to community (B-1)

D. Religion program
   1. To emphasize Catholic values and doctrine in non-religious subject matter (C-1)
   2. "Justice and rights" program (C-1, P-1)
   3. Quality of faith education (knowledge, practice, service) should be monitored by the diocese (C-1)
   4. Healthy spiritual Catholic formation (C-1, P-1)
   5. Encourage clergy to teach in religion program *if* they are qualified (C-1, O-1)
   6. Trained teachers (MA in theology) to teach religion (C-1, P-1)
   7. Religious education is primary in relation to other subjects taught (C-2, E-2, B-1)
   8. Offer world religion class in junior and senior high school (E-1)
   9. Diocese recommend religion texts following new Catholic catechism (P-1)

10. More courses in morals and ethics (P-1)
11. Weekend retreat for fifth or sixth graders to come between those for first communion and confirmation (P-1)
12. Involve school in the community (E-1)
13. Coordinate school religion program with CCD program (P-2, B-2, O-1)

E. Methodology
    1. Innovative teaching and course offerings (C-2, E-6, P-1, B-1, O-1)
    2. Use of multimedia to instruct children (C-1, O-1)
    3. Team teaching approach (E-3, P-1)
    4. More hands-on experience for students, especially in science (E-2)
    5. More cooperative learning (E-2, B-1)
    6. Encourage a variety of approaches in teaching subject matter (E-1, O-1)
    7. Departmentalize different subject areas (E-1)
    8. "Whole language" and "whole math" approach (E-1)
    9. Heterogeneous grouping, flexible grouping, ability grouping (E-2)
    10. More interaction between grade levels within a school (P-1, O-2)
    11. Avoid "fad" teaching styles and subjects (P-1)
    12. Focus on enduring skills, not latest technology which keeps changing (P-1)
    13. Investigate multi-age programs in lower grades with a team of teachers (P-1)
    14. Peer tutoring (E-1, P-1)

F. Instructional setting
    1. Class size 20-25 max (C-1, P-1)
    2. Rotating schedules in junior high similar to senior high (C-1)
    3. Longer school year: August 1 - June 30 (C-1, B-1)
    4. Longer school day: 1 hour (C-1, E-1, P-2, B-1)

G. Materials/facilities/resources
    1. Textbooks
        a. Update textbooks (C-2, E-12, P-4, B-3)
        b. Same textbooks throughout diocese (C-1, P-1, O-2)
        c. Diocese have list of approved texts (C-1)
        d. Use textbooks that foster and respect multi-culturalism (E-1)
    2. Long-range planning to acquire *technology* for the classroom (C-1, E-2, B-2, O-1)
    3. Upgrade and modernize facilities and equipment (E-1, P-3)
    4. Better use of equipment we already have (B-1)
    5. More use of community resource people (C-1)
    6. Teacher input as to their classroom needs (C-1)
    7. Share specialty teachers among the schools (C-1)
    8. Rent out YMCA for gym programs (E-1)
    9. Parents lobby for up-to-date non-religion texts from the state (P-1, O-1)
    10. Latest technology must be available (B-1)

H. Diocesan responsibilities
    1. Diocese provide quality resource person/committee for curriculum enhancement and updating services to schools (C-1, E-6, P-1, B-1, O-2)
    2. Diocesan guidance in textbook selection, esp. science and math (E-1)
    3. Curriculum task force to define a curriculum of the future for our students (E-4, P-1, B-1)
    4. Diocese monitor the curriculum (E-1, O-1)

5. Diocesan grant writing team to seek funds to strengthen the curriculum (E-2, P-2, B-1, O-1)
6. Diocese focus on a need throughout the diocese and implement plan to improve (E-1)
7. Appoint person to work with the public education system to keep abreast of everything (P-1)
8. Vicar of education should be more actively involved with the schools (P-1)
9. Diocesan athletic program director (P-1)
10. Incentive program awards given by diocese: school of the year, teacher of the year (P-1)
11. Compare/contrast academic programs of top national schools and modify RI curriculum as required (P-1, B-1, O-2)
12. Sponsor regional gifted and talented days, competitions, etc. (P-1)
13. Sponsor math meets, spelling and geography bees, writing contests (P-1)
14. Diocesan financial pool to support/maintain/update materials (B-1)
15. Greater support from diocese in science fields (B-1)
16. Need diocesan board of education (O-1)
17. Special diocesan curriculum team for each subject area (O-1)
18. Diocese demand excellence in all areas of the curriculum (E-1)

II. Personnel

A. Principals

1. Professional competence
   a. Knowledgeable of new trends and creativity in implementing them (E-1)
   b. Continued professional development (E-1)
   c. Freedom to make adjustments according to the needs of students (P-1)
   d. Merit pay for excellence (B-1)
   e. Ensure that administrators are accountable to parents, teachers, and students (P-1)
   f. Qualifications for principals equal to those of public school principals (P-2)

2. Leadership
   a. Provide incentives for teachers and students to excel (E-1)
   b. Discipline plan for the school and stick to it (E-1)
   c. Seek parents and community *professionals* to help with curriculum areas as adjuncts (E-3)
   d. Educate parents *beforehand* of changes that are coming (P-1)

3. Teacher evaluation
   a. No tenure policy: how do we let teachers go who are unsatisfactory? (E-3)
   b. Serious ongoing teacher evaluation (E-1, P-2, B-2, O-1)
   c. Ineffective teachers need to be removed (E-1, B-1)
   d. Evaluation of teachers geared to their production of academic results (P-1, O-1)
   e. Review teacher qualifications periodically (P-1)
   f. Reward good teachers (P-1)
   g. Look at successful teachers to see what they are doing right (P-2)
   h. Classroom visits to encourage new teachers (E-1)
   i. Maximize teacher strengths and minimize their weaknesses (E-1, P-1)

4. Principals and teachers encouraged to be on local government school boards (P-1)
5. Special consideration given to principals of regional schools (P-1)

B. Teachers

1. Qualifications
   a. Mastery of subject matter (C-3, E-3, P-2, B-2)
   b. Mastery of teaching techniques (C-3, E-1)

    c. Certification required (C-1, E-4, P-6, B-1, O-3)
    d. Quality teachers (C-1, E-1, P-1, B-1, O-2)
    e. Especially excellent math, science, computer teachers (E-1)
    f. Student teaching requirement (E-2)
    g. Hire teachers with a minor in a specialized field (E-1)
    h. Require teachers to obtain further education (P-1)

2. Spirituality
    a. Teachers must be committed teachers living the faith (C-2, P-1, O-1)
    b. Foster sense of mission and role modeling (C-1)
    c. Foster sense of teaching as a vocation (C-1)
    d. Required updating in religion (P-1)
    e. Standard religion training for all teachers (P-1)
    f. Flexible teachers with good spirituality (P-1)

3. Professionalism
    a. Subject specialization in junior high (C-1)
    b. Teachers must be supervised and evaluated (C-3)
    c. Board of teachers to review and update curriculum every few years (E-1)
    d. Teacher input into curriculum development (E-2, P-2, B-1)
    e. Teacher input into curriculum evaluation (E-2)
    f. Teacher input into textbook choice (E-1)
    g. Code of ethics for teachers (O-1)
    h. Ways for teachers to share viable working ideas with each other (E-1)
    i. Freedom to be innovative and creative (P-1)
    j. Merit system for excellence (E-1, B-1)
    k. Develop master teacher program in cluster areas (E-1)

4. Increase salaries to attract and keep quality teachers (E-8, P-7, B-1, P-1)

5. Incentives to attract and keep quality teachers (E-2, P-3, O-3)

6. Training/in-service
    a. Workshops to keep updated, learn new methods, ideas, techniques, etc. (E-9, P-3, B-2, O-3)
    b. Meetings to share ideas and experiences (C-1, E-1, P-1, O-1)
    c. Workshops in subject-specific and grade-specific areas (P-1)
    d. Computer workshops (E-5)
    e. Teachers invited to public school in-service free of charge (E-1, O-1)
    f. Creatively challenge teachers to keep updated (E-1)
    g. Work with Salve and PC to develop inexpensive programs for teachers (C-1, E-7)
    h. *Insist* on ongoing development (C-4, E-3, P-1, B-1, O-1)
    i. Workshops to clarify programs and objectives and create ownership of the curriculum (E-1)

7. New teachers
    a. More preparation time before September (E-1, P-1)
    b. Support system to improve skills (E-1, P-1)
    c. Hire minority teachers (O-1)

8. Diocesan policies
    a. Diocesan hiring policy defining academic and religious requirements (C-1)
    b. Provide incentives for updating (E-15, P-2, B-3, O-1)
    c. Diocesan pool of specialized teachers to go from school to school either for in-service or for teaching courses (E-2)

C. Students
   1. Encourage students to participate in outside contests, projects, etc. (E-3, P-2, B-1)
   2. Student input at each school for sixth, seventh, and eighth graders to give their views on things (P-1)
   3. Investigate gender bias in the classroom (P-1)
   4. Bring excitement and fun to students' lives via excellent activities, programs, field trips, arts, etc. (P-2, B-1, O-1)
   5. Raise student awareness of relevancy of Catholic education using graduates as role models (P-1)
   6. Definite community involvement (P-1)
   7. Catholic universities provide scholarships for students who commit themselves to teach in Catholic schools for "X" number of years (P-1)
   8. Involve students in advisory positions at all levels (P-1)

D. Staffing
   1. Seek out retired master teachers who will teach at reduced salary (C-2, P-1)
   2. Outside speakers on curriculum matters (E-1)
   3. Resource people from government, professionals, alumni (P-1)
   4. Outside speakers to highlight curriculum: Holocaust survivor, Vietnam vet, research scientist, etc. (P-1)
   5. Part-time teachers (P-1)
   6. Parent volunteers (P-1, O-1)
   7. Provide teacher aides (B-1)

E. Diocesan responsibilities
   1. Provide conferences for principals and assistant principals to review and revise curriculum yearly (P-1)
   2. Diocesan teacher evaluation (B-1, O-1)
   3. Teacher recognition in parishes (B-1)
   4. Establish "Peace Corps"-type program for Catholic college grads to serve the schools, not just teaching (B-1)

III. Other
A. High schools
   1. Work with high schools to meet their requirements (E-1)
   2. Work study programs (E-1, P-1)
   3. Partner program with colleges (E-1)
   4. Catholic colleges share courses with high schools (B-1)
   5. Create magnet schools (P-1)
   6. High school student input to grade schools (P-1)

B. School committees
   1. Meet before school begins to adjust curriculum (parents/teachers/principals) (E-1)
   2. To update course of study in each subject area (E-1)
   3. Review curriculum at faculty meetings (E-1)
   4. Curriculum planning meetings between teachers in same school or same grade, different school (E-1)

I. Tuition

A. Tuition policies

1. Tuition rates

a. Standard diocesan tuition rates for all areas (C-5, E-3, P-6)

b. Standard tuition rates for all schools in an area (C-2, P-2)

c. Set minimum and maximum tuitions (C-1, E-1, P-1)

d. Families pay at least 50 percent of tuition (C-1, E-1)

e. Tuition set at per-pupil cost (E-4, B-1, P-1)

f. Tuition based on income/ability to pay/sliding scale/fair share (C-2, E-6, P-2, O-1)

g. Tuition break for multi-child families (E-1, P-8)

h. Tuition reduction for active parish families (C-1, E-2)

i. Inactive Catholics, out-of-parish, and non-Catholics pay full per-pupil costs (E-1)

j. Eliminate higher rates for non-Catholics (E-1)

k. Cap tuition to encourage enrollment (E-1)

l. Keep tuition at a rate people can afford in a given area (C-1, E-1, P-3)

m. Tuition should be main source of income (B-1)

n. Reduced tuition for parents who supply needed services to the school (E-1)

o. Minimum parish collection contribution to qualify for in-parish tuition rate (E-1)

2. Tuition payment plans

a. Alternate payment plans (E-1)

b. Tuition incentive plan (E-1, B-1)

c. Allow parents to pre-pay tuition for two to three years at first-year rates (O-1)

d. Split tuition between parents/parish/diocese (P-1)

e. Encourage participation in tuition payment plans: FACTS, SMART (P-1)

f. Parents donate services in lieu of all/part of tuition (E-5, P-6)

g. Parents' fund raising over a certain amount could be deducted from tuition (E-1)

h. Student loan programs: establish a loan agency to allow parents to pay off loans over a longer time period (P-5, B-1)

i. Enforceable diocesan policy for collecting delinquent tuition (E-2, P-2)

B. Tuition assistance/scholarships

1. Create a school fund for scholarships (P-1)

2. Advertise funds available (P-2, B-1, O-1)

3. Provide more scholarships based on need (P-5, O-1)

4. Provide separate scholarships for academics and need (E-1, P-1)

5. Provide scholarships for

a. Minorities (B-1, O-1)

b. Poor families (E-1, P-2, B-1, O-1)

c. Multi-children families (E-1)

d. Secondary as well as elementary school students (P-1)

e. Young families (E-1)

6. Sources of funds/scholarships

a. St. Vincent de Paul/K of C/Catholic organizations (E-1, P-1, O-1)

b. Expand/alter Warde Fund (C-1, E-4, P-1)

c. Abolish Warde Fund and have "adopt-a-local school" within deanery (C-1)

d. Warde Fund be available to all, not just the poor (E-1)

e. Non-Catholics/non-active parishioners should not receive money from the Warde Fund (C-1)

    f.   Advertise Private School Aid Fund (E-2, B-1)

    g.   Diocesan annual collection (E-5, P-1, B-1)

    h.   "Educational Godparent" program (B-1)

    i.   Business/corporations (C-1, E-17, P-9, B-6, O-4)

       (1) Work/study programs (E-1, O-1)

       (2) Matching funds programs (E-2, P-1, B-1)

       (3) Catholic CEOs (E-1, B-2)

       (4) Bishop solicits (B-1)

    j.   Parish

       (1) Set up fund (C-1, E-5, P-1)

       (2) Parish collection once a year (E-2, P-2, B-1)

       (3) Parish collection once a month (E-5, P-2)

       (4) Parish endowment fund for tuition (E-1)

    k.   Parishioners/private individuals/benefactors: Mr. Feinstein (E-1, P-5, B-2)

    l.   Alumni (C-5, E-12, P-5, B-4, O-2)

       (1) Seek alumni donations, begin/strengthen alumni organizations (C-2, P-1, B-2, O-1)

       (2) Alumni agreement to donate to school (P-1, O-1)

    m. Diocesan fund for poor families (E-1, P-1)

    n.   Diocesan loan program (E-1)

    o.   Special fund-raising programs (P-1)

7.   Criteria for determining financial aid

    a.   Develop systematic way to determine financial aid eligibility for entire diocese (P-2)

    b.   Recognize financial limitations of parents (C-1, P-1)

    c.   Based on need, not across the board (C-2, B-1)

8.   Begin special programs (through business, parish, individuals, parish groups, groups of individuals)

    a.   Adopt-a-school (C-2, E-7, P-6, B-2, O-2)

    b.   Adopt-a-student (C-2, E-12, P-11, B-6, O-1)

    c.   Adopt-a-family (E-3)

9.   Real need to help the poor

    a.   Make Catholic education available to anyone (C-2, E-4, P-2, O-1)

    b.   One economically disadvantaged student per grade gets free tuition (B-1)

    c.   Budget assistance to delinquent families (C-1)

10. Tuition assistance offered through tenth grade, at which point student gets a part-time/summer job to pay; otherwise, we are subsidizing cars and good times (B-1)

II. Subsidies

A. Parish funds

   1. Parish collections

    a. Have parish-wide support collections exclusively for schools yearly/monthly/weekly (E-2)

    b. Missionary attitude/tithing/stewardship program in parishes (C-4, E-6, P-4, O-4)

    c. Tax all parishioners evenly (O-1)

    d. Tax all parishioners, more for those with no children in the school (E-1)

    e. Monthly parish collection—75 percent to school, 25 percent to CCD and RCIA (E-1)

   2. Parish subsidies

    a. Define parish subsidy (C-1, E-1, P-1)

    b. Establish uniform diocesan guidelines for parish subsidy (P-4)

    c. Limit parish subsidy (to 40 percent) of parish income (C-1, E-1, P-1)

    d. Subsidize individual students by parish (P-1)

    e. Increase parish subsidy (C-1, E-1, P-1, B-1)

   f. Recognize financial limitations of parish (C-1)

 3. Tuition assistance assessment

   a. Renew the 7 percent assessment (E-1)

   b. Enforce the 7 percent assessment (E-8, P-7, O-2)

   c. Increase the 7 percent assessment (C-1, E-2, O-1)

   d. Reduce the 7 percent assessment for those parishes with schools (C-1)

   e. All 7 percent be given to school, not parents; parents pay full tuition (C-1)

   f. Direct tuition assistance to school based on real per-pupil cost (C-1)

   g. Parishes without schools contribute *substantial* amount to diocesan education fund (C-1, P-1)

 4. Educate parishioners re

   a. How money for the schools is an investment in the parish and its future (C-2, E-2, P-2, O-1)

   b. Responsibility to help poor families in parish (E-2)

   c. "Ownership" of schools (C-1, P-1)

   d. Disclosure: publish budget information for all parishioners/parents to see (C-1, E-3, P-7, B-2)

 5. Schools should not bankrupt parish (C-1)

 6. Mutual understanding that school is but one of other equally important parish ministries (C-1)

 7. Accountability to parents and parish who subsidize the system (C-1)

 8. Limit subsidy and challenge parents to raise the rest (C-1, E-1)

 9. Understanding that tuition is not enough to finance the school (E-1, P-1)

B. Diocesan monies

 1. Diocesan funds

   a. Greater share of Catholic Charities Fund and central funds for Catholic schools (E-3, B-1)

   b. Parishes with school keep a portion of Catholic Charities Fund (E-1)

   c. More equitable/greater diocesan subsidy for schools (C-1, P-3, O-1)

   d. Diocese-wide commitment that all Catholics should support the schools (E-2)

   e. More diocesan help for schools in trouble (C-1, E-1, P-1, B-1)

 2. Diocese take over schools in financial trouble (C-1)

III. Financial Planning

A. Development

 1. Establish a strong central development office (C-1, E-5, P-1, O-2)

   a. Devoted to fund raising (E-1)

   b. Devoted to grant writing (C-1, E-5, P-2, O-3)

   c. Devoted to seeking materials, equipment, etc., from government sources (E-1, O-1)

   d. Devoted to training local personnel in grant writing (E-1, P-2, O-1)

   e. Diocesan campaign to raise money for *all* schools (E-3)

   f. Use expertise of board members (E-1)

 2. Hire professional development groups (E-1)

 3. Establish local development offices (C-1, E-1)

 4. Share development director within an area (E-1, P-1)

 5. Develop sources of major contributors for each parish (C-1)

6. Establish school development committees (E-2, P-2)
7. Development program that allows tax-deductible contributions (P-1)
8. Funds needed for materials, books, equipment, services (P-1, O-1)
9. Appeal to sense of investment in their own future (O-1)
10. Expertise (P-1)
11. Sources
    a. Book company donations (O-1)
    b. Diocesan development fund (C-1, E-3, P-2, B-1)
    c. Establish fund similar to Kansas City Fund (P-1)
    d. Wills (P-1)

B. Endowments
   1. Ways to develop (C-2, E-2, P-1, B-2)
   2. Present as responsibility of all in gratitude for past and vision for the future (C-1)
   3. Parish-based (C-1, P-1)
   4. Diocese-based (C-1)
   5. Establish endowments for
      a. Student aid/scholarships (C-1, P-1)
      b. Teacher salaries (C-1)
         (1) From alumni (B-1)
      c. Schools (E-1, P-2)
   6. Catholic education fund (E-2)
   7. Grandparents endowment fund (B-1)
   8. For each school (C-1)

C. Financial planning
   1. Administration
      a. Financial managers to use existing funds efficiently (P-2)
      b. Diocese-wide school resource group to allocate funds/resources from haves to have nots (P-1)
   2. Funds
      a. Keep meticulous financial records at all levels (P-1)
      b. Diocese hold all funds in one account, invest, spend income across the board (E-1)
      c. Invest funds in mutual funds, bonds, etc. (E-1)
   3. Local
      a. Establish local school finance committees (C-4, B-1)
      b. Parents/teachers/pastors work together on budget and curriculum (E-1)
      c. School boards and financial boards work together (B-1)
      d. Use parishioners with financial/business expertise (P-1)
      e. Use regional efficiency experts to minimize expenditures and maximize use of current resources (O-1)
      f. Every school should follow a budget (C-2, P-2)
      g. Financial accountability in all schools (C-2)
      h. Use financial experts to oversee the financial operations of the school (C-1)
      i. Financial committees should have teacher representation (E-1)
      j. Use trained financial personnel to manage funds (C-1)
      k. Long-range planning (P-3, B-2)

4. Diocesan
   a. Develop a replenishable emergency spending fund (C-1)
   b. Provide financial consultant to the schools (P-1)
   c. Central purchasing: diocese take over all purchasing of supplies (P-5, B-1, O-2)
   d. Catholic Schools Week collection (P-1)

IV. Alternative Sources of Funding
A. Staffing
   1. Develop volunteer corps of teachers: live in community, take temporary vows, work for less (P-1)
   2. Develop corps of retired teachers, senior citizens to augment the needs of the schools (P-2, O-1)
   3. Develop corps of volunteers from parishioners (P-2)
   4. Return religious to the schools as teachers (C-1)
   5. Catholic universities (B-1)
   6. Train clergy and staff in financial matters (E-2, P-1)

B. Funding
   1. Parish set up savings plan and use interest (P-1)
   2. Special collection for school by decreasing the number of diocesan collections (C-2, B-1)
   3. Rent out unused buildings/rent after hours (P-1, B-1, O-3)
   4. Install new programs: pre-K, before/after school, summer school (E-1)
   5. Set aside money from Catholic Charities for schools (C-1)
   6. Diocese-wide annual fund drive (P-6, B-1, O-1)
   7. Parents must not be the sole supporters of the school (P-1)

C. Other
   1. Invest in a lottery (E-3)
   2. Schools conserve resources: paper, lights, recycle (P-1)
   3. Keep academics #1; sports and clubs funded by participants (P-1)
   4. Generate funds without tapping parents (P-1)
   5. Build a casino (O-1)

V. Fund Raising
A. Who should raise funds
   1. Parents must be more involved in fund raising (C-2, P-1, B-1, O-1)
   2. Fund raisers must be joint parish/school efforts (E-2, P-1)
   3. Diocese, not parish or school, should have the burden of fund raising (P-1)
   4. Need professional help (P-1, B-1)
   5. PTO generate funds for unbudgeted needs (B-2)
   6. Catholic organizations, so more funds stay with the school (O-1)

B. What should be done
   1. How many?
      a. One/two major fund raisers per year: golf tourneys, auction/dinner (E-2, P-1)
      b. More small fund raisers during the year (C-1, P-1)
      c. Have several *diocesan* fund raisers (E-1, P-1)

     d. Annual *parish* fund raiser devoted to the school (E-2)
     e. Parents agree to give set sum in lieu of fund raising (B-1)
     f. Have some regional fund raising activities (E-1)
  2. What?
     a. Desperately need creative ideas (E-4, B-1)
     b. Telethon/walkathon/phonathon/marathon (B-1)
     c. National "Give Back" program (E-2)
     d. Fund raisers that appeal to larger community: carnivals, ethnic dinners, sports days (E-1, P-2, B-1)
     e. Choose "fun" family activities rather than always selling things (E-1)
     f. Diocesan lottery for schools (E-1)
     g. Separate fund raisers for children and adults (E-1)

VI. Interparish Support and Cooperation

A. Area schools
  1. Regionalize (E-5, P-1) [within city (B-1)]
  2. Consolidate (C-2, E-4, P-1, B-1, O-1)
  3. Merge in a given area to save money (E-3, P-1, B-2, O-1)
  4. Area schools, by grade level or specialty (C-1)
  5. Evaluate the number of schools in a given area (E-1)

B. Support and cooperation
  1. Educate parishes to the fact that one parish–one school is no longer possible (P-1)
  2. Merge schools that are not cost-effective/self-supporting (C-1, E-1)
  3. Non-school parish adopt a school (E-2)
  4. Parishes without schools give aid to their students desiring a Catholic education (E-2)
  5. Educate all parishioners to support Catholic schools (E-3)

C. Sharing resources
  1. Share resources and ideas regionally (C-1, E-2, B-1, O-1)
  2. Bulk purchasing, at least regionally (C-1, P-3, B-2)
  3. Sister schools: inner-city with middle-class schools (P-1)
  4. Consolidate schools in poor areas so resources can be pooled (C-1)
  5. Share business management and maintenance services (C-1)
  6. Pool chapter funds to benefit cluster schools (P-1)
  7. Establish sharing network among Catholic schools (B-1)

VII. Teacher Salaries and Benefits

A. Salaries
  1. Equitable, just salary and benefits (C-1, E-9, P-5, O-2)
  2. Need outside source to fund teacher salaries (not tuition); establish diocesan fund to support teacher salaries (E-1, P-1)
  3. Have uniform teacher salaries across the diocese (C-4, E-9, P-2, B-1, O-1)
  4. Explore merit pay/incentive pay for teachers (E-1, B-1)
  5. Add salary for those who teach special courses, after-school programs (E-1)

B. Benefits
  1. Diocese maintain health plan and add dental plan (E-1)
  2. Teachers' children attend Catholic schools free or at reduced tuition (E-2, P-1, O-1)
  3. Seek other "benefits" besides money and health plan (E-1)
  4. Financial breaks for teachers (B-1)

C. Programs with PC and Salve for upgrading teachers at reduced rates (E-1)

D. Provide funds for teacher enrichment with time commitment to pay back (C-1)

E. Financial incentives for teachers to earn masters' degrees (C-2)

VIII. Capital Improvements and Maintenance
A. Establish plan/budget for replacement (E-1)
B. Seek competent advice for building maintenance (E-1)
C. Preventive maintenance schedule (C-1)
D. Use parish/community volunteers to help with routine maintenance (E-2, P-1, O-1)
E. Capital improvement fund in each school (E-1)

IX. Government Assistance
A. Current funding
   1. Seek and utilize all government (city, state, federal) monies available to us (C-1, E-7, P-6, B-2, O-1)
   2. Seek funds for mandated services (B-1)
   3. Seek funds for the poor (B-1)
   4. Seek funds for materials and equipment (E-2)
   5. Insist local school boards follow state requirements to (Catholic) schools (B-1)
   6. Lobby to keep funds and services we already have (C-1, P-2)

B. Additional funding
   1. Government (general) (E-1)
   2. City (P-1, B-1)
   3. State pay teacher salaries (B-1)

C. Pursue tax credits/voucher system at all levels for all families (C-8, E-15, P-16, B-5, O-1)

D. Lobby actively for government funds (C-1, E-4)
   1. Parents (C-2, E-3, P-2, B-1)
   2. Catholic Bishops' Conference: national push (C-1)
   3. Parish (E-1)
   4. Inter-denominational lobby (C-1, P-1)
   5. Support political candidates who favor vouchers (E-1)

E. Avoid government vouchers to ensure integrity of Catholic schools (P-1)

F. Close all non-public schools for one week to make our point (E-1)

G. Catholic school representation in local government (P-1)

H. Creation of task force to make recommendations in case state aid for busing and books is eliminated (B-1)

I. Work out a transportation system that does not rely on government assistance (O-1)

X. Alternative Solutions to Catholic Schools
A. Close schools to make public aware of Catholic contributions (C-1, E-1, P-1, B-1)
B. Centralize all schools (C-1)
C. Create school districts where each parish contributes a certain amount/year to go to equal subsidies, teacher pay, benefits, etc. (E-1)

XI. Central Office

A. Pooling of all funds in central office, no parish responsible for a school (E-1, P-1, B-1, O-1)
B. Central office must establish priorities for all the funds demanded of it, with education at or near the top (P-1)
C. Commitment of Catholic Church to Catholic education (B-1)
D. End concept of parish school and establish idea of church school (E-1)
E. Less money spent on high-powered consultants (B-1)
F. More diocesan support for elementary schools (P-4, B-1)
G. Stronger leadership from bishop to increase enrollment (B-1)
H. More central services (O-1)
   1. Purchasing (E-5, P-2, B-1, O-1)
   2. Marketing (E-3, O-1)
   3. In-service training (E-1, P-1)
   4. Salaries (E-1)
   5. Curriculum: with flexibility (E-3, O-1)
   6. Physical plant maintenance (E-1)
I. Seek privatization of some services: food, recreation (O-1)
J. Diocese assume all financial responsibility: payroll, purchasing, tuition collection, subsidies (C-1)
K. Diocese should contract for outside services (consultants, health) and offer them to all schools (E-1)
L. Diocesan administrator to disperse funds equitably (P-1)

XII. Other

A. Campaign to increase enrollment (P-3, O-1)
B. Bring back non-practicing Catholics (P-1)
C. Continuing evaluation of performance at all levels (C-1)

Governance Solutions

I. Diocesan Leadership

A. Catholic education
   1. More commitment from bishop and priests to Catholic education (E-8, P-4, B-1)
   2. Mission statement which reflects Catholic education as a top priority (E-1, P-3, B-1)
   3. Identify strong leaders on diocesan and parish level who can rally people and resources to support Catholic schools (E-2, P-2, B-1)
   4. Must convince all that all Catholics are responsible for Catholic schools (E-4, P-2, O-1)
   5. Leadership training for all pastors and principals so as to involve constituents of community in governance (E-2, B-2)
   6. Improve management skills of administration, board members, pastors (E-2)
   7. Organized outreach and communication re: educational needs (E-1)
   8. More visible superintendent (P-1)

B. Central office/school relationships
   1. Reorganize Catholic school office (CSO) to make it more effective in helping schools (E-1, P-1, B-1)
   2. What kind of authority resides in the superintendent's office? (C-1)
   3. Expand diocesan office to include assistant superintendent in deanery areas (C-1)
   4. Power to hire principals (C-1)
   5. Troubleshooters to help schools (E-1, P-2)

6. More control by central office/superintendent (E-1, P-2, B-1)
7. Develop strong guidelines for schools and *enforce* them (P-1)
8. More authority for CSO (centralized policies) (E-1, P-1, O-2)
9. Diocese oversee problems (E-1)
10. In-service workshops to define/explain roles of CSO, school boards, pastors, principals (E-1)
11. CSO formulates policy; schools and parishes implement them (P-1)
12. Focus on modern *management techniques* (P-1)
13. Accountability—to whom, by whom—and everyone should know (priests, administrators, faculty, parents) (E-2)
14. CSO be source of ideas and support (P-1)
15. Be careful of too much central "top-down" authority when our strength has been the reverse (O-1)

C. Planning
   1. Follow demographics of Catholic population (E-2)
   2. Evaluate diocesan staff/hire more to implement results of this study (E-1)
   3. Regular meetings between diocese and parish/school representatives to troubleshoot (P-1)

D. Regional planning
   1. Must be *teeth* in diocesan support for regional schools (C-2)
   2. Diocesan standards to regulate regionalization and school closings (C-1)
   3. Uniformity in governing regional schools (C-1)
   4. Regional planning by geographical areas/population shifts (C-1, P-1)
   5. Successful ideas and policies should be shared (P-1)
   6. More cooperation among pastors and parishes for responsibility of schools (P-1)
   7. Regional directors to facilitate communication and sharing resources (B-1)
   8. Emphasize what has made us successful: site-based management, quality, accountability (P-1)

E. Governance issues
   1. Clear diocesan policies on governance (structure and roles) (C-1, E-2)
   2. Move from parish-run schools to diocesan-run schools (C-3, B-1)
   3. One school system (GWCRS) (C-3, E-11, P-7, B-3, O-2)
      a. Uniform throughout (E-3, P-2, B-1)
      b. Same governing laws and constitution (E-1)
      c. Retain on-site management (E-1)
      d. Need conformity in some areas (tuition, salaries), but *not* in curriculum (E-2, B-1)
      e. United structure other than individual elementary schools (E-2)
      f. Each school should govern itself with parish board (P-1)
   4. Run schools as a business (E-1)
   5. Review governing process every two years (B-1)
   6. Standardize more of the governing groups (P-1)

F. Personnel
   1. All involved in governance must be *qualified* and *committed* to Catholic schools (E-1)
   2. All Catholic school office personnel should be expert and knowledgeable about diocesan resources so we don't need outside consultants (E-1)
   3. Administration must see to needs of whole diocese (E-1)
   4. All personnel must be accountable (E-1)
   5. Involve teachers in decision-making at appropriate levels (E-2)

6. Mandate priest involvement in school life (P-1)
7. More parents participate in school governance (B-1)
8. College and university professionals assist with governance (B-1)
9. Pool of personnel available to schools (fine arts teachers, counselors, etc.) (B-1)
10. When regionalization happens, keep commitments to teachers (E-1)

G. Other
1. To always have policies in place that withstand political changes (E-1)
2. General newsletter from diocese re: ideas, activities, etc. (E-1, P-1)
3. Analyze role of Catholic school office (E-1)
4. More help from Catholic school office to meet requirements of curriculum and physical plant (E-1)
5. Regional centers for services (marketing, purchasing, in-service training) (P-1, B-1)

II. Parish/School Relationships

A. Parish
1. Greater commitment from pastors and parishioners to Catholic school system (C-1)
2. Encourage parishioners to take greater interest in the school (C-1)
3. Greater involvement/interest of pastor and parishioners without schools (C-1, P-1)
4. Generate broad-based support from parish and parishioners (C-1)
5. Acknowledge pastor difficulty with Catholic school always operating at a deficit (P-1)

B. School
1. Develop set policies for each school (P-1)
2. Each school should have a management plan (P-1)
3. School should be accountable to parish and parents (P-1)
4. School is cornerstone of parish (P-1)

C. Consider focusing resources on family-centered religious education (P-1)

III. Local Leadership

A. Pastor-school
1. Assign only pastors who support schools to parishes with schools (C-4, E-4, P-2, B-1, O-4)
2. Clearly defined roles for pastors in the schools (C-3, E-1, P-1)
3. Pastors should have less responsibility in school governance (C-1)
4. Pastors should meet regularly with school personnel to create a spirit of cooperation (C-1, E-1)
5. More *visible* presence of pastor and priests in the school (E-5, P-3)
6. More support and commitment from pastors (E-5, P-5, B-1)
7. Ongoing training of pastors in support of Catholic education (E-1)
8. Pastor should attend school board meetings (E-1)
9. Pastors not in support of Catholic schools must be heard (E-1)
10. Pastor and school board run the school (E-1)
11. Pastor and principal govern the school (P-2)
12. Pastors are not educators (P-1)
13. Pastors responsible for establishing diocesan policies in the schools (O-1)

B. Principal-school
1. Principal responsible for total operation of the school and is answerable to the school board (C-1, E-1, P-1, B-1)
2. Rotate principals after a specific term (C-1)

3. Must have well-trained administrators (C-1)
4. Principals must have clearly defined roles (C-1)
5. School administration must be tailored to the needs of the geographical area (C-1)
6. Principals must be certified in administration (C-1)
7. Principal selected by search committee, not pastor (C-1)
8. Need dedicated principals with strong Christian life (E-2)
9. Training programs for principals re: how to work with school boards and other advisory groups (E-1)
10. Mandate periodic updating in areas of school law, finance, budgeting, marketing (E-1)
11. Strong leader who can make and enforce decisions (E-1)

C. Schools
   1. Don't close a school if no other school in area (E-1, P-1)
   2. Increase communication between school board and finance board (E-1)

IV. Interparish Relationships
   A. Equal distribution of assistance from all parishes in regional schools (C-1)
   B. Define parish responsibilities for support and maintenance of school (E-1, P-1)
   C. Every parish must declare affiliation to and sponsorship of a Catholic elementary school (E-4, B-1)
   D. Encourage more support among parishioners/pastors involved in regional schools (E-1, P-3, B-1)
   E. Pastors without schools should have a say in governance when they subsidize students to a particular school (E-1, P-1)
   F. Ensure sufficient input from pastors/clergy without schools (O-1)

V. School Boards
   A. General
      1. Composition
         a. Interested persons who have no children/grandchildren in the school (C-1)
         b. Only committed people (P-1)
         c. Define qualifications for members (P-2)
         d. Members with various backgrounds (B-1)
      2. Need for *limited jurisdiction* school boards (C-1)
      3. Term limit for members (C-1, E-1, B-1)
      4. Enforce all guidelines governing school boards (C-1)
      5. Define roles of school board on each level (C-1, E-2, P-2, O-1)
      6. Incorporate school boards independently (E-1)
      7. Diocesan-level training for all school boards to ensure unity of mission, roles, philosophy, responsibilities (C-1, E-1, B-1)
      8. Empower boards with governing, not just advisory status (P-2)
      9. Define authority of school board (E-1)
      10. Define duties of members (E-1, P-3, O-1)

   B. Diocesan school boards
      1. Establish diocesan board advisory to superintendent (C-1, E-5, P-2)
      2. Establish diocesan board representing different geographical areas (C-1, P-1)
      3. Diocesan board mandate salaries, books, curriculum, finance, subsidy, fund raising (E-1, P-2)
      4. Elected and appointed members (E-1)

5. Leadership to minimize competition among schools (P-1)
6. Lay/parent representation on board (P-1)
7. Ensure each school is run in a uniform manner (B-1)

C. Regional-vicariate school boards
1. Representatives from all parishes involved in regional school (C-2, E-4)
2. Representatives should be pastors, principals, teachers, parents, others (C-2, P-1)
3. Decide allocation of resources (E-1)
4. Set tuition, salaries, budget (E-1)
5. Advise on curriculum, not necessarily mandate it (E-1)
6. Absolute competence and commitment from regional board (O-1)

D. Parish school boards
1. Every school should have a school board (C-2, E-8, P-1, B-2, O-1)
   a. Advisory to the principal C-2, E-3)
   b. With clout (P-3, B-1)
   c. Should board be advisory or governing? (E-1)
2. Membership
   a. Parents only (P-1)
   b. Pastor, principal, teachers, parents, parishioners, high school students (E-5)
   c. Parents/non-parents (E-2, O-2)
   d. Serve at request of pastor (E-1)
   e. Principal non-voting member (E-1)
   f. More teachers on school board (E-1)
   g. Elected school board (E-1, O-1)
   h. Representative of school community (E-1, O-1)
3. Better communication between parents and school board (P-1)
4. School board independent from other school/parish groups (E-2)
5. School board and finance committee must work together (E-1, P-1)
6. Twice-a-year meetings to evaluate principal and school (C-1)
7. Site-based management by school board (B-1)
8. Accountable to diocesan school board (O-1)
9. Set tuition, budget (B-1)

VI. **Alternative Models**
A. Regionalization
1. Establish regional schools (C-1, E-5, P-5, B-3, O-3)
   a. Especially in urban areas (C-1)
   b. Elementary and middle schools (C-1, P-3, B-2)
   c. For financial reasons (C-1, E-3, P-4)
   d. Junior high in feasible areas (E-3, B-1, O-1)
   e. Only if enrollment is down (E-5, P-4, O-1)
   f. For more compelling reasons than finance (P-1, O-1)
   g. Create a middle school system (O-1)
   h. Establish regional middle school with local elementary schools (E-2)
2. All regional schools should be co-ed (P-1)
3. Share resources, teachers, facilities (C-1, E-2, P-1)
4. Uniform tuition, salaries, financial aid (P-1)
5. Regional schools implemented and enforced by bishop and Catholic school office (P-1)
6. Regionalize all schools including, to some degree, private schools (B-1)

7. Provide transportation to regional schools (P-1)
8. Non-participating parishes have no governing rights (B-1)
9. Abolish parish schools, make all regional (C-1, E-1, P-2, O-2)
10. Parish schools with more than 200 students should not be forced to regionalize (E-1)
11. Define firm and clear rights and obligations for parishes involved (E-1)
12. Method of financing must be clear *before* regionalization occurs (P-1)
13. Consider needs of all areas (P-1)
14. (Prior) commitment from all parishes (P-2)
15. Regionalize where there are no Catholic schools (B-1)

B. Consolidation
1. Especially in urban areas (C-1)
2. Geographically proximate schools with fewer than 150 students (C-1)
3. In regions with multiple schools (C-1, P-2)
4. Consolidation of nearby and weak schools must be mandated (C-1, B-1)
5. Not enough neighborhood schools (E-1)
6. Consolidate to preserve viability: "Church" schools vs. "parish" schools (E-1)
7. Look at ways to avoid consolidation (P-2)
8. Consolidate *parishes* to save money (P-1)

C. Area schools
1. Determine if new schools are needed (C-1, E-1)
2. See if parents support ideas (C-1)
3. Establish area schools: pre-K, 1-3, 4-5, etc. (C-1, E-4, B-1)
4. Schools that meet a variety of needs (E-1)
5. Separate middle schools from elementary schools (E-2)
6. Avoid closing a school completely, but try area schools by grade level (P-1)
7. Where middle school is unsuccessful, add middle school grades to high school (P-1)

D. Clusters
1. Attach each parish to a school (Baltimore) (C-1)
2. Cluster schools in various regions (E-2, P-1)
3. Establish new schools where needed (E-1)
4. Expand into suburbs (E-1)

E. Regional planning councils
1. Pastors and principals must work together in regions (C-1, E-1, B-1)
2. Meetings to share ideas and strategies (E-2, B-1)
3. Regionalize, consolidate, close, open schools to meet needs and maximize resources (E-3)
4. Superintendent for each grade area meet to address needs of each group (E-1)
5. Need more pre-K programs (E-1)
6. Eliminate competition between schools (E-1)
7. Need to offer summer programs (E-1)
8. Need to offer day care (P-1)

VII. Study Process
A. Resolve problems *together* with meetings such as this (E-1)
B. Follow through on recommendations of this study (E-1)

VIII. Other
    A. Survey successful educational models (NCEA) (C-1, E-3, P-2, B-1, O-2)
    B. More parental involvement in governing boards (E-2)
    C. Unified force to represent us in the legislature (C-1, E-2, P-2)
    D. Teacher organization to ensure just and fair voice in governance (E-1)
    E. Please include suggestions from white paper (P-1)
    F. Discuss the situation of *no* Catholic schools (P-1)

Parent Solutions

I. Parental Involvement
    A. Increasing parental involvement
        1. Commitment
            a. Parents must commit themselves (contracts) to spiritually and financially support the school when they enroll their children and be held to that commitment (C-1, E-2, P-4, B-3)
            b. Parents who register their children must be clearly informed of their responsibilities toward involvement and ownership: Mass attendance, practice of faith and values taught by school, support school in its activities, meetings, etc. (C-4, E-1, P-1)
            c. Mandate parent involvement in specific areas (C-3, E-4, P-3, B-1)
            d. Have pastor interview each family at registration time to secure commitments, both spiritual and material (C-1)
            e. Develop a policy of commitment (E-3)
            f. Develop a parent handbook delineating rights and responsibilities for parents (E-1)

        2. Ways to increase involvement
            a. Parents who value Catholic education must promote their enthusiasm and conviction (C-2, P-1, B-1, O-2)
            b. Educate parents to the need for their involvement (disclosure policies) (C-1, E-2, P-2, B-1)
            c. Create a feeling of *ownership* for the schools (C-1, E-1, P-2)
            d. Encourage the formation of strong PTOs to serve the school and the parents (E-4, P-8, B-1)
            e. Offer incentives for parent participation, especially tuition breaks (P-5, B-1, O-1)
            f. Parent group to welcome new parents (E-2, P-2)
            g. More recognition of parent contributions by pastors and principals (E-3, P-1)
            h. Suggestion boxes (P-1)
            i. Principal/core parent group to contact all parents and get them involved (C-1, P-7, B-1)

    B. Encouraging parent attendance
        1. At meetings
            a. Fewer, but well-run, mandatory meetings (C-1, E-2)
            b. Have speakers/agenda to make meetings attractive (C-3, E-5, P-1, B-1, O-1)
            c. Reach-out program from PTO to encourage attendance/telephone tree (E-4, P-1)
            d. Support services for parents: babysitting, car pools, etc. (O-1)
        2. At-school activities
            a. Encourage classroom visits from parents (E-2)
            b. Encourage/develop/invite parent participation in school activities (C-1, E-5)
            c. More back-to-school/open house days (E-1, P-3, B-1, O-2)
        3. Support parents and they will support the school (B-1, O-2)

C. Encouraging parent volunteers
1. Use parental talents and expertise for school betterment (C-1, E-13, P-5, B-1)
   a. Classroom aides/subject matter (C-1, E-7, P-4)
   b. Governance/law/finance (E-1, B-1)
   c. Repair/maintenance (C-1, E-4, P-1, B-1)
   d. Extracurricular activities (E-3, P-3)
   e. Career days (E-1, O-1)
2. Use grandparent volunteers (E-4, P-1, B-2)
3. Use retired persons as volunteers (B-2)
4. Fund raising
   a. Downplay fund raising as the only parent contribution (O-1)
   b. More cooperation in fund-raising events (C-2, E-1, P-1)
   c. Fund raising needs handled by parents (P-1)
   d. Be more creative in fund-raising events involving parents (P-1)
   e. Involve parents in fund-raising decisions (E-2)
5. Establish school stewardship program with annual sign-up (C-1, E-1, P-2)
6. Involve core groups of parents in various areas: development, fund raising, public relations (P-1)
7. Specific tasks which parents could sign up for (P-1)
8. Parents must actively support at least one function of the school (P-1)
9. Make after-work volunteer opportunities for working parents (P-3)
10. Enlist parents of one grade to be responsible for a specific event (B-1)
11. Overcome parent feeling that paying tuition is enough (B-1)
12. Parents and children work together on projects for the school (B-1)

D. Involving parents in parish life
1. Involve parents in parish life as lectors, eucharistic ministers, ushers, etc. (C-1, P-5, B-1)
2. Have family parish activities to encourage parent involvement (C-1, E-4, P-3, B-3, O-2)
3. Have a family requirement for *service* to parish community (P-1)

E. Involving parents in decision-making
1. Involve parents in governance structure at all three levels (C-2, E-4, P-7, B-1, O-2)
2. Create diocesan parent board to share information, problems, ideas (E-2, B-2)
3. Schools
   a. Ask for parent input on school issues (C-1, E-12, P-8, B-1, O-2)
   b. Invite parents in to explain program changes (E-1)
   c. Create parental advisory board, separate from PTA, to give input to school board (E-1)
   d. Give parents more information about what it takes to run the school (E-1)
4. Let parents know their input is necessary and important (C-1, E-2, P-3)
5. Include parents on finance committees (E-3)

II. **Religious Commitment**
A. Practice of the faith
1. Spiritual abuse occurs when parents fail to model Catholic faith (C-1)
2. More opportunities for parents to practice their faith (C-2, E-4, P-1, O-1)
   a. At home with their children (C-1, E-4, P-3, O-1)
   b. At school with their children (E-3, P-2)
3. Evangelization of parents (C-1, E-1)
4. Strengthen Catholic family life (E-1, P-6, B-1)
5. Commitment statement that parents are actively practicing the faith with their children (E-1, P-1)

6. Parents take responsibility for the religious education of their children (P-2)
7. Meet with "lapsed" Catholics/non-involved parents to find out what kinds of things might draw them back to the Church (C-1, E-1)
8. Liturgy commission in each school to plan family liturgies (P-1)
9. Reinstate communion breakfast for different small groups of families during the year (B-1)

B. Increase parental understanding
1. Workshops to discuss value of Catholic education (C-3, E-6, P-10, B-3, O-1)
2. Parents are the *primary educators* of their children (C-2, E-4, P-3)
3. Education without a moral background is worse than morally indifferent education (C-2, E-3)
4. Parents must perceive Catholic education as a priority for their families (C-3, E-6)
5. Parents must be committed to Catholic education, not to a "safe" place (E-3)
6. Diocese must educate parents to show them that Catholic education is an extension of their families and a central part of their child's development (B-1)

C. Actively involve parents
1. Realize that all Catholics will not be advocates of Catholic schools (C-1)
2. Stress to parents their responsibility to parish/church for what they have received (C-3, E-1, P-1, B-2)
3. Expand *sacramental* program to include bringing back non-involved parents (C-1, E-2, P-1)
4. Mandate family retreats (E-1)
5. Involve grandparents in faith-sharing days (E-1)

III. Adult Education
A. Religious education
1. Promote spiritual enrichment: Marriage, Engaged Encounters; Cursillo (C-1)
2. Formation in catholicity (C-3, E-5, P-2 O-1)
3. Enrichment for parents involving parish and parishioners (C-1)
4. Use radio and TV to reach parents with Catholic teachings (C-1)
5. "Religious" activities to bring families and parishioners together (P-2)
6. Educate parents in the same values as those taught to their children (P-1)

B. Parenting
1. Parents need to be firm authority/guidance figures for their children (C-2, E-1, P-1)
2. Encourage parents to monitor children's TV and music for undesirable moral values (C-1)
3. Parents, not children, should make important choices (which school) (C-1)
4. Sponsor support groups to discuss family life issues (C-1, E-3, B-1)
5. Classes on modern family life issues: drugs, teen pregnancy, divorce (E-4)
6. Devise a school-based response to the needs of families of divorce (C-1)
7. Teen/parent workshops (E-1, P-1, B-1)
8. Educate parents to the importance of participating in their child's educational life (E-3)
9. Develop a family service directory (P-1)
10. Provide a video library for excellent parenting tapes (O-1)

C. Language barrier
1. ESL and literacy programs for parents (P-1, B-1)
2. Outreach to minority parents (O-1)

D. Support groups/services
   1. On educational matters, *how* to actively participate in child's learning: homework, studying at home (E-1, P-2)
   2. Parent "hotline"; parents who can help/support other parents (E-1)
   3. Diocesan programs for preschool parents to introduce them to the Catholic educational program (P-1)

E. Leadership
   1. Parents must teach children about "pay back" obligation for education received (E-1)
   2. Support and assist needs of immigrant and needy families (E-1)
   3. PTOs which extend outreach to community (E-1)
   4. PTOs which visibly support Catholic education (E-1)

IV. Communication
A. Pastor/faculty/parents
   1. Parents need to hear pastor vocally support the school (C-2, P-2, B-1, O-1)
   2. Parents need to feel support of entire parish/parishioners (C-1, O-1)
   3. Increase communication to parents re: real circumstances and needs of the school (P-1)
   4. School write a letter to parents assuring them of its commitment to the religious, moral, and academic education of their children (C-1, P-1)
   5. Keep parents informed as to the reasons for practicing faith at home, fund raising, etc. (P-2)

B. Parent/teacher/principal
   1. Parents support teachers when child is having difficulty (C-1, P-1)
   2. Monthly newsletter/calendar of events to increase communication between parents/school (E-5, P-4)
   3. Section in newsletter written by parents for parents (E-1, P-1)
   4. Formal and informal communication (E-3, P-3)
   5. Make clear guidelines for parental communication when things go wrong (E-1)
   6. Policy which requires principal/teacher response to parental inquiry within 24 hours (E-2)
   7. Give parents the sense that they *matter* in the life of the school (E-1)
   8. System of communication between school and parents (E-4)
   9. Mandate parent/teacher meetings when student is failing (E-1)
   10. Parent representatives from each class work as a group to foster communication with other parents (E-1)
   11. Exit interviews for those who graduate and those who leave (P-1, B-1)
   12. Parent/teacher rap sessions (P-1)
   13. Seek information from parents about what children talk about regarding happenings in school (P-1)

C. Newsletters/phone calls in native languages (E-1, O-1)

D. Communication with parish
   1. Newsletter/bulletin to keep parish informed of school activities, achievements, etc. (E-1, P-1, B-4)
   2. Promote parish athletics (P-1)
   3. Need to recruit families from CCD program into the school (P-1)
   4. Regard school and parish as "us," not "we" and "them" (P-1)

5. Connect parish with school through scholarships, adopt-a-family, prayer partners (P-1)
6. School/parish involvement
   a. "Invite a parishioner" luncheon for students (B-1)
   b. "Invite a parishioner to coffee" with principal and faculty (B-2)
   c. Parishioners become mentors (B-1)
   d. Parish-sponsored family activities (O-1)
   e. Students/parents speak to parish about school activities (O-1)
   f. Programs to involve parishioners in the school (B-1)
   g. Parish announce school activities (O-1)
   h. Catholic education as a form of parish involvement (O-1)
   i. School used by parish as a chance to reach out to larger community (O-1)
   j. Parishes emphasize development of family life as part of what Catholic school gives children (B-1)

V. Political Action

A. Rally parents around a cause: busing, vouchers (E-1, P-2)
B. Parents become more involved in political process (E-4)
C. PTO be watchdog over state services (E-1, B-1)
D. Everyone view Catholic/private education as a *civil right,* not a threat to public education, but a complement to it (O-1)
E. Establish regional parental units to lobby for vouchers (C-2, B-1)

VI. This Study

A. Keep parent task force intact as a group to model for other areas (E-1)
B. Keep parents informed as to what is happening with this study (E-1)
C. More publicity and parent involvement in this study (C-1)

Public Relations/Marketing Solutions

I. Personnel/Structures

A. Bishop/clergy
   1. Bishop, pastors, priests be more vocal and visible in their support of the schools (E-7, P-7, B-1)
   2. Pastor and priests constantly support the good work of the school from the pulpit (E-6, P-3)
   3. Bishop and clergy respond clearly, take a stand on public moral issues and government/state policies on education (C-2, P-1)
   4. Bishop tour the schools (E-1, P-1)

B. Public relations
   1. Hire professional help (C-4, E-9, P-7, B-1, O-1)
   2. Make use of *current* marketing skills (C-1)
   3. Learn from other schools what makes them attractive (C-1)
   4. Promote Catholic schools in toto, not single schools (C-2)
   5. Have a school registry with enrollment, vacancy, financial information (P-1)
   6. Each school should devise its own PR/marketing plan (C-2, E-4, P-2, O-1)
   7. Establish liaison with public schools to strengthen shared programs (C-1)
   8. Conduct campaign for elementary schools similar to the secondary school one (E-3)
   9. Use media spots throughout the year, not only during Catholic Schools Week (P-1)
   10. PR should be the *last* concern on the list of priorities (O-1)

C. Diocesan concerns
1. Publish appreciation for teachers and educators at diocesan level (C-3, E-3)
2. Create a uniquely Catholic award for outstanding counter-cultural activities (C-1)
3. Create a "Great Contributions Award" for Catholic parents or educators who contribute substantially to a school (C-1)
4. Survey successful PR programs in other dioceses (C-1)
5. Diocesan implementation of marketing strategies (E-1)
6. Establish diocesan speakers bureau (P-1)
7. Publish more about our schools (E-1)
8. Yearly *diocesan* workshop for administrators on PR (C-2, E-2, O-1)
9. Diocesan statewide parent group to exchange ideas and knowledge (P-1)
10. Stop closing schools: bad press (P-1)

D. Development
1. Marketing director as part of Catholic school office (C-1, E-9, P-3, B-1)
2. Establish diocesan office for development (C-3, E-8, P-2, B-1, O-3)
3. More unified approach to marketing (E-4, P-3, B-2, O-1)
4. *Diocesan* marketing strategy (C-2, E-8, P-7, B-1)
    a. Seek funds/expertise from businesses (E-5, P-5)
    b. Newsletter to corporations and individuals (E-2)
    c. Development office personnel visit schools (E-2)
    d. Development office personnel train local personnel (E-3, P-2, O-1)
    e. Grant writing (P-1)
    f. Make contacts with media (E-1)
    g. Make mailings to households (P-1)
5. Create diocesan recruiting (B-1)
6. Diocesan recruiters go to parishes without schools to recruit (E-1)
7. Put school consolidations in positive light, seen to improve quality, answer special needs, offer something unique (C-1)
8. PR officer named for each school board (C-1)
9. *Diocesan* competitive scholarships (C-1)
10. Provide PR training for parents and students (E-1)
11. Promote cooperation among schools, not competition (E-3, P-1)
12. Diocese make schools more competitive in athletics and extracurricular activities (E-1)

E. Finances
1. Establish a PR line item for each school budget (C-1, E-1, B-1)
2. Publish annual report for each school (C-1)
3. Coordinated efforts, to share costs in PR/marketing (E-3, P-2, O-1)
4. Devise less costly ways to market the schools (E-1)
5. Utilize resources not yet tapped (E-1)
6. Spending lots of money is unnecessary if we use informal, day-to-day PR/marketing opportunities (E-1)
7. Make clear the *costs* and the *financial help* available to parents (C-1, E-1)
8. Advertise that we have scholarships available (P-3)

II. **"Ambassadors"**
A. Students
1. Be ambassadors for the schools via appearance and conduct (C-1, E-1)
2. Be visible in their service to the parish and larger communities (C-3, E-7, P-9, O-1)

3. Take part in local and state competitions, contests, events (E-2, P-1, O-1)
4. Determine why our students choose Catholic schools and stress this (P-1)
5. Happy students make good PR (P-1)
6. Students in uniforms be present at Masses as ushers, etc. (B-1)

B. Teachers/principals
1. Professionalism in word, deed, appearance (C-1, P-1)
2. Project a positive image (E-1, P-1)
3. One teacher in each school be responsible for PR (E-1)
4. Principal is best PR person and therefore should embody what we stand for (O-1)

C. Parents
1. Speak at all Masses to endorse Catholic schools (C-3, E-1, P-2)
2. Speak at all Masses at parishes without schools to endorse the schools (C-2, P-1)
3. Use PR talents of parents (E-2, P-2)
4. Each school have parent group to provide information and personal contact (P-2)

D. Use senior citizens and grandparents to promote the schools (C-1, E-1, P-1, B-1)

E. Parishes
1. "Adopt Catholic school child" program (C-1)
2. Total parish community must support and advertise the school (C-1, P-4, O-1)
3. Encourage parishioners to lobby state legislature (C-1)
4. Seek out parishioners with PR expertise (C-1, E-1, O-1)
5. Catholic education Sunday in all parishes, with a collection (C-1, P-1)
6. List of Catholic school-educated parishioners to show numbers and quality (C-1)
7. Internal marketing of schools in parishes (E-2, P-1, B-1)
8. CYO be ambassadors to promote schools (E-1)
9. CYO coaches recruit in upper grades (E-1)

F. Schools
1. Open schools to the community
   a. Put on school awareness night in parishes (C-1)
   b. Showcase different schools each Saturday (P-1)
   c. Open houses, evenings as well (C-2, E-9, P-8, O-3)
   d. Invite people in to see the school in operation during the day (C-1)
2. Improve visibility of the school in the parish through school news in parish bulletins (C-2, E-7, P-6)
3. Stress that we have room in our schools for overcrowded communities (C-1)
4. Put "best foot forward": student conduct, building appearance, etc. (C-1)
5. School video to be shown to parishes (C-1, E-1)
6. Have successful secondary and post-secondary schools help elementary schools (E-1)
7. Invite public school children to spend a day at your school (E-1)
8. Write up "brag letters" and mail to parishioners (P-1)
9. Sponsor events which attract students (P-1)
10. PR person in each school (P-1)

G. Alumni
1. Highlight successful alumni (C-3, P-2, B-3, O-1)
2. Use any alumni expertise in PR (C-2, E-1, P-1)
3. Establish an active alumni list (C-1)

4. Build network of supportive alumni (E-3, P-2, B-1, O-1)
5. "Sell" influential Catholics on the schools (E-1)

III. Getting the Word Out
A. Message
  1. General
     a. Aggressively promote our achievements (C-1, E-2, P-1, O-1)
     b. Accent the positive, remove negative image of schools (C-1, E-3, P-5)
     c. Respond immediately to negative images of our schools (P-1)
     d. Educate the public more about our schools (E-1, P-1)
     e. Update image of Catholic schools (E-3, P-1, O-1)
     f. Better PR to sell *existing* programs (P-2)
  2. Specific
     a. Present schools as a preferred method for education, not a "second choice" (P-1)
     b. Promote schools as a *safe*, supportive environment where Catholic/Christian *moral* values are taught (C-4, E-6, P-12, B-2, O-1)
     c. Schools are not to be used as a *safe* haven (P-1)
     d. Stress caring teachers, nurturing family spirit (E-2, P-3)
     e. Promote survey results which show that Catholic education produces quality results (C-1, E-1, P-5)
     f. Offset notion that schools do not promote good social development (C-2)
     g. Publicize our efforts to update and modernize equipment (C-1, E-4, O-1)
     h. Advertise the unique aspects of each school (C-2, P-3)
     i. Emphasize per-pupil cost compared with public schools (C-1)
     j. Market our junior highs as alternatives to troubled public junior highs (E-1, P-1, B-1)
     k. Promote schools which meet specific needs (E-1)
     l. Stress discipline and quality over catholicity of schools (P-1)
     m. Publish statistics comparing our schools with public schools (P-1)
     n. Do not compare ourselves with public schools, but stress *our* strengths (P-2)
     o. Stress that we are not just for Catholics, but for all families interested in value-laden education (P-1, B-1)
     p. Best message is well-stated and well-lived mission statement (O-1)
     q. Stress the number one purpose of the schools is to teach the Catholic faith (P-1)

B. Means
  1. Use of available media
     a. TV, cable, radio spots year-long (C-3, E-10, P-11, B-2, O-3)
     b. Develop personal contact with media personnel (E-1, P-1)
     c. Local newspapers for activities, achievements, advertising (C-5, E-18, P-18, B-1, O-3)
     d. *Providence Visitor,* more prominence (E-3, P-1, O-1)
     e. Billboard advertising, esp. during Catholic Schools Week (C-1, E-4, P-1, O-1)
     f. Posters to distribute to local businesses (E-1)
     g. Well-designed videos to distribute to real estate offices, libraries, doctors' office (E-4, P-1)
  2. Bilingual advertising to reach non-English-speaking families (C-1)
  3. Well-designed, informative professional brochures for each school (C-2, E-3, P-4)
  4. "Word of mouth" campaign (C-1, E-5, P-3, B-1)
     a. By students (E-1, P-1, B-1)
     b. By teachers/principals (P-2, B-1)
     c. By parents (E-9, P-4, B-1, O-1)
  5. Create media event focusing on different schools' participation (C-1)
  6. Sell clothing with school/diocesan logos (E-1, P-1)

7. Direct mail campaigns to young families: Scituate, Foster, Gloucester (E-1)
8. Begin exchange program with public schools (P-1)

C. Accomplishments
   1. Promote survey results which show that Catholic education produces results (C-4, E-2)
   2. Publish accomplishments of graduates (E-3, P-3)
   3. Cite accomplishments of Catholic education in general (P-4)
   4. Cite good things about our current schools and students (P-1)
   5. Create logo of excellence (P-1)

D. Targets/recruitment
   1. Those areas of state with large numbers of families with young children (C-1)
   2. Direct advertising campaign to specific audiences (E-4, P-3, B-1)
     a. Nursery schools, day care (E-3, P-1, B-1)
     b. Include all races, creeds, ethnic groups (E-1, O-1)
     c. Non-Catholics (B-1)
   3. Keep tabs on changing demographics (E-1)
   4. Keep tabs on changing needs of families (E-1)
   5. Baptismal program, to establish contact with families of preschool children (E-4)
   6. School children "adopt-an-infant" (P-1)
   7. Mailings to families with school-age children to promote/explain the school (E-1)
   8. Develop feeder system: elementary school to middle school to high school (P-1)
   9. Need to actively recruit (P-1)
  10. Survey parents who switched from public school to Catholic school (P-1)
  11. Strong incentives to draw and keep families (P-1)

Purpose

The purpose of the task force is to develop detailed recommendations for addressing the major issues in its area of responsibility as initially defined by the participants at the problem element meeting on (specify date).

To accomplish this primary purpose, the task force should perform the following tasks:

1. After studying the information from the problem element meeting, define the major issues the task force will address in its work.

2. Study a variety of sources for possible solutions for each major issue, including:
   a. Proposed solution elements from the solution element meeting of (specify date)
   b. Current practices in the diocese and in other dioceses
   c. Innovative strategies being tested anywhere in the United States or other countries (including other religious denominations)
   d. Current state-of-the-art thinking about the issues in scholarly or popular literature

3. Develop possible solutions for each major issue and assess
   a. Strengths and weaknesses of each solution
   b. Feasibility for implementation in the diocese
   c. Costs and benefits associated with implementing the proposed solution compared with maintaining the status quo

4. Develop recommendations for each major issue, documenting the above steps and rationale for the recommendations.

5. Select several members of the task force to present recommendations and participate with the diocesan planning committee in deciding which to propose to the bishop for his consideration and approval.

End Product

The task force will prepare a written document that should include the following elements for each major issue:

1. Definition of the issue and brief presentation of its context

2. Listing of possible solutions that were considered

3. The major advantages and disadvantages of each solution

4. The solution that is recommended and the rationale for recommending it

5. Projected anticipated impact of the recommendation, including benefits, costs, potential problems, and strategies for dealing with problems

6. Suggestions for the implementation of the solution, describing proposed steps for phasing in the recommended solution

Progress Reports

The task force will present a preliminary report to the diocesan planning committee in (specify month) (tentative dates are_____) and a final report in (specify month) . In addition, prior to each diocesan planning committee meeting at which there is no scheduled task force presentation, the chairperson of the task force or the liaison to the task force from the diocesan planning committee will communicate the progress of the task force to the chairperson of the diocesan planning committee or to the study director.

Chairperson

The chairperson of the task force
1. Presides over the meetings of the task force
2. Appoints subcommittees and their chairpersons
3. Ensures that someone acts as recording secretary and keeps accurate records
4. Maintains communication with the diocesan planning committee
5. Oversees the preparation of the final report

Some Suggestions

As soon as possible after its formation, the task force should develop an operational plan that addresses
1. Specific major issues to be addressed
2. Identification of key tasks
3. Timeline for accomplishing key tasks
4. Meeting schedule for the task force
5. Identification of appropriate subcommittees
6. Identification of resources and support services that may be needed

Confidentiality

The task force members will maintain appropriate confidentiality with regard to the discussions and recommendations of the task force, as well as any sensitive materials they review. Materials used and recommendations being considered need to be kept confidential to preserve the integrity of the work and prevent distortion or unnecessary polarization within the diocese.

Directions: Each family should complete one questionnaire. Your responses will assist the parish planning committee in developing recommendations concerning Catholic schools in this area of the diocese.

Part I: Attitudes and Opinions

Using the following scale, circle the code corresponding to how you feel about each statement:

SA=Strongly Agree   A=Agree   U=Uncertain   D=Disagree   SD=Strongly Disagree

1. Catholic schools are an essential part of the Church's educational mission.   SA   A   U   D   SD

2. Catholic schools are needed more today than twenty-five years ago.   SA   A   U   D   SD

3. Salaries of teachers in Catholic schools should be increased substantially.   SA   A   U   D   SD

4. I would contribute to a special fund to provide more support for Catholic schools.   SA   A   U   D   SD

5. The religious education program (CCD) of the parish is functioning well.   SA   A   U   D   SD

6. There are too many Catholic schools in this area of the diocese.   SA   A   U   D   SD

7. An additional elementary school is needed in this area of the diocese.   SA   A   U   D   SD

8. A new Catholic high school is needed in this area of the diocese.   SA   A   U   D   SD

9. Catholic schools can provide an effective Catholic education with all lay teachers.   SA   A   U   D   SD

10. The Catholic schools in this area of the diocese have a good reputation.   SA   A   U   D   SD

11. I would increase my weekly parish contribution to show support for Catholic schools.   SA   A   U   D   SD

12. The diocese should establish an endowment fund for Catholic schools.   SA   A   U   D   SD

13. The public views Catholic schools as being among the best schools in the area.   SA   A   U   D   SD

14. The tuitions charged by the Catholic schools in the area are affordable.   SA   A   U   D   SD

15. I am familiar with the reputation and program of the nearest Catholic school.   SA   A   U   D   SD

16. Our parish should (circle one letter)
    a. Sponsor (or continue to sponsor) its own Catholic school
    b. Join with neighboring parishes to sponsor an interparish or regional school
    c. Not sponsor a school, but financially assist parents who send their children to a Catholic school
    d. Not financially assist parents who send their children to a Catholic school

17. Which of the following is most important to you if you were considering sending your child to a Catholic school? (circle one letter)
    a. Academic program of the school
    b. Religious atmosphere and value orientation of the school
    c. Both of these are equally important

18. What do you consider the major reason people choose not to send their children to a Catholic school? (circle one letter)
    a. Inability to afford the tuition
    b. Dissatisfaction with a Catholic school's academic program
    c. Dissatisfaction with a Catholic school's religious education program
    d. Desire to have their children educated in the public schools
    e. Other (Specify)_____

Part II: Demographic Information

19. How many years have you lived in the parish?_____

20. How many children under age 18 do you have?_____

21. Do you currently have a child in a Catholic school? _____Yes _____No

22. Do you anticipate sending a child to a Catholic school in the next few years? _____Yes _____No

23. Did any of your children ever attend a Catholic school? _____Yes _____No

24. Check the Catholic schools you have attended: _____None   _____Elementary
                                                   _____Secondary   _____College/University

25. Check your race/ethnicity:
    _____American Indian/Alaskan Native   _____Asian/Pacific Islander
    _____Black, non-Hispanic   _____Hispanic   _____White, non-Hispanic

26. Check your annual family income:
    _____Under $10,000   _____$10,000-$20,000   _____$20,001-$30,000
    _____$30,001-$40,000   _____$40,001-$60,000   _____$60,001-$80,000
    _____$80,001-$100,000   _____Over $100,000

Comments:

Catholic Identity Proposals

Catholic schools provide a choice for parents seeking both academic and spiritual growth for their children in an atmosphere that emphasizes religious formation and values. "The special character of the Catholic school and the underlying reason for its existence is precisely the quality of the religious instruction integrated into the overall education of the students" (*Catechesis in our Time*, no. 69).

Catholic schools are faith communities, in addition to being academic communities. The establishment of the faith community within the school assists the parish community in its endeavor to provide for the spiritual and moral development of its young parishioners. The faith community also is a vital force for preparing future church and civic leaders. Although the Catholic school is primarily established for the education of Catholic students, non-Catholic students are welcomed. Thus, the school has an important evangelization mission.

"The very reason for the existence of Catholic schools, why they were established in this nation and in particular in this diocese was to maintain and foster the growth of the Catholic faith. This reason still exists today, for all responses to the various surveys, both school parent input and general parishioner input, cry out for strong leadership in the faith with clear and unwavering teaching of our Roman Catholic beliefs, in doctrine and in living out of the doctrine in our school community" (*Diocese of Providence Catholic Identity Task Force*).

1. Each school shall develop and publish a mission statement, which shall include a statement of its Catholic identity. The mission statement shall be modeled on the diocesan mission statement that will be developed by the diocesan board of education (confer proposal 11).

2. Each school shall be thoroughly Catholic in identity and in teaching. To this end, both Catholic and non-Catholic students shall participate in religious instruction that clearly presents the doctrinal and moral teachings of the Catholic Church.[1]

3. In order to help develop a strong faith community, each school shall provide students with an opportunity to participate in their own religious formation by periodically scheduling eucharistic liturgies and other religious functions as part of the school program.

4. The physical environment of each school shall contain identifiable religious symbols, such as crucifixes and religious art.

5. Each school shall develop a program of apostolic service to the parish and the community. In the case of a parish school, activities shall emphasize the close connection between the mission of the parish and the mission of the school.

6. The importance of the relationship between Catholic schools and their sponsoring parishes, as well as the schools' contribution to parish life, shall be recognized and cultivated by all parishes and schools.

7. The pastor of a parish with a school is responsible for supervising the school's religion curriculum, which shall emphasize the necessity of regular and active participation in the eucharist and

---

1. "Not all students in Catholic schools are members of the Catholic Church; not all are Christians. . . . The religious freedom and the personal conscience of individual students and their families must be respected, and this freedom is explicitly recognized by the Church. On the other hand, a Catholic school cannot relinquish its own freedom to proclaim the Gospel and to offer a formation based on the values to be found in Christian education; this is its right and its duty. To proclaim or to offer is not to impose, however; the latter suggests a moral violence which is strictly forbidden, both by the Gospel and by church law" (*The Religious Dimension of Education in a Catholic School*, 6).

the sacrament of reconciliation by Catholic students, as well as the importance of religious services for all students.

8. The priests of the parishes that sponsor schools shall take an active part in the life of the schools by visiting them frequently and by participating in their religious formation and liturgical programs.

9. The pastor of a parish with a school shall foster the mutual cooperation of the school's religious education program and the parish's religious education program. Whenever possible, facilities, activities, curriculum, and teachers shall be shared.

Governance Proposals

Diocesan Leadership

The Diocese of Providence requires strong leadership for Catholic schools to ensure their future viability. This leadership must provide direction in the areas of policy making, governance, financing, development, public relations, strategic planning, and periodic evaluation.

10. The bishop shall establish a diocesan board of education, which shall be consultative[2] to the bishop, the vicar for education, and the superintendent of schools in the areas of educational policy for the Diocese of Providence, strategic planning, structural organization and governance (including the opening and closing of schools), financing and development, marketing and public relations, and evaluation of educational programs. The board shall include nine to sixteen members, who shall be selected on the basis of their expertise and interest in Catholic education.

11. The diocesan board of education shall develop a diocesan mission statement for Catholic schools, which shall form the basis of the mission statement that each school is requested to develop (confer proposal 1).

Interparish/Regional Schools[3]

12. For each school (regional or interparish) formally associated with more than one parish, the relationship among the cooperating parishes and the school will be determined by a formal agree-

---

2. A consultative board acts in an advisory capacity and does not establish policy. A consultative board, however, differs from an advisory board in that the decision maker must consult a consultative board in the areas of the board's jurisdiction prior to establishing and enacting policy, whereas the decision maker is not required to consult an advisory board. For example, the parish finance council is consultative in that the pastor must confer with it in matters dealing with parish finances. The parish pastoral council is an advisory group, which, if a parish has one, provides advice to the pastor concerning parish issues, but with which the pastor is not required to consult before acting.

3. The Diocese of Providence has five types of schools: parish, interparish, regional, diocesan, and private.

    A **parish school** is operated and financially supported by one parish. The pastor and the principal of the school co-administer the school. A consultative parish school board provides advice to the pastor and principal concerning the finances and policies of the school.

    An **interparish school** is jointly operated and financially supported by more than one parish. The school is co-administered by a designated pastor, who normally is the pastor of the parish that hosts the school, and the principal. A consultative interparish school board, which has representation from the sponsoring parishes, provides advice to the designated pastor and principal of the school concerning the policies of the school and to the pastors of all the cooperating parishes concerning the finances of the school.

    A **regional school** is jointly sponsored by designated parishes within a specified region of the diocese. A regional school may be located at a single site or at multiple sites. A board of limited jurisdiction, which has representation from the sponsoring parishes, formulates and enacts the policies of the school, including the approval of the school's budget. The school's administrator, who is the principal in the case of a single-site regional school, is accountable to the board and responsible for overseeing the implementation of school policies.

    A **diocesan school** is owned by the diocese and is part of a diocesan corporation. Each diocesan school is educationally administered and managed by the principal, who is responsible to a school board of limited jurisdiction and the diocesan corporation.

    A **private school** is owned and operated by a religious congregation or incorporated under a board of trustees. In order to call itself Catholic, a private school receives formal approval from the bishop and commits itself to follow the diocesan policies concerning Catholic schools that are contained in the diocesan policy manual. The principal is responsible to the congregation's administrators and/or to the board of trustees.

---

ment or a series of agreements. Parties to this agreement shall be each of the parishes involved and, for regional schools, the school board. The vicar for education or his delegate, the superintendent of schools, in the name of the bishop, shall be responsible for certifying the agreement. The agreement will include at least the following provisions:

    a. A mission statement, including a statement of its Catholic identity, that unites the efforts of the parishes to promote the goals of Catholic education by collectively sponsoring a school

    b. A policy governing student admissions to the school, including who receives priority admission when a school is at or near capacity

    c. A policy on tuition assistance eligibility

    d. The financial responsibility each parish has for the school, as well as the financial responsibility the school has for the parishes

    e. Processes for making major decisions concerning the school

    f. Processes for allocating capital improvement costs among the parishes

    g. The non-school use of the buildings and the pro-ration of associated costs

    h. The rental of parish buildings for the use by the school

    i. Representation of each parish on the interparish/regional school board

    j. The coordination of fund-raising responsibilities

    k. The coordination of religious education activities including sacramental preparation

    l. A mechanism for resolving disputes

Local Governance

13. Within one year after promulgation of these recommendations, each elementary school shall have a school board.

    a. The parish school shall have a consultative board that advises the pastor and the principal.

    b. The interparish school shall have a consultative board that advises the designated pastor and the principal of the school.

    c. The regional school board shall govern within the model of limited jurisdiction. The specific powers of the board shall be defined in the formal agreement among the sponsoring parishes, with the approval of the vicar for education or his delegate, the superintendent of schools.

    d. Pastors and principals shall ensure that local boards include representatives of those committed to the mission of the school, especially parents, but also alumni(ae), parishioners, and individuals in the community.

    e. The boards shall adopt constitutions and by-laws that clearly indicate the authority and responsibility of the members.

    f. The boards shall have appropriate (consultative or limited jurisdiction) responsibilities in at least the following areas:

        i. School policies, within the framework of diocesan policies

        ii. Preparation of the school budget

        iii. Short-range and long-range goals for the school

        iv. Financial development, public relations, and fund raising

    g. Board members shall be willing to attend and participate in workshops that deal with the role of boards in Catholic education.

14. The Catholic school office shall develop clear guidelines for boards, noting in particular purpose, membership, term of office, areas of responsibility, and committee structure.

15. The Catholic school office shall offer to local school communities in-service programs for the establishment of boards and for the evaluation of existing boards. The in-service programs shall include discussion of various governance models, which ensure that authority and responsibility are invested in those committed to the school's mission.

Diocesan Commitment

The priority accorded Catholic schools in the Diocese of Providence goes beyond fiscal support and extends to the appointment of parish leaders, who are essential to the success of Catholic schools. The bishop also provides witness to this priority by assigning the responsibility for assisting parishes with their schools to the vicar for education and the superintendent of schools and by charging the Catholic school office to take a proactive stance in helping to secure the future vitality of each Catholic school.

16. Because Catholic schools are essential to the educational mission of the Church and thus require generous support from the entire Catholic community, each parish must either have its own school or participate pastorally with at least one Catholic school and financially contribute to the support of Catholic schools according to diocesan guidelines (confer proposals concerning parish funds).

17. In making personnel decisions, the bishop and the personnel board, in consultation with the superintendent of schools, shall consider the sentiments of priests toward Catholic schools and their willingness to support the schools enthusiastically. In particular, pastors assigned to parishes with schools or to parishes that sponsor an interparish or regional Catholic school should demonstrate a strong commitment to Catholic schools.

18. The Catholic school office shall assist in providing information and strategies to promote Catholic schools to priests, deacons, seminarians, and other diocesan personnel. The Catholic school office shall particularly assist pastors of parishes with schools to deal with the complex responsibilities and challenges that having a school entails.

19. A pastor who is newly assigned to a parish that has responsibility for a Catholic school of a type (parish school, interparish school, or regional school) that the pastor has not previously experienced shall participate in an orientation program conducted by the Catholic school office. The orientation program shall include information concerning the financing and governance of Catholic schools, as well as the nature and function of school boards.

Proposals Concerning School Programs and Planning

The schools of the Diocese of Providence will maintain a curriculum that fosters high, yet attainable, standards for their students. The development of a challenging curriculum in all academic areas and careful strategic planning are keys to the future of Catholic schools. The curriculum must recognize the spiritual, intellectual, moral, emotional, and physical needs of each student. The quality of the academic offerings in the areas of language arts, mathematics, social studies, science, and the fine arts shall be continuously maintained. Strategic planning will ensure the maintenance of a school's academic and fiscal well being, which are essential to its viability.

20. Each school shall develop and maintain a current five-year strategic plan that covers the areas of curriculum, maintenance, upgrade of facilities, recruitment, public relations, and development, with the view of assuring the future viability of the school.

21. Each school shall develop with its sponsoring parishes and maintain a five-year plan regarding capital costs. The parishes and schools shall review their plans annually.

22. Each school shall implement strategies designed to foster the following conditions associated with effective Catholic schools:
    a. A principal who is a person of vision and a strong instructional and spiritual leader
    b. Clear instructional standards for monitoring and assessing performance
    c. High expectations for all students
    d. An orderly and supportive environment that is conducive to learning
    e. A strong community among administrators, teachers, students and parents

23. The parishes and schools in contiguous geographic areas of the diocese shall work more closely with each other regarding long-range planning and sharing of resources. The leadership of parishes and schools shall have regular meetings with each other to achieve these ends.

24. The Catholic school office, in conjunction with local school boards, shall monitor the religious, academic, demographic, and financial viability of each school through the following means:
    a. The successful completion of a diocesan-approved accreditation process and the annual review by the Office
    b. Participation in assessment programs, such as CTBS, McGraw-Hill, and ACRE
    c. An enrollment that ensures the financial stability of the school
    d. Demographic data that indicate the school-age population shall remain at a level sufficient to justify the future continuation of the school

25. Normally, a school shall satisfy at least the following criteria to ensure its viability:
    a. A K-8 enrollment of at least 198 (22 per class on average)
    b. A per-student cost within $500 of the diocesan median,[4] unless the higher costs result from a deliberate decision by the school to limit enrollment
    c. At least 70 percent of its operating budget generated from sources other than the parish and/or the diocese
    d. Less than 40 percent of a parish's gross income required to support the school
    e. Enrollment declines no greater than 20 percent annually or 50 percent over a five-year period

26. For a school that fails to meet one or more of the criteria in the above proposal, the superintendent of schools shall appoint an intervention team that shall meet with the pastor or pastors, principal, and school board to discuss the development of a plan to improve the school's academic, financial, and enrollment status. In the absence of special circumstances, such as a school that is traditionally small, and after a reasonable period of such assistance, two years in most cases, should a school continue to fail to meet one or more of the established criteria, the superintendent of schools, in conjunction with the pastor in the case of a parish school, the designated pastor in the case of an interparish school, and the school board in the case of a regional or diocesan school, and in consultation with the principal of the school, its parents, and the parishioners of the parishes involved, shall make a recommendation to the bishop concerning the future of the school.

    Low or sharply declining enrollment is not always a sufficient reason to consider a school in need of intervention. Some schools in the diocese traditionally have been small and some may have purposely reduced their enrollment to achieve certain educational objectives. On the other hand, low enrollment often brings financial instability, and sharply declining enrollment is often symptomatic of academic or leadership problems, rapid changes in the demographic composition of an area, or increases in tuition beyond the ability or willingness of most families to pay.

27. No school shall close or significantly modify its grade structure by adding or deleting grades without prior consultation with the diocesan board of education and the Catholic school office and without the permission of the bishop.

28. The local school communities, with the assistance of the Catholic school office, shall develop diocesan minimum standards in the areas of student outcomes, curriculum, technology, resource materials, library, specialized personnel (art teacher, music teacher, reading specialist, counselor, and so forth) and extracurricular activities.

29. The curriculum of each school shall promote multicultural understanding and appreciation and foster awareness of the contributions of diverse populations.

---

4. The median cost per student for elementary schools currently is approximately $1,770.

Proposals Concerning Administrators and Teachers

The Diocese of Providence has historically been blessed with dedicated and high-quality religious and lay administrators and teachers. The planning committee's surveys of administrators and teachers revealed a high level of commitment to the mission and goals of Catholic schools. In addition to exercising their professional role as educators, individuals work in Catholic schools to serve the Church, to share their faith and their values, and to fulfill their special ministry. At the same time, it is increasingly difficult for some to continue to work in Catholic schools because of financial concerns. Clearly, the quality of the academic and religious education programs depends upon the quality of the administrators and teachers that the schools are able to attract and retain. Because of the special nature of Catholic schools, administrators bring an extra dimension to their leadership role, which is to lead their faculty in understanding what it means to be a Catholic school and how the philosophy of a Catholic school informs the entire school program.

30. To ensure the selection of quality professionals, the Catholic school office shall continue to be progressive by monitoring and improving, if necessary, the screening process for principals and teachers.

31. All administrators and teachers in a Catholic school shall understand and accept the school's philosophy, policies, mission statement, and statement of Catholic identity and participate actively in their implementation.

32. All administrators and teachers in Catholic schools shall participate in programs of spiritual formation and professional development, especially those sponsored by the Catholic school office.

33. Religion teachers in Catholic schools shall be practicing Catholics, who are qualified to fulfill that role and who have completed or are in the process of completing diocesan religion teacher certification.

34. In seeking to attract and retain qualified administrators and teachers for Catholic elementary schools, the Catholic school office, individual pastors, and schools shall continue to give attention and action to three areas: (a) financial factors (salaries and benefits); (b) recognition factors (acknowledging excellence and length of service); and (c) training factors (continued efforts to upgrade the skills of teachers).
    a. Compensation for administrators and teachers must be thoroughly examined in the light of their professional responsibilities, preparation, experience, and service to the Church, as well as the principles of Catholic social justice. An ad hoc committee appointed by the superintendent of schools shall develop salary scales for administrators and teachers that account for years of service, academic preparation, continuing education, and certification status. No school shall pay less than the established salary scale.
    b. The Catholic school office, individual schools, and parishes shall find ways to recognize publicly the professional excellence, length of service, and commitment to the Church of administrators and teachers.
    c. The Catholic school office shall continue to provide programs for the in-service training of administrators and teachers in Catholic schools. The goal of this training shall be to have the curriculum reflect the best of current knowledge in the field and to prepare teachers to utilize sound teaching strategies and principles based upon current educational research.

Proposals Concerning Parents and Their Involvement

Parents as the primary educators of their children must be actively involved in their education. The principal involvement of parents is in the home, where they have the opportunity and responsibility to reinforce what the children learn in school. However, it is also critical that parents become more involved in the life of the school itself. Research shows that the active participation of adults, both teachers and parents, in the school community is a major reason for the effectiveness of a Catholic school.

35. In recognition of parents' role as the primary educators of their children and their individual talents and gifts, each school shall establish a structure to increase the involvement of parents in the school.

36. Each school shall have a parent organization, such as a home and school association, which will (1) serve as a forum for communication between parents and the school, (2) promote service activities in the school, and (3) keep abreast of the political issues affecting the schools.
    a. Each parent organization shall have a constitution and by-laws, which are in accordance with diocesan guidelines, that describe its mission and clearly differentiate it from the school's consultative board or board of limited jurisdiction.
    b. Each school shall provide space to the parent organization to facilitate its meetings and support its activities.

37. The Catholic school office shall encourage and promote parental participation in the educational process by providing information and support to parents, parent organizations, and educators throughout the diocese.

38. The Catholic school office shall coordinate the formation of parent groups that will join state and national networks of parent groups, particularly the newly established Office for Catholic School Parent Associations at the United States Catholic Conference, to lobby federal and state legislatures for the purpose of securing tax-supported financial assistance for the education of their children.

39. As close as possible to the opening day of school, each school shall provide parents with an orientation to the school and its "culture." This is especially appropriate for parents new to the school, as a means of welcoming them. During this orientation the principal and school staff shall
    a. Help parents understand the school's mission and philosophy by describing the programs and activities that demonstrate its religious and academic priorities
    b. Present their expectations of the students and parents
    c. Give parents an opportunity to express their concerns and expectations

40. As a service to families and the local community, each school shall determine the need and the feasibility of offering or sponsoring apart from the normal school program the following programs and services:
    a. Pre-K and extended-day services, which include before- and after-school programs
    b. Parental religious education programs offered in conjunction with the sponsoring parish or parishes, which are designed to help parents reinforce the religious instruction provided by the school
    c. Additional educational programs for children, which may include tutoring, remedial programs, and enrichment programs
    d. Extracurricular activities and clubs, which may include sports programs, dance lessons, music lessons, art, journalism, and drama

Finance Proposals

Tuition

Tuition is the primary source of revenue for Catholic schools; however, tuition does not cover the entire cost of educating a child. The rest of the cost is covered by fund raising, investment income, and parish subsidy. Parishes have the responsibility to help families that contribute to the support of the parish by offering them parishioner tuition rates and/or by offsetting part of their tuition payments through tuition assistance.

41. The budgeted cost per student shall be calculated as follows:
    a. Estimate the anticipated total operating cost
    b. Add a premium for capital expenditures, emergencies, and family tuition plans (confer proposal 44) to obtain an adjusted operating cost
    c. Divide the adjusted operating cost by a low estimate of the anticipated number of students

42. Parish elementary schools shall have two tuition rates:
    a. A preferred rate equal to the budgeted cost per student at the school less the anticipated average revenue per student from fund raising, parish subsidy, and other sources of income. Families that are formally registered in, contributing to, and attending church in the parish are eligible for consideration to receive the preferred tuition at the school.
    b. A standard rate equal to the budgeted cost per student at the school less the anticipated average revenue per student from fund raising and other sources of income, but excluding parish subsidy. Families that do not regularly contribute to the support of the parish shall pay the standard tuition.

43. The tuition at a parish school shall normally equal at least 70 percent of the cost per student.

44. As a sign of its support for families, a parish school may have a family tuition plan, which provides tuition discounts for a second child and additional children from the same family that attend the school. The family tuition plan shall apply to families who qualify for the preferred tuition rate. The family tuition plan may be extended to those who pay the standard rate. A family tuition plan is a form of tuition assistance to families.

45. Catholic families who regularly contribute, as determined by the pastor, to a parish without a school shall qualify for the preferred tuition rate at a parish school, provided that the home parish pays the difference between the preferred tuition rate and the standard rate at the school.

    Possible Methodologies:
    a. *A family receives from its home parish a certificate that states the parish's willingness to pay the difference between the preferred and standard tuitions; the school then bills the parish.*
    b. *A parish collects the entire tuition and sends it to the school.*

46. The formal agreement among the participating parishes shall specify how regional and interparish elementary schools determine their tuition and the kind of family tuition plan that may be offered (confer proposal 12).

47. Schools that now have tuition rates different than those proposed shall gradually adjust them over the next three years.

Diocesan Funds

The Diocese of Providence shares with parishes the responsibility for the financial support of Catholic schools. The diocese exercises that responsibility by making Catholic schools a financial priority, through organizing diocesan development efforts to raise funds for tuition assistance and by providing diocesan funds for the support of a limited number of schools.

48. The Diocese of Providence shall assume a co-responsibility with the parishes to provide funds for the support of Catholic schools. To this end, the bishop shall seek to increase substantially the funds for the Frances Warde Fund.
    a. The diocese shall increase the public's awareness of the Frances Warde Fund and seek substantial contributions to it from individual major donors and corporations.
    b. Contributions to the Frances Warde Fund from major donors and corporations shall be held in the principal of the fund, and only interest shall be disbursed annually.
    c. The Frances Warde Fund shall provide grants for tuition payments for Catholic elementary schools to families who need additional tuition assistance beyond what is available from their parishes.
    d. Once the principal from the Frances Warde Fund reaches $20 million, the fund shall provide grants for tuition payments for Catholic secondary schools to families who need additional tuition assistance beyond what is available from the school.

49. The diocese shall continue an annual allocation of at least $550,000 from the Catholic Charity Appeal to provide tuition assistance funds to high schools and, as a sign of its commitment to the poor, a subsidy to a limited number of elementary schools, designated as "special mission schools," that serve families of limited means and whose parishes are unable to provide sufficient financial support. The following criteria will be considered in designating schools as special mission schools that are eligible to receive a diocesan subsidy and/or financial support from parishes throughout the diocese (also confer proposal 57):
    a. At least 50 percent of the students are eligible for free or reduced milk.
    b. At least 25 percent of the students come from single-parent households.
    c. The school is affiliated with a parish whose annual income is less than $200,000.
    d. The school is located in a neighborhood in which at least 25 percent of the population does not speak English well or at all.
    e. The school is located in a neighborhood in which at least 25 percent of the adult population does not have a high school diploma.

Parish Funds

The Church has repeatedly called attention to the preeminence of its teaching mission and the importance of Catholic schools in carrying out this mission. Because of the importance of Catholic schools to the future of the diocese, the financial support of schools must be a normal responsibility for all parishes. The support of a Catholic school presents a parish with a financial challenge, however, and requires it to set priorities for the allocation of its resources. Because of local circumstances, the responsibility to support Catholic schools will be met in different ways and to different degrees by each parish. Those parishes that have schools are asked to provide direct financial support for the operation of their schools. All parishes are asked to continue to provide tuition assistance to families in financial need and to help capitalize a diocesan tuition assistance effort. In deciding whether a family qualifies for financial assistance, it is expected that pastors, tuition assistance committees, or school boards will require a 1040 Form or some other documentation of the family's financial need.

50. A parish with a parish school shall provide a subsidy to the school equal to at least 10 percent of the school's operating costs.

51. In addition to a subsidy, a parish with a parish school shall budget funds for tuition assistance for families in financial need.

52. The total of a parish's subsidy to a school and its tuition assistance to families shall not exceed 40 percent of the parish's gross income, without the permission of the bishop.

53. A parish without a parish school shall pay the difference between the preferred tuition rate and the standard tuition rate at a parish school for each child who attends that school as long as the child's family regularly contributes to the financial support of the parish, as determined by the pastor.

54. The Catholic Elementary Education Assessment Program should be continued indefinitely. Each parish that does not have a parish school, including all parishes associated with a regional school, will continue to contribute annually a minimum of 7 percent of its income, calculated on the same basis as the diocesan assessment, for the tuition assistance of families in financial need who send their children to Catholic elementary schools.

55. Until a diocesan development effort generates sufficient revenues for a substantial Catholic school endowment, each parish with a parish school that does not distribute at least 10 percent of its income annually in subsidy to schools or tuition assistance to individual students, and each parish without a parish school that does not distribute at least 7 percent of its income annually in tuition assistance to students in financial need, shall contribute the difference to the Frances Warde Fund. When the school endowment is realized, the need for parish contributions to the Frances Warde Fund shall be re-evaluated.

56. Since the Frances Warde Fund is limited to elementary school students, parishes are encouraged to provide tuition assistance to high school students, even though such assistance would not be included in the 7 percent assessment.

57. All parishes, particularly those without a financial obligation to a specific school, are encouraged to help financially support one of the "special mission schools" in the diocese.

Marketing and Development

The diocese, individual parishes, and schools must give the highest priority to the establishment and maintenance of a well-organized, professional marketing and development program for Catholic schools. Development is not simply fund raising, but a strategy to secure commitment to Catholic schools and, thus, to ensure the schools' financial well-being. The diocesan effort in marketing and development must have dynamic leadership and should come under the auspices of the diocesan board of education.

58. The bishop shall establish a diocesan development program for Catholic schools, which could be a part of the diocesan development office. The development effort for the support of Catholic schools must be adequately staffed by experienced development professionals whose responsibilities shall include:
    a. Formulating and implementing a multifaceted action plan to target external sources of revenue for the support of Catholic schools, particularly for schools that serve low-income students
    b. Assisting parishes and individual Catholic schools in their efforts to establish their own development programs

59. The bishop shall establish a diversified endowment and scholarship portfolio, which shall contain separate endowment and scholarship funds. The aggregated goal of the portfolio shall be at least $30 million.
    a. The major part of the diversified portfolio, at least $20 million, shall be the Frances Warde Fund as an endowment that provides tuition assistance for elementary and secondary school students.

b. Restricted funds may be established for students from specific populations, such as the children of Catholic school teachers and administrators and those of parish employees, children from inner-city schools, high school students, and other groups.

c. The portfolio shall contain funds to support capital needs and special school projects.

60. The diocesan development program for Catholic schools shall be responsible for (a) soliciting major gifts from principal benefactors, (b) preparing the prospectus or the "case statement" for major gifts, (c) planning and supervising major campaigns to provide funds for the Frances Warde Fund and other endowment funds, (d) assisting schools to initiate development programs, and (e) coordinating with schools that have development directors. In addition, the program will promote estate planning and deferred giving for current and potential donors to schools. In particular, donors will be encouraged to designate a school as a beneficiary in their will or life insurance policy.

61. Each parish, in conjunction with its own parish school or the regional school with which it is associated, shall establish an endowment fund for the support of the school. This must be done in coordination with the diocesan development program for Catholic schools. Revenues raised shall be centrally invested in order to gain a more favorable interest rate; however, each parish shall retain ownership of the corpus of the endowment fund and completely control access to the interest from it. Disbursements from the endowment fund could be used to help families in financial need with tuition grants to Catholic schools and to pay for special school projects and programs. Some examples of sources of income for the endowment fund are

a. Offerings by parents from the parish whose children attend a Catholic school and who are financially able to contribute more to the cost of educating their children

b. Donations by parishioners in special collections taken by the parish or in response to a solicitation by the pastor, the school principal, or a member of the school board

c. Special gifts and bequests that are given to the parish for the school

d. Proceeds from an annual appeal that is targeted to specific constituencies, such as parishioners who are graduates of the school, other alumni of the school, grandparents of children in the school, other relatives of the children, and the like

Budgets

Planning and budgeting for the future requires reliable and accurate accounting information. School budgets must be consistent in their treatment of revenue sources and expenses and in their allocation of costs between parish and school.

62. To assist in establishing a program of sound financial management, current standardized accounting definitions and methodologies need to be re-evaluated and improved by the Catholic school office in consultation with diocesan officials and implemented by all parishes and schools.

63. Each school shall prepare a detailed expense and income budget for proper financial planning. All school budgets and financial reports shall be formulated according to the diocesan accounting system and will account for all funds used in the operation of the school.

64. Budgets and financial reports shall clearly show the use of parish, interparish, and diocesan funds for their approved purposes.

65. The cost of the use of the school building by parish groups and community groups shall be allocated (cost accounted) to the parish and not charged to the school's operating expenses. The cost of the school and the cost of the parish shall be accounted for separately.

Public Relations Proposals

A good public relations program provides to families with school-age children information about the benefits of a Catholic school education and about the programs in individual schools. The people of the diocese need to be informed of the merits of Catholic schools and see tangible evidence that the Church in Rhode Island does indeed value Catholic schools. Catholic schools must be kept in the public eye as much as possible. The public relations program, as in the case of development, must be taken beyond the Catholic community to the general public. The public needs to be informed about the value of Catholic schools in helping to educate the citizens of Rhode Island, how Catholic schools complement the public schools in the community, and how Catholic schools provide a savings to the taxpayers of the community.

66. Catholic schools shall be a diocesan public relations priority. As a sign of this priority, the bishop shall establish in the Catholic school office a public relations program with a professional staff that shall coordinate the diocesan promotion of Catholic schools and assist individual schools in their public relations efforts.

67. The public relations program, in conjunction with the diocesan board of education, shall develop an overall marketing and promotional plan for Catholic schools. The plan should emphasize the religious nature, academic quality, value-centered curriculum, discipline, and supportive community of the schools.

68. The Catholic school office shall advertise for a public relations firm to provide consulting and other services on a pro-bono basis, with a small out-of-pocket expense on the part of the diocese.

69. The diocesan public relations effort on behalf of Catholic schools shall use multiple methods, which may include the following:
    a. An elementary and secondary school marketing kit
    b. Radio and print advertising
    c. A toll-free 800 information hotline
    d. Cable TV advertising
    e. A diocesan information/media kit
    f. A speakers program
    g. Use of selected billboards
    h. Press releases and feature story efforts
    i. Use of radio talk shows
    j. Videos on Catholic education and/or specific schools
    k. Special events
    l. Parish/pastor communications program

70. The major diocesan public relations effort shall be funded by a fee charged to each student by each elementary and secondary school in the diocese. It is anticipated that this fee would range from $4.00 to $8.00 annually.

71. Each parish shall develop a program for proclaiming the Church's commitment to education and the parish's commitment to Catholic schools. The proclamation concerning Catholic schools will include a review of
    a. The special character of a Catholic school
    b. The importance and necessity of Catholic schools
    c. Catholic schools' relationship to the evangelization mission of the parish
    d. The sponsored school's mission statement and statement of Catholic identity
    e. The cost to educate a child in the parish-sponsored school
    f. The parish contribution to the support of its school and other Catholic schools

g. The specific financial needs of its school and of Catholic schools in general

h. Ways parishioners can assist their school and Catholic schools in general

72. The parish bulletin shall regularly contain articles emphasizing the positive achievements of students in Catholic schools. Parishioners should be made aware through the bulletin that the school contributes to the life of the parish by reinforcing traditional Catholic values and by promoting parish-wide activities.

73. Each school shall develop specific and systematic public relations and recruitment strategies.

a. Each school shall examine its religious formation and academic programs in the light of the characteristics and needs of the parishes and of children in the neighborhood and make appropriate adjustments to attract students.

b. Each school is encouraged to use available media, such as *The Providence Visitor*, local newspapers, radio, and television, to publicize the benefits of a Catholic school education and the accomplishments of its students and graduates.

High School Chart 1: Student Recruitment Analysis: Four-Year History

Year	Inquiries	Visits	Applied	Accepted	Enrolled	%

High School Chart 2: Recruitment Inquiry Analysis by Zip Code and by Inquirer's School

Zip Code of Inquirer	About Gr 9	About Gr 10	School of Inquirer	About Gr 9	About Gr 10

High School Chart 3: Enrollment Percentages by Ethnic/Religious Composition

Grade 9

Year	Asian	Black	Hispanic	White	Other	Catholic

Grade 10

Year	Asian	Black	Hispanic	White	Other	Catholic

Grade 11

Year	Asian	Black	Hispanic	White	Other	Catholic

Grade 12

Year	Asian	Black	Hispanic	White	Other	Catholic

High School Chart 3 (continued)

Total School

Year	Asian	Black	Hispanic	White	Other	Catholic

High School Chart 4: Enrollment Trend: Four-Year Tracking by Grade

Year	Grade 9	Grade 10	Grade 11	Grade 12

High School Chart 5: Enrollment Pattern of Student Body by Zip Code

Zip Code	Gr 9 %	Gr 10 %	Gr 11 %	Gr 12 %	Total

High School Chart 6: Enrollment Pattern of Student Body by Feeder Schools

School Attended In Eighth Grade	Gr 9 %	Gr 10 %	Gr 11 %	Gr 12 %	Total

High School Chart 7: Attrition Rate—Three-Year History

School Year: _____

Grade	By 10/1 Enrolled	Moved	Not Returning After 10/1 Counseled Out	Drop Out	Transfer	Rate Attrition %*
9						
10						
11						
12						

School Year: _____

Grade	By 10/1 Enrolled	Moved	Not Returning After 10/1 Counseled Out	Drop Out	Transfer	Rate Attrition %*
9						
10						
11						
12						

School Year: _____

Grade	By 10/1 Enrolled	Moved	Not Returning After 10/1 Counseled Out	Drop Out	Transfer	Rate Attrition %*
9						
10						
11						
12						

*Divide total of those not returning after 10/1 by 10/1 enrollment.

High School Chart 8: Parent Reasons for Withdrawing Students
(Sources of information: exit interview, follow-up survey, conversation, hearsay, etc.)

Reasons Given by Parents	Source(s)
1.	
2.	
3.	
4.	
5.	

High School Chart 9: Student Reasons for Leaving the School
(Sources of information: exit interview, follow-up survey, conversation, hearsay, etc.)

Reasons Given by Students	Source(s)
1.	
2.	
3.	
4.	
5.	

High School Chart 10: Schools Receiving Transferred Students

School	Tuition of School
1.	
2.	
3.	
4.	
5.	
6.	

High School Chart 11: Student Profile
(last academic year)

Grade	% on Honor Roll All Four Quarters	% with Less than C- Cumulative Average	% Perfect Year Attendance
9			
10			
11			
12			

High School Chart 12: Student GPA Profile
(last academic year)

Grade	Average GPA	Top 10%	Bottom 10%
9			
10			
11			
12			

High School Chart 13: Student SAT/ACT Profile: Five-Year History

Year	# Gr 12	% took SAT/ACT	Average Verbal	Average Math	Average Total

High School Chart 14: Five-Year Graduate Profile History

Year	Seniors as of September	Graduates in June	% to College	% to Work

High School Chart 15: Graduate Honors

Year	# Seniors	# Grads	Total $ Earned in Scholarships	Special Honors

High School Chart 16: The Five Colleges Graduates Most Frequently Attended

Last Year		Two Years Ago		Three Years Ago	
College	N	College	N	College	N

High School Chart 17: Student Work Responsibilities

Grade	% with a Job Outside School	% Work at School	% Pay All/Part of Tuition
9			
10			
11			
12			

High School Chart 18: Student Participation Analysis by Grade

Grade	Sports	Academic Clubs	Service Clubs	Drama/Music/Fine Arts	Other
9					
10					
11					
12					

High School Chart 19: Student Participation Analysis by Gender and Ethnic/Minority

Organization/Activity	Students in the Activity	% Female	% Minority

High School Chart 20: Mother's Education Profile

Grade	Less than High School	Completed High School	Completed College	Graduate Degree
9				
10				
11				
12				
Total				

High School Chart 21: Father's Education Profile

Grade	Less than High School	Completed High School	Completed College	Graduate Degree
9				
10				
11				
12				
Total				

High School Chart 22: Present Family Background Profile
(* Disrupted: = divorced, separation, death, remarried, etc.)

Grade	Total Families	% Dual Working	% Single Working	% Disrupted Families
9				
10				
11				
12				
Total				

High School Chart 23: Mother's Occupation

Occupation	Gr 9	Gr 10	Gr 11	Gr 12	Total
Parent Absent					
Unknown					
Unemployed					
Disabled					
Laborer/Factory/Sales					
Business/Clerical					
Professional/Technical					
Homemaker					
Other					

High School Chart 24: Father's Occupation

Occupation	Gr 9	Gr 10	Gr 11	Gr 12	Total
Parent Absent					
Unknown					
Unemployed					
Disabled					
Laborer/Factory/Sales					
Business/Clerical					
Professional/Technical					
Other					

High School Chart 25: Parent Participation Profile
(last year)

Grade	% Fund Raisers	% Volunteers	Ave. Hours	Other
9				
10				
11				
12				

High School Chart 26: School Financial Profile

Year	Per-Pupil Cost	% From Tuition	% From Fund Raising	% From Subsidy	% From Other

High School Chart 27: Tuition and Financial Aid History

Year	Tuition and Fees	Amount Uncollected	Number of Students Aided	$ Aid Granted

High School Chart 28: Enrollment/Staffing Average

Year	Total Enrollment	# Total Faculty	Pupil-Teacher Ratio	Average Class Size	Range of Class Size

High School Chart 29: Enrollment/Staffing/Cost/Income

Year	# Faculty Full-Time	# Faculty Part-Time	Total Staff Salaries & Benefits	Total Collected Tuition/Fees

High School Chart 30: Financial Data: Teachers

Year	Total Salaries	Starting	Median	Highest

High School Chart 31: Salary Scale

Experience	BA	MA	MA+30 credits
0 years			
1			
2			
3			
4			
5			
6			
7			
8			
9			
10			
11			
12			
13			
14			

High School Chart 32: Staffing Profile
(Include all professional personnel—librarians, counselors, etc.)

ID #	Years This School	Total Years	Degree	Certified	Full-Time

High School Chart 33: Discussion Guide for Use by Religious Community/Board/Parish

Assets/Strengths

Liabilities/Weaknesses

Future Prognosis

Reasons for Continued Need for School

Obstacles for Community/Board/Parish Support

Recommendations/Plan for the Future

Elementary School Chart 1: Enrollment Trend by Grade

Year	PK	K	1st	2nd	3rd	4th	5th	6th	7th	8th	Total

Elementary School Chart 2: Total Enrollment by Zip Code

Zip Code	Year ___	Year ___	Year ___	Year ___	Year ___

Elementary School Chart 3: Racial/Ethnic Enrollment by Years

Race/Ethnicity	Year____	Year ____	Year ____	Year ____	Year ____
American Indian/Alaskan Native					
Asian/Pacific Islander					
African American/Black					
Hispanic/Latino					
White/Non-Hispanic					
Other (List Specific Subgroups)					

Elementary School Chart 4: Feeder Parish and Non-Catholic Enrollment by Years

Parish	Year___	Year ___	Year ___	Year ___	Year ___
Non-Catholic					
Catholics (Total)					

Elementary School Chart 5: Financial Data by Years

Financial Category	Year___	Year ___	Year ___	Year ___	Year ___
Tuition for Parishioners					
Tuition for Non-Parishioners					
Tuition for Non-Catholics					
Cost per Student					
Total Operating Expenses					
Salaries and Benefits: Total					
% Operating Expenses					
Total Revenue					
Revenue from Tuition					
% Total Revenue					
Revenue from Parish Subsidy					
% Total Revenue					
Revenue from Fund Raising					
% Total Revenue					
Other Revenue					
% Total Revenue					
Total Tuition Assistance					

Benson, P. L., and M. J. Guerra (1985). *Sharing the Faith: The Beliefs and Values of Catholic High School Teachers.* Washington, D.C.: National Catholic Educational Association.

Benson, P. L., R. J. Yeager, P. K. Wood, M. J. Guerra, and B. V. Manno (1986). *Catholic High Schools: Their Impact on Low-Income Students.* Washington, D.C.: National Catholic Educational Association.

Bryk, A. S., P. B. Holland, V. E. Lee, and R. A. Carriedo (1984). *Effective Catholic Schools: An Exploration.* Washington, D.C.: National Catholic Educational Association.

Bryk, A. S., V. E. Lee, and P. B. Holland (1993). *Catholic Schools and the Common Good.* Cambridge, Mass.: Harvard University Press.

Buetow, H. A. (1988). *The Catholic School: Its Roots, Identity, and Future.* New York: The Crossroad Publishing Company.

Cibulka, J. G., T. J. O'Brien, and D. Zewe (1982). *Inner-City Private Elementary Schools.* Milwaukee: Marquette University Press.

Ciriello, M. J. (ed.) (1993). *The Principal as Educational Leader.* Washington, D.C.: United States Catholic Conference.

Ciriello, M. J. (ed.) (1994a). *The Principal as Spiritual Leader.* Washington, D.C.: United States Catholic Conference.

Ciriello, M. J. (ed.) (1994b). *The Principal as Managerial Leader.* Washington, D.C.: United States Catholic Conference.

Coleman, J. S., and T. Hoffer (1987). *Public and Private High Schools: The Impact of Communities.* New York: Basic Books.

Coleman, J. S., T. Hoffer, and S. Kilgore (1982). *High School Achievement: Public, Catholic, and Private Schools Compared.* New York: Basic Books.

Congregation for Catholic Education (1977). *The Catholic School.* Washington, D.C.: United States Catholic Conference.

Congregation for Catholic Education (1982). "Lay Catholics in Schools: Witnesses to Faith." *The Pope Speaks,* no. 28: 45-73.

Congregation for Catholic Education (1988). "The Religious Dimension of Education in a Catholic School." *Origins,* no. 18(14): 213, 215-228.

Convey, J. J. (1989). "Catholic Schools, Research on." In Marthaler, B. (ed.) *The New Catholic Encyclopedia,* vol. 18, 73-78. Palatine, Ill.: Jack Heraty and Associates.

Convey, J. J. (1991). "Catholic Schools in a Changing Society: Past Accomplishments and Future Challenges." In *The Catholic School and Society.* Washington, D.C.: National Catholic Educational Association.

Convey, J. J. (1992). *Catholic Schools Make a Difference: Twenty-Five Years of Research.* Washington, D.C.: National Catholic Educational Association.

Delbecq, A. L., and A. Van de Ven (1971). "A Group Process Model for Problem Identification and Program Planning." *The Journal of Applied Behavioral Science,* no. 7: 466-492.

Delbecq, A., A. Van de Ven, and D. Gustafson (1975). *Group Techniques: A Guide to Nominal and Delphi Processes.* Glenview, Ill: Scott Foresman.

Greeley, A. M. (1982). *Catholic High Schools and Minority Students.* New Brunswick: Transaction Books.

Greeley, A. M. (1989). "My Research on Catholic Schools." *Chicago Studies,* no. 28: 245-263.

Guerra, M. J., M. J. Donahue, and P. Benson (1990). *The Heart of the Matter: Effects of Catholic High Schools on Student Values, Beliefs and Behaviors.* Washington, D.C.: National Catholic Educational Association.

Harkins, W. (1993). *Introducing the Catholic Elementary School Principal: What Principals Say About Themselves, Their Values, Their Schools.* Washington, D.C.: National Catholic Educational Association.

Kotler, P., and P. E. Murphy (1981). "Strategic Planning for Higher Education." *The Journal of Higher Education,* no. 52: 470-489.

Lee, V. E. (1985). *1983-84 National Assessment of Educational Progress Reading Proficiency: Catholic School Results and National Averages.* Washington, D.C.: National Catholic Educational Association.

Lee, V. E. (1987). *1983-84 National Assessment of Educational Progress Writing Proficiency: Catholic School Results and National Averages.* Washington, D.C.: National Catholic Educational Association.

Lee, V. E., and A. S. Bryk (1986). "Effects of Single-Sex Secondary Schools on Student Achievement and Attitudes." *Journal of Educational Psychology,* no. 78: 381-395.

Lee, V. E., and C. Stewart (1989). *National Assessment of Educational Progress Proficiency in Mathematics and Science 1985-86: Catholic and Public Schools Compared.* Washington, D.C.: National Catholic Educational Association.

Lunenburg, F. G., and A. C. Ornstein (1991). *Educational Administration: Concepts and Practices.* Belmont, Calif.: Wadsworth Publishing Company.

Marks, H. M. , and V. E. Lee (1989). *National Assessment of Educational Progress Proficiency in Reading 1985-86: Catholic and Public Schools Compared.* Washington, D.C.: National Catholic Educational Association.

McCune, S. D. (1986). *Guide to Strategic Planning for Educators.* Alexandria, Va.: Association for Supervision and Curriculum Development.

National Conference of Catholic Bishops (1972). *To Teach as Jesus Did.* Washington, D.C.: United States Catholic Conference.

National Conference of Catholic Bishops (1979). *Sharing the Light of Faith: National Catechetical Directory for Catholics of the United States.* Washington, D.C.: United States Catholic Conference.

National Conference of Catholic Bishops (1990). *Statement of the United States Bishops in Support of Catholic Elementary and Secondary Schools.* Washington, D.C.: United States Catholic Conference.

O'Brien, J. S. (1987). *Mixed Messages: What Bishops and Priests Say About Catholic Schools.* Washington, D.C.: National Catholic Educational Association.

Patterson, J. L., S. C. Purkey, and J. V. Parker (1986). *Productive School Systems for a Nonrational World.* Alexandria, Va.: Association for Supervision and Curriculum Development.

Popham, W. J. (1993). *Educational Evaluation.* (3rd ed.) Boston: Allyn and Bacon.

Reck, C. (1988). *The Small Catholic Elementary School: Advantages and Opportunities.* Washington, D.C.: National Catholic Educational Association.

Reck, C., and R. J. Yeager (eds.) (1984). *Elementary School Finance Manual.* Washington, D.C.: National Catholic Educational Association.

Riordan, C. (1990). *Girls and Boys in School: Together or Separate?* New York: Teachers College Press.

Sheehan, L. (1990). *Building Better Boards: A Handbook for Board Members in Catholic Education.* Washington, D.C.: National Catholic Educational Association.

Tarr, H. C., M. J. Ciriello, and J. J. Convey (1993). "Commitment and Satisfaction Among Parochial School Teachers: Findings from Catholic Education." *Journal of Research on Christian Education,* no. 2: 41-63.

Van de Ven, A., and A. L. Delbecq (1971). "Nominal Versus Interacting Groups for Committee Decision-Making Effectiveness." *Academy of Management Journal,* no. 14.

Van de Ven, A., and A. Delbecq (1974). "The Effectiveness of Nominal, Delphi, and Interacting Group Decision-Making Processes." *Academy of Management Journal,* no. 17: 605-621.

Vitullo-Martin, T. (1979). *Catholic Inner-City Schools: The Future.* Washington, D.C.: United States Catholic Conference.

Warren, E. K. (1966). *Long-Range Planning: The Executive Viewpoint.* Englewood Cliffs: Prentice-Hall.

Yeager, R. J. (ed.) (1984). *Elementary School Finance Manual.* Washington, D.C.: National Catholic Educational Association.

Yeager, R. J., P. L. Benson, M. J. Guerra, and B. V. Manno (1985). *The Catholic High School: A National Portrait.* Washington, D.C.: National Catholic Educational Association.